THE MODERN AMERICAN MILITARY

THE MODERN AMERICAN MILITARY

EDITED BY
DAVID M. KENNEDY

OXFORD
UNIVERSITY PRESS

OXFORD

UNIVERSITY PRESS

Oxford University Press is a department of the University of Oxford.
It furthers the University's objective of excellence in research, scholarship,
and education by publishing worldwide.

Oxford   New York
Auckland   Cape Town   Dar es Salaam   Hong Kong   Karachi
Kuala Lumpur   Madrid   Melbourne   Mexico City   Nairobi
New Delhi   Shanghai   Taipei   Toronto

With offices in
Argentina   Austria   Brazil   Chile   Czech Republic   France   Greece
Guatemala   Hungary   Italy   Japan   Poland   Portugal   Singapore
South Korea   Switzerland   Thailand   Turkey   Ukraine   Vietnam

Oxford is a registered trademark of Oxford University Press
in the UK and certain other countries.

Published in the United States of America by
Oxford University Press
198 Madison Avenue, New York, NY 10016

© Oxford University Press 2013

Library of Congress Cataloging-in-Publication Data
The modern American military / edited by David M. Kennedy.
pages cm
Includes index.
ISBN 978-0-19-989594-6 (hbk. : alk. paper)   1. United States–Armed Forces.
2. United States–Military policy.   3. National security–United States.
I. Kennedy, David M.
UA23.M5854 2013
355.00973–dc23
2012050996

1 3 5 7 9 8 6 4 2
Printed in the United States of America
on acid-free paper

CONTENTS

CONTRIBUTORS

David M. Kennedy is the Donald J. McLachlan Professor of History, Emeritus, at Stanford University, where he is also Director of the Bill Lane Center for the American West and a Senior Fellow in the Woods Institute for the Environment. His publications include *Over Here: The First World War and American Society* (1980) and *Freedom from Fear: The American People in Depression and War, 1929–1945* (1999), for which he received the 2000 Pulitzer Prize in History.

Deborah Avant is the Sié Chéou-Kang Chair for International Security and Diplomacy and Director of the Sié Chéou-Kang Center for International Security and Diplomacy at the Josef Korbel School of International Studies, University of Denver. Her publications include *Political Institutions and Military Change: Lessons from Peripheral Wars* (1994), *The Market for Force: The Consequences of Privatizing Security* (2005), and *Who Governs the Globe?* (with Martha Finnemore and Susan Sell, 2010).

Andrew J. Bacevich is Professor of History and International Relations at Boston University. His publications include *The New American Militarism: How Americans Are Seduced by War* (2005), *The Limits of Power: The End of American Exceptionalism* (2008), and *Washington Rules: America's Path to Permanent War* (2010).

Charles J. Dunlap, Jr. is Executive Director of the Center, on Law, Ethics and National Security at Duke University Law School where his teaching responsibilities include a course on criminal law in the armed forces. He holds a B.A. from St. Joseph's University, a J.D. from Villanova University, and is a distinguished graduate of the National War College. He is retired Air Force major general having served in the Judge Advocate General Corps for more than 34 years. While on active duty he served as a prosecutor, defense counsel, and military judge in scores of courts-martial, and also taught military justice at the Air Force Judge Advocate General's School. In 2010 he was appointed by the Secretary of Defense to serve on the Uniform Code of Military Justice Committee, an advisory body established by 10 U.S.C. §946.

Karl W. Eikenberry is the William J. Perry Fellow in International Security at Stanford University's Center for International Security and Cooperation. He served in Afghanistan as the U.S. Ambassador from 2009 to 2011 and Commander of the American-led Coalition forces from 2005 to 2007. He enjoyed a thirty-five-year career in the U.S. Army, retiring with the rank of lieutenant general. His military assignments included postings with mechanized, light, airborne, and ranger infantry units in the continental United States, Hawaii, Korea, Italy, and Afghanistan. He also served as the U.S. defense attaché in Beijing and as a senior officer at NATO Headquarters in Brussels. He is a graduate of the U.S. Military Academy, earned master of arts degrees from Harvard University in East Asian Studies and from Stanford University in political science, and was awarded an Interpreter's Certificate in Mandarin Chinese from the British Foreign Commonwealth Office.

Lawrence Freedman has been Professor of War Studies at King's College London since 1982, and Vice-Principal since 2003. Elected a Fellow of the British Academy in 1995 and awarded the CBE in 1996, he was appointed Official Historian of the Falklands Campaign in 1997. He was awarded the KCMG in 2003. In June 2009 he was appointed to serve as a member of the official inquiry into Britain and the 2003 Iraq War. Professor Freedman has written extensively on nuclear strategy and the Cold War, as well as commentating regularly on contemporary security issues. His most recent book, *A Choice of Enemies: America Confronts the Middle East*, won the 2009 Lionel Gelber Prize and Duke of Westminster Medal for Military Literature.

Robert L. Goldich is a defense consultant and military historian. He served for more than thirty-three years as a defense analyst for the Congressional Research Service (CRS) of the Library of Congress. He has published articles or book reviews in *Army*, *Armed Forces and Society*, *Military Review*, and *The Journal of Military History*, as well as dozens of CRS studies and analyses of U.S. military manpower policy. He is currently writing a book on the history of conscription from the first human civilizations to the present, tentatively titled *Conscription in History: Organization, Administration, and Context*.

Lawrence J. Korb is a Senior Fellow at the Center for American Progress and an adjunct professor at Georgetown University.

Brian McAllister Linn is Professor of History and Ralph R. Thomas Professor in Liberal Arts at Texas A&M University. His publications include *Guardians of Empire: The U.S. Army and the Pacific, 1902–1940* (1997) and *The Philippine War, 1899–1902* (2000), both of which received the Society for Military History Distinguished Book Award, and *The Echo of Battle: The Army's Way of War* (2007). His current project is *Elvis's Army: Transformation and the Atomic-Era Soldier, 1946–1965*.

Thomas G. Mahnken is the Jerome E. Levy Chair of Economic Geography and National Security at the U.S. Naval War College and a Visiting Scholar at the Philip Merrill Center for Strategic Studies at Johns Hopkins University. From 2006 to 2009 he served as the Deputy Assistant Secretary of Defense for Policy Planning. His most recent book is *Technology and the American Way of War since 1945* (2008).

Renée de Nevers is an Associate Professor of Public Administration at the Maxwell School of Citizenship and Public Affairs at Syracuse University. Her publications include *Regimes as Mechanisms for Global Governance* (1999), *Comrades No More: The Seeds of Change* *in Eastern Europe* (2003), and *Combating Terrorism: Strategies and Approaches* (with William Banks and Mitchel Wallerstein, 2007).

William J. Perry is a senior fellow at the Hoover Institution and the Freeman Spogli Institute of International Studies. He is the Michael and Barbara Berberian Professor at Stanford University and serves as codirector of the Nuclear Risk Reduction initiative and the Preventive Defense Project. He is an expert in US foreign policy, national security, and arms control. He was the codirector of CISAC from 1988 to 1993, during which time he was also a half-time professor at Stanford. Perry was the nineteenth secretary of defense for the United States, serving from February 1994 to January 1997. He previously served as deputy secretary of defense (1993–94) and as undersecretary of defense for research and engineering (1977–81). Perry currently serves on the Defense Policy Board, the International Security Advisory Board, and the Secretary of Energy Advisory Board.

Michelle Sandhoff is a Ph.D. candidate in sociology at the University of Maryland. Her dissertation, "Service, Sacrifice, and Citizenship: The Experiences of Muslims Serving in the U.S. Military," examines the experiences of Muslim service members in the post-9/11 era. Her recent publications include "Sexuality in the Military" (*International Handbook of the Demography of Sexuality*, 2013, with Karin De Angelis, Kimberly Bonner, and David Segal) and "Gender Issues in the Transformation to an All-Volunteer Force: A Transnational Perspective" (in *The New Citizen Armies*, 2010, with Mady Wechsler Segal and David Segal). Her master's research focused on gender in the Israeli military. She is an instructor of sociology at the University of Maryland.

David R. Segal is Professor of Sociology and Director of the Center for Research on Military Organization at the University of Maryland.

Mady Wechsler Segal earned her Ph.D. at the University of Chicago. She is Professor Emerita of Sociology at the University of Maryland, where she has been Distinguished Scholar Teacher, faculty affiliate of the Women's Studies Department, Associate Director of the Center for Research on Military Organization, and Associate Dean for Undergraduate Studies. Her recent publications include "Moving with the Military: Race, Class, and Gender Differences in the Employment Consequences of Tied Migration" (in *Race, Gender and Class*, 2011, with Richard Cooney and Karin De Angelis). She is currently working on a paper with David G. Smith titled "On the Fast Track: Dual Military Couples Navigating Institutional Structures" and a paper with Karin De Angelis, "Transitions in the Military and the Family as Greedy Institutions: Original Concept and Current Applicability" (for a book titled *Military Families on Mission, Comparative Perspectives*, edited by Manon Andres, René Moelker, Gary Bowen, and Philippe Manigart).

Jonathan Shay was a staff psychiatrist at the Boston DVA Outpatient Clinic for twenty years, and is author of *Achilles in Vietnam: Combat Trauma and the Undoing of Character* (1994), and *Odysseus in America: Combat Trauma and the Trials of Homecoming* (2002), with a joint foreword by Senators Max Cleland and John McCain. He has been a MacArthur Fellow. He has done the following with U.S. forces (partial list): 1999–2000, Commandant of the Marine Corps Trust Study; 2004–2005, Chair of Ethics, Leadership, and Personnel Policy in the Office of the U.S. Army Deputy Chief of Staff for Personnel; 2009 Omar Bradley Chair of Strategic Leadership, U.S. Army War College; and various activities with Canadian Forces, UK Royal Marines, UK Royal Navy, Bundeswehr, and other NATO personnel.

James Sheehan, a Fellow of the American Academy of Arts and Sciences since 1992, is the Dickason Professor in the Humanities and Professor of Modern European History, Emeritus, at Stanford University. His publications include *Where Have All the Soldiers Gone? The Transformation of Modern Europe* (2008), *Museums in the German Art World from the End of the Old Regime to the Rise of Modernism* (2000), and *German History, 1770–1886* (1989).

Jay Winter is Charles J. Stille Professor of History at Yale University. He is the author of *Sites of Memory, Sites of Mourning: The Great War in European Cultural History* (Cambridge University Press, 1995);

Remembering War (Yale University Press, 2006) and *Dreams of Peace and Freedom* (Yale University Press, 2006); and, with Antoine Prost, *René Cassin et les droits de l'Homme: Le projet d'une génération* (Paris: Fayard, 2011); the English version will be published by Cambridge University Press in 2013 under the title *René Cassin and Human Rights: From the Great War to the Universal Declaration*. In 1996, he won an Emmy Award for best television series of the year as coproducer and cowriter of the eight-hour *The Great War and the Shaping of the Twentieth Century*.

FOREWORD

William J. Perry

The dropping of nuclear bombs on Hiroshima and Nagasaki ended World War II but ushered in an entirely new form of conflict that came to be called the Cold War. During the Cold War, the United States and the Soviet Union each built up enormous arsenals of nuclear weapons designed to deter the other from launching a conventional military or nuclear attack. At the time, deterrence worked in the sense that the United States and the Soviet Union did not come into direct military conflict with each other. But these vast nuclear arsenals did not deter the Soviets from using conventional military force in Czechoslovakia, Hungary, or Afghanistan. They did not deter the United States from using military force in Korea and Vietnam. And they did not preclude both sides from amassing large conventional forces in Europe.

When the Cold War ended, many hoped that a new era of peace would replace the threat of large-scale nuclear war breaking out at any moment. At the time, many believed that this peace would be accompanied by a significant global reduction in nuclear weapons. Instead, new challenges to world security arose. Regional instabilities led to threats of war between India and Pakistan, on the Korean Peninsula, and in the Mideast. These threats contributed to and were exacerbated by the proliferation of nuclear weapons in these regions. Additionally, catastrophic terrorism arose as a new threat to world security, with large-scale attacks on civilian populations in the United States, Russia, India, Spain, the United

Kingdom, and Indonesia. And nuclear terrorism—the conflation of those two dangers—loomed as a new and grave potential security threat.

The possibility of another global war breaking out, however real, still seems remote. Militarily, the United States is in a class of its own. Today there is no peer competitor for America's military forces. Yet the public debate in Congress and the Pentagon surrounding future U.S. military planning still focuses on the potential conventional military threats emerging from a modernized China or resurgent Russia. China has been making truly impressive and sustained gains in its economy and is devoting a significant portion of its GDP to modernize its military. However, China is very far from being a peer military competitor to the United States. And war between China and the United States appears unlikely, with leaders from both countries recognizing that a military conflict would be disastrous for both societies. And while Russia has a large nuclear force similar to that of the United States, its conventional forces are substantially less capable than those of the United States.

Since the end of the Cold War, four successive presidential administrations have been unclear as to how the U.S. military should be restructured to respond to this new security environment. Although we cut back our conventional forces by about one-third during the 1990s, we have started to rebuild our ground forces this past decade in response to the ongoing military operations in Iraq and Afghanistan. In particular, we have made substantial increases in our Special Operations Forces capabilities. Our nuclear arsenal has been reduced by 84 percent from its peak during the Cold War, but we still retain 2,150 deployed nuclear warheads, as well as thousands more in reserve or storage. In addition, we retain nuclear weapons development facilities capable of building new weapons or modernizing old ones. The most recent U.S. Nuclear Posture Review, released in May 2010, states that as long as other nations have nuclear weapons, the United States should ensure the reliability and effectiveness of our deterrent force through a Life Extension Program and a science-based Stockpile Stewardship Program. In the meantime, both China and Russia are developing new nuclear weapons.

In the first half of the twenty-first century, we will face security dangers very different from those of the first half of the twentieth century (two world wars fought with massive conventional forces), or the second half of the twentieth century (a Cold War characterized by the buildup of enormous nuclear arsenals).

The security dangers we face today must be dealt with at least as much with political, social, and economic strength (soft power) as with military strength (hard power). Our need to exert military power can no longer be met by the large conventional forces used during World War II, or the large nuclear forces accumulated during the Cold War. Today, our armed forces have been reconfiguring to meet these new demands, but many more changes are required. We need to further downsize our conventional forces and at the same time reconfigure them to be more agile. Our ground troops need to focus on further developing expeditionary forces that can be moved quickly to distant locations and do not need established military bases nearby to conduct operations. Our air forces should focus on strengthening their long-range strike and unmanned capabilities. Our naval forces should continue to focus on their mission of establishing sea control that can be projected worldwide on relatively short notice. Also, all our military services must become more proficient in operating in an environment of cyber threats to military technologies.

So while the U.S. military will never be going back to the large conventional forces required during World War II, or the large nuclear forces amassed during the Cold War, its operations will continue to be stretched worldwide, and it will have to deal with new emerging unconventional threats such as insurgents, terrorists, and pirates. At the same time, it will have to maintain effective command and control in the face of potential cyber attacks.

All these changes will take place while profound technological changes are occurring in society. Some of these technological changes can be used against us (cyber attacks on our military command and control, or on our civil infrastructure). However, they can also be used to our advantage, as was the case during the so-called revolution in military affairs (RMA), which led to quantum leaps in the effectiveness of technology used to detect enemy targets, avoid detection of U.S. warplanes by enemy radars through use of stealth technology, and provide more accurate readings of location through the development of Global Positioning System (GPS) technology. This RMA gave the U.S. military a major advantage over other militaries, as was demonstrated convincingly in Operation Desert Storm at the beginning of 1991. Unfortunately, these technologies have not been effective in dealing with urban insurgencies or global terrorism, and other technologies have not yet been developed to give our military a compelling advantage against these threats. In the meantime, an entirely new application of technology—social networking—is having a profound effect on political developments throughout the world, and could affect global military developments as well.

The American military has, since World War II, depended on U.S. industry for building most of its weapons, including those developed during the RMA. This has worked very well, since our country's most advanced technologies are created in the private sector. But as the need for weapons fluctuates, and, in particular, as future needs remain uncertain, it is difficult to maintain a stable defense industry. And as military specifications and procurement regulations continue to diverge from those in the commercial sector, more and more military procurement will rely on companies dedicated solely to military work.

During the wars in Iraq and Afghanistan, our military complicated this military-industry collaboration by heavily relying on private security personnel from defense contractors deployed in the battle space to conduct operational tasks usually reserved for members of the armed forces. With these private security contractors operating outside the traditional command structure of the military, their use resulted in significant command and discipline problems. As a result, the U.S. military in the future will need to exercise tighter control over what operational functions can be performed by contractor personnel.

Another kind of technology—medical technology—has had a profound effect on preventing battlefield casualties. Our wounded soldiers in Iraq and Afghanistan have had far better medical treatment than in any other war, resulting in a high percentage of soldiers surviving wounds that would have been fatal in earlier wars. However, the presence of advanced weapons on the battlefield has also resulted in a much higher number of veterans with long-term disabilities, including post-traumatic stress disorder. The need for more and better treatment facilities has never been greater.

Besides the profound changes to the international threat environment and advances in military technology, there have been equally profound changes in the political, economic, and social environment within the United States over the last century. Politically, the American people and their Congress are not as directly engaged with the U.S. military as they were during World War II or the Cold War. Today, fewer than 1 percent of American families have a family member in active military service; only 22 percent of U.S. senators and congressional representatives have ever served in the military. Our military force is composed entirely of volunteers, which has many real benefits, especially in the training and discipline of the force. But it also has one great liability: the American people and their elected representatives are more detached from their military than at any time this past century. As our body politic makes decisions about how to use its military force, these decisions should be made with the understanding that the people whose lives are being risked are the sons and daughters of their constituents (or their own sons and daughters). There is a potential danger that our all-volunteer force could eventually be seen by Congress as a "mercenary" force.

Congress, under Article 1, Section 8, of the U.S. Constitution, is granted the authority to "raise and support Armies ... To provide and maintain a Navy. To make Rules for the Government and Regulation of the land and naval Forces." Over time, Congress has manifested this responsibility by passing laws that set specific standards for civilian control of the military, for civil-military interfaces, and for establishing a military structure that enables effective joint-service operations. The Goldwater-Nichols Act of 1986, which restructured civil-military relations in the Pentagon and put into place a culture of "jointness" between the military services, has been a successful example of military legislation, and lawmakers are currently considering new legislation to bring the act up to date.

Along with these external and domestic political changes, our military is shaped by the evolution of society and our educational systems. These changes affect the capabilities and attitudes of recruits for the all-volunteer force. A declining quality of K–12 education will result in a declining quality of potential recruits at a time when the technological demands on military personnel are only getting higher and more complex. This in turn will increase the need for the military services to do their own training, possibly including remedial training to compensate for inadequacies of the K–12 education system. Society is also becoming less tolerant of gender and racial inequality, and these changes will be reflected in today's military services. The military for many decades has been open to all races. Women are now accepted in all services and with increasing responsibilities. Congress recently amended the law to allow gays to openly serve. All these changes will bring the face of the military to look more like the face of America.

Finally, America's economic power has strongly influenced its military strength. U.S. government spending on the military forces has increased over time, paralleling our economic growth. As a result, we have by far the largest military budget in the world; in fact, ours is about equal to the rest of the world's combined military budgets in real terms. But we are also the only nation that takes on global responsibilities for security. Our nuclear umbrella over many allied countries allows them to remain nonnuclear, which is a benefit to world security, including our own. And our naval and air forces in the Pacific have contributed to peace in that historically troubled part of the world, to the benefit of East Asian countries and to our trade with them.

The present economic difficulties facing the United States will generate strong pressures to decrease defense spending. Military and civilian leaders will increasingly be pressed to answer the question: How much spending is enough to meet the requirement? That question could be answered by returning to our historical estimate of appropriate defense spending based on a percentage of GDP. For the last sixty years, our defense budget has been about 3 to 6 percent of our GDP, excluding defense spending during the years of the Korean and Vietnam Wars, where it reached a high of 11 percent.

Alternatively, defense spending can be measured by an assessment of the threat we face, but that is a highly subjective measurement that can be endlessly debated. But the wind-down of military operations in Iraq and Afghanistan may still create an opportunity to decrease military spending without compromising U.S. national security or interests.

The world has been changing in very important ways since the end of the Cold War, and new and dangerous threats are emerging every day. But, against all odds, the world has not had a nuclear bomb used in anger since World War II; there has not been, nor is there likely to be, a World War III; and the average standard of living worldwide has increased since the end of the Cold War. The U.S. military has played an important role in these positive results and will be called upon to continue to play that positive role in the future. In order to do this, the U.S. military will have to adapt to economic, political, technological, and social changes, as well as evolve to meet the changing global threat environment.

Introduction

David M. Kennedy

Parvi enim sunt foris arma, nisi est consilium domi.

Cicero, *De Officiis**

This volume surveys the evolution, character, missions, and possible futures of the modern U.S. armed forces. It concentrates on the period since the creation of the all-volunteer force (AVF) in 1973. It proceeds from the conviction that today's American military is at once increasingly prominent as an instrument of national policy and increasingly detached from and poorly understood by the civilian society in whose name it is asked to fight—and perhaps coming dangerously unmoored from venerable systems of civilian political control. As a U.S. Army general at Fort Lewis, Washington, asked in 2007: "How can it be that the Army is at war but the nation is not?" Admiral Michael Mullen, then chairman of the Joint Chiefs of Staff, put it this way in his address to West Point graduates in May 2011: "I fear they [civilian Americans] do not know us. I fear they do not comprehend the full weight of the burden we carry.... We're also fairly insular, speaking our own language of sorts, living within our own unique culture."

The U.S. armed forces today are by many measures a unique historical phenomenon. A majority of today's service members are married, many of them to other service members, giving rise

---

*"Arms are of little value in the field unless there is wise counsel at home"; Cicero, *De Officiis*, Book I, XXII, par. 76.

to references at once proud and anxious about the military as a "family business." Since President Truman desegregated the force in 1948, the military has arguably been the most effective institution in American society for promoting racial equality and nurturing career opportunities for minorities. The AVF in particular has opened the doors to higher education for hundreds of thousands of veterans who would not otherwise have been able to afford it. And those who have served in the last several decades, especially in the post-9/11 years, have brought to their tasks a level of professionalism—as well as robust, unapologetic patriotism—that has earned them the richly deserved respect of their countrymen.

Today's American warriors also wield unprecedented firepower and hold in their hands an almost incalculable capacity for focused violence. Not since the time of the Roman Empire have a single country's arms weighed so heavily in the global scales. The United States today accounts for nearly half of the planet's military spending, more than the next ten rank-ordered countries combined. But if America's AVF looms enormously large on the world stage, it is, paradoxically, almost vanishingly small in the context of American society and the American economy. The active-duty force numbered just 1.4 million in 2012: 544,000 in the Army, 328,000 in the Air Force, 318,000 in the Navy, 198,000 in the Marine Corps, and 41,000 in the Coast Guard. Those numbers amount to less than 0.5 percent of the American population. In World War II, by comparison, nearly 9 percent of all Americans served in uniform; in the Vietnam War, about 2 percent. What's more, in the behemoth $15 trillion U.S. economy, total military spending of some $700 billion (in 2012) adds up to only 20 percent of the federal budget and about 4 percent of gross domestic product (GDP)—whereas military expenditures soaked up the lion's share of the federal budget and almost 40 percent of all economic production during World War II, and ran at nearly 50 percent of federal spending and 8–10 percent of GDP for much of the Cold War. The United States, in short, has developed an armed force that can be sent into battle on behalf of a society that scarcely breaks a sweat—demographically, economically, or financially—when the force is deployed. In vivid contrast with the experience of almost all other societies throughout history, the United States today can wage prodigiously effective warfare without asking the great mass of its citizens to make any contribution—let alone sacrifice—whatsoever.

Today's force, of course, is also an all-volunteer force—and for precisely that reason it is not representative of the society as a whole. African Americans are substantially overrepresented (nearly 20 percent of the military but only 12.6 percent of the relevant age cohort in civil society). Hispanics are markedly underrepresented (more than 17 percent of the eighteen-to forty-year-olds in civil society, but only about 13 percent of the military). Women compose 51 percent of eighteen- to-forty-four-year-olds, but only 14 percent of the armed forces. And while 23 percent of all Americans were registered Republicans in 2011, 36 percent of post-9/11 veterans were so registered; 21 percent of veterans identified as Democrats, compared with 34 percent in the voting-age population at large. And unlike almost every other major institution in America today—Congress, the courts, the media, the churches, professional sports—the military enjoys exceptionally high measures of the public's admiration and trust.

It would be an irresponsible exaggeration to suggest that the cultural divide that now separates the military from the civilian sectors in the United States is a precursor to the emergence of an American *Freikorps* or *Fasci di Combattimento*—the veterans' organizations that helped bring Hitler and Mussolini, respectively, to power in the wake of World War I. But the distance that separates those who serve from those who do not undoubtedly exacerbates the festering social tensions that palpably threaten America's social comity. This volume aims not only to measure the range of that distance, but to help close it. It also seeks to advance national thinking about the complex interrelationship between the structure of the armed forces and the effectiveness of inherited mechanisms for civilian control of the military and political accountability for its use.

The creation of the AVF, combined with some impressive technological innovations documented in the pages that follow, has allowed the United States to rely on an ever-smaller proportion of its citizens to shoulder its military burdens. Today's U.S. military is a standing professional force with formidable capacities to prevail in virtually any conceivable battle space. Whether those developments should be celebrated or lamented is a question that animates many of the chapters to follow, but all contributors agree that this is a situation with slender precedent in the history of the American republic. "A standing army, however necessary it may be at some times, is always dangerous to the liberties of the people," warned American Revolutionary leader Samuel Adams. "Soldiers are apt to consider themselves as a body distinct from the rest of the citizens.... Such a power should be watched with a jealous eye." For nearly two centuries thereafter, the United States accordingly embraced the principle of the citizen-soldier. Deeply rooted in antiquity, that principle was axiomatic in the organization of America's armed forces well into the twentieth century. It held that all who were able and deemed fit for service were liable to serve. As George Washington put it in 1783: "It may be laid down as a primary position, and the basis of our system, that every citizen who enjoys the protection of a free government, owes not only a proportion of his property, but even of his personal services, to the defense of it."

To be sure, the citizen-soldier principle was more an ideal than a reality for much of the nineteenth century, when the military usually consisted of a modestly scaled professional force largely confined to frontier Indian-fighting and occasional constabulary duties. But the ideal remained robust and had a powerful effect in shaping the great conscript armies that the United States fielded in World Wars I and II, Korea, and Vietnam.

But since the close of the Vietnam era, the United States has sought to wage major expeditionary wars with a relatively small professional force. That kind of force used in that way is something new in the American experience; small wonder that soldiers and civilians alike remain ambivalent or just plain uninformed about the structure of today's armed forces and the purposes for which they are used.

The advent of the AVF also severed the link between citizenship and service. No American today is obligated to serve in the military. Indeed, the ranks of the armed forces now include tens of thousands of noncitizens, who receive accelerated access to citizenship on the basis of their service. So service can earn citizenship, but citizenship does not require service. The implications of that curi-ous asymmetry inform the analysis in several of the chapters in this volume.

In December 2004, Secretary of Defense Donald Rumsfeld said: "As you know, you go to war with the Army you have. They're not the Army you might want or wish to have at a later time." His now-notorious comment underscored the truth that the Army (and Navy, and Marine Corps, and Air Force) that this or any country has at any given time is the product of both history and prophecy. The size of the force, the configuration of its combat and support arms, the missions for which it is trained and equipped: all are guided by lessons distilled from the experience of the past and by guesses about what the future might hold. And because modern weapons systems and training regimes take years, even decades, to develop, the inexorable logic of inertia shapes the military's state of readiness at any given moment, even while the nature of the eventual mission might be largely unanticipated. A timeless issue, this phenomenon has become decidedly more pronounced in an age of exponentially accelerating social and technological change.

Recent years have seen striking disjunctions between the nature of the force and the tasks it has been assigned. The authors in this volume seek to explain just how history has deposited the U.S. armed forces where they are today, to clarify what is new and what is not about the twenty-first-century military and its missions, to under-stand the demography and the psychology of those who serve, and to judge the appropriateness of the force to the missions at hand. They also do their best to foresee the kinds of adaptations that are likely to be necessary going forward. This volume thus aims to shed light both on what today's military *does* and what it *is*, as well as on what it might *become*.

Beginning with the foreword by former secretary of defense William J. Perry, all the chapters that follow take a historical approach to their various parts of the subject. They share the prem-ise that American forces today are by no means your grandfather's or even your father's military. They explore the strategic, techno-logical, and cultural factors that have made the modern American armed forces distinctive, with respect to both their own national

antecedents and other nations' contemporary military establishments. They emphasize the ever-changing political and fiscal con-
texts in which the armed forces are recruited, trained, and deployed,
and the constantly shifting objectives that they are tasked to achieve,
especially in the post–Cold War and post-9/11 environment. Authors
examine threat assessments, strategic doctrine, force configuration,
composition, and training, as well as questions about who serves
and why; the peculiarly challenging nature of modern warfare; the
tactical challenges and ethical dilemmas it can generate; gender,
legal, and medical issues in the battle space and beyond; the relation
of the military to civil society, including the ways it is depicted in
popular culture, and, notably, the health of command-and-control
systems; and its role in the institutional structure that constitutes
the national security apparatus.

All consideration of these topics, of course, begins with an
understanding of the threats for which the military thinks it
must prepare and the means it deems appropriate for coping with
them. Lawrence Freedman documents the advent of the high-tech
revolution in military affairs, or RMA, that drove doctrinal and
weapon-system changes in the closing years of the twentieth century. He takes both the military and civilian leadership to task for
embracing the RMA too uncritically, especially in the post–Cold
War era when protracted, large-scale conventional warfare among
advanced industrial nation-states seemed decreasingly likely. He
dwells on the inappropriateness of RMA-driven weapons and tactics in counterinsurgency warfare and the effort, led by General
David Petraeus among others, to devise an effective way to wage
"fourth-generation warfare," or "war among the people." He pre-
dicts a considerably diminished role for conventional military
forces in the coming years.

Brian McAllister Linn expands on Freedman's contribution
by focusing on the uniformed "military intellectuals" who write
about strategic doctrine. He tracks the debate within military
circles about fourth-generation warfare and ends with a discussion of how the Petraeus counterinsurgency doctrine has been
promulgated and implemented. Thomas G. Mahnken also puts
the accuracy-and-technology-driven RMA at the center of his

analysis, including the advent of unmanned military vehicles like the Predator drone. He describes the adaptive responses to the RMA as either "emulative" or "countervailing," with special emphasis on the latter. He shares Freedman's view that the architects of the RMA did not adequately anticipate what the counterresponses would be, especially the emergence of asymmetrical warfare. He provocatively speculates that the evolutionary pathway of these weapons and the tactical innovations they have spurred on the part of adversaries may drive American war-fighting doctrine back to a greater or renewed reliance on nuclear weapons.

Turning from what the military is asked to do to who actually does it—to the human face of the force—Robert L. Goldich examines the widely held notion that today's recruits come from the least advantaged corners of American society, and he comes up with some surprising answers. He also invokes the example of the Roman legionaries to argue that a potentially dangerous gap has opened between military and civilian cultures. He focuses not only on the socioeconomic differences between the civil and military sectors but also on the possible divergence in values between service members and civilians, particularly with respect to attitudes about the legitimacy of violence and force. David R. Segal and Lawrence J. Korb address some of the same issues in the immediately succeeding contribution. They examine the demographic and fiscal characteristics of the AVF, with special attention to the financial implications of measures taken to meet recruitment and retention goals. They are particularly critical of the fact that military health and pension benefits have not been budgeted on an accrual basis. They raise the troubling question of whether it might be desirable to restore conscription, or at least to enforce compulsory Selective Service registration. They also advocate reforms in veterans' medical benefits, along the lines that Secretary of Defense Robert Gates suggested in January 2011.

Deborah Avant and Renée de Nevers call attention to that part of the overall force that is not in uniform: the surprisingly large numbers of civilian "contractors" who have taken over a range of traditional military duties, including construction and supply, but armed combat roles as well. In Iraq and Afghanistan the number of contractors at times equaled or exceeded the number of uniformed troops. Avant and de Nevers probe the implications of those numbers for civilian perceptions of the size of the force commitment and the political ease of defending that commitment (since its true scale is not altogether apparent). They also analyze issues of command, control, and accountability that arise from such heavy reliance on an "irregular" force component, while noting that the Defense Contract Management Agency, in charge of overseeing those contractors, has actually downsized rather remarkably since 2002.

Jay Winter and James Sheehan open the supremely important subject of the military's relation to civil society at large. Winter asks how the public on the home front forms its image of warfare on the distant fighting front. He discusses some widely read war novels but focuses on that most accessible and influential of all popular media, film, from the era of the silents to the present. He finds a persistent tension between the rendition of war as spectacle and war as the setting for psychological and moral drama, with an increasing tendency in our time to focus on stories that are less about war per se than about individual warriors and their interior lives. Sheehan rehearses the role of the military in state formation in Europe over the last two centuries, showing how most Western European nations have now become "civilian societies," with a much-diminished role for the military. Meanwhile, across an ill-defined but discernible boundary, on the eastern side of which lie many of the successor Soviet states, as well as Turkey, the military remains a powerful institution, largely relying on conscription. Sheehan's comparative analysis casts the United States into clearer perspective as an anomalous hybrid of the Eastern and Western European models: it has a small and relatively inexpensive military that commands unprecedented destructive power, and it is a civilian state with significant military obligations—indeed, a greater weight and range of such obligations than any other nation.

Andrew J. Bacevich takes Sheehan's argument about the relation of the American military to the civilian state still further. He decries what he sees as the ascendant power of the military in national security decision making, what he calls "inside the Beltway" civil-military relations. Turning to the "beyond the Beltway" dimensions of the subject, he revisits the long-running debate about the political implications of force configuration among military intellectuals and policy makers from Emery Upton and Elihu Root in the early twentieth century to John McCauley Palmer and George C. Marshall in the World War II and Cold War eras. He asks how the tradition of the citizen-soldier or its functional equivalent might somehow be restored, as a way of buttressing civilian engagement with the military and underwriting political accountability for decisions to resort to force.

Retired lieutenant general Karl Eikenberry, also a former U.S. ambassador to Afghanistan, offers some especially trenchant reflections on the current state of civil-military relations. He notes in particular the historically novel paucity of military experience among members of Congress—as well as among the general public—and the consequent emergence of a culture of uncritical deference to the armed forces that threatens the historic foundations of civilian control over military operations. He also raises some unsettling questions about the ways in which "war among the people" has redefined the roles of military officers from managers of violence to nation builders and community organizers, tasks that depart markedly from traditional definitions of the soldier's duties, and for which satisfactory performance metrics remain to be developed.

Charles J. Dunlap Jr. brings to bear his experience as deputy judge advocate general of the United States Air Force, to explicate the Uniform Code of Military Justice and its relation to civil society's jurisprudential norms and practices. He notes that since antiquity, the cardinal purpose of military justice systems has been, quite simply, to enforce discipline. As he puts it: "Unlike its civilian counterpart it is designed to help execute if necessary, the difficult—and melancholy—task of getting human beings to kill, in the name of the state." Yet as in so many other realms, the armed forces feel pressure to adapt to evolving changes in civil society. Military justice officials struggle with efforts to "civilianize" their procedures, rebalancing the demands of fairness and discipline, not least with respect to cases of sexual assault. Dunlap also sheds light on the volatile subject of whether military tribunals or civilian courts are the more appropriate venues for trying terrorism suspects.

Michelle Sandhoff and Mady Wechsler Segal examine yet another issue residing at the intersection of inherited military traditions and broader changes in societal values: the chronically vexed issue of women—and sexual and gender issues more generally—in the military. The advent of the AVF in 1973 coincided with seismic shifts in American culture concerning women's roles and, eventually, matters of sexual identity. Those shifts are still playing out in the twenty-first century, and with special urgency in the historically masculine precincts of the armed forces. From debates over women's combat assignments to the development of Female Engagement Teams in the context of counterinsurgency warfare—as well as the torturous controversy surrounding homosexual service members, apparently resolved by the Obama administration's repeal of the controversial "Don't Ask, Don't Tell" policy—gender issues are nowhere more prominent than in today's armed forces.

Jonathan Shay, a clinical psychiatrist who has written extensively about post-traumatic stress disorder (PTSD), concludes this volume with reflections on war's aftermath for the men and women who wage it, and the wounds, physical and psychological, it has inflicted on them. Distinguishing between "primary" and "secondary" physical wounds, he points out that most battle deaths have historically resulted from the latter—from infection and exsanguination, for example—and that modern battlefield medicine has sharply reduced the incidence of secondary effects. He explores the implications of those improved battlefield medicine techniques that have, in effect, substituted long-term disability for mortality for tens of thousands of service people. (By some estimates, if the armed forces had practiced Vietnam-era battle medicine procedures in Iraq, the U.S. military death toll would have been well over 20,000, rather than the 4,486 dead counted by mid-2012.) He then draws a parallel with psychological trauma, arguing that the secondary, or post-battle, effects of what he terms "moral wounds" are less well understood and currently receive inadequate attention from the military and the medical profession.

Taken together, the chapters in this volume paint a comprehensive portrait of the American armed forces today. They raise several urgent questions, which may be summarized as matters of military efficiency, political accountability, and social equity. Does the United States have a well-articulated national security doctrine that is relevant to the challenges ahead, and are the armed forces properly configured for those challenges? Are the mechanisms that throughout American history have ensured civilian control of the military, and held civilian leaders properly accountable for the decision to shoulder arms, still operating properly? Does the recruitment of today's force honor American notions of fairness and shared obligations? Perhaps most important, how faithful are we to Cicero's ancient dictum that arms are of little value in the field unless there is wise counsel at home? On the answers to those questions hang not only the security of the Republic but its political and moral health as well.

1 :: The Counterrevolution in Strategic Affairs

Lawrence Freedman

Abstract: Claims from the 1990s about a revolution or transformation in military affairs are assessed in light of the experience of the 2000s in Iraq and Afghanistan. The importance of considering political as well as military affairs is stressed. Though the United States developed evident predominance in capabilities for regular war, it was caught out when drawn into irregular forms of warfare, such as terrorism and insurgency. The United States significantly improved its counterinsurgency capabilities. It does not follow, however, that the United States will now engage more in irregular conflicts. Indeed, the military circumstances of the past decade were in many ways unique and led to an exaggeration of the strategic value of irregular forms and the need for the United States to respond. Meanwhile, the political legacy of the experience is likely to be a more limited engagement with the problems associated with "failed" and "rogue" states.

War, as Carl von Clausewitz reminds us, is governed by politics, which provides its purpose, passion, and accounting. Yet politics is often treated in military theory as an awkward exogenous factor, at best a necessary inconvenience and at worst a source of weakness and constraint—a disruptive influence interfering with the proper conduct of war. This outlook has featured prominently in American military thought. There has long been a clear preference, reflected in force structure and doctrine, for big, regular wars against serious great-power competition. With the end of the Cold War, this preference came under pressure. The United States had no obvious "peer competitor," and many in the military apparently felt that the sort of operations coming into vogue—tellingly described as "operations other than war"—were beneath them. There was an evident lack of enthusiasm as the United States was drawn into the series of conflicts connected with the breakup of the former Yugoslavia, culminating in the 1999 campaign against Serbia over Kosovo. The withdrawal from Somalia in 1994, like that from Beirut a decade earlier, was taken as a cautionary tale about the folly of such involvements. In these conflicts, the military could not simply take political direction and then get on with the fighting; rather, it found every move full of political sensitivity and its freedom of action restrained at each turn.

As a symptom of the attitude toward operations of this type, the proposition that shaped high-level thinking in the U.S. defense establishment during the 1990s and into the 2000s disregarded them entirely. The proposition held that a "revolution in military affairs" was under way, involving a step change in the nature of war. It gained sufficient acceptance for the abbreviation RMA to become familiar shorthand for what appeared to be an irreversible trend, an inexorable phenomenon to which all military establishments must respond. Those that mastered the RMA most effectively would have a sure route to victory.

The roots of the revolution were assumed to be technological rather than political. Thus, the United States, which was demonstrably to the fore in the relevant information and communication technologies, would be in the vanguard. Even better, the logic of the revolution anticipated that the conduct of military affairs would be pushed in a direction that most suited the United States: one favoring high-tempo conventional warfare.

These predictions further reinforced the presumption that the United States could maintain its "hyperpower" status for decades to come. The effect was to play down the importance of the political dimension in shaping contemporary conflict. Making sense of what has changed over the past decade, therefore, requires looking not only at the lessons of warfare but also at the changing geopolitical environment. This chapter is concerned with "strategic" rather than purely "military" affairs. First, I consider political changes and, in particular, the shifting relationship between the United States and the states that used to be known collectively as the third world. Next, I address the problems with the RMA and the asymmetrical responses that promotion of the strategy naturally encouraged. As these reactions included forms of irregular warfare, notably terrorism and insurgency over the last ten years, I then explore whether the intervention in Afghanistan set a pattern for the future in terms of both its objective and its conduct. (The specific origins of the Iraq intervention render that conflict almost sui generis, although the conduct there reinforces the lessons of Afghanistan.) I argue that, on balance, Afghanistan does not set a precedent. Combined with the political changes discussed in the first section of the chapter, the situation in Afghanistan suggests a much more limited engagement with the problems associated with "failed" and "rogue" states. I conclude by considering whether the United States will now refocus on big wars between great powers as a result of the rebalancing of American strategy, prompted by the combination of budget cuts, the prospective conclusion of operations in Afghanistan, and concern about China's growing military balance.

The term "third world" was coined in France in the early 1950s to describe countries that were economically underdeveloped, politically unaligned, and therefore at a distance from the liberal capitalist first world and the state socialist second world. The long-forgotten inspirational model for the term was the "third estate" of French commoners, who eventually, in 1789, revolted against the first and second estates of priests and nobles. The term therefore captured an idea of a coherent group, a coalition of the disadvantaged, that might one day overthrow the established order. It came to include many states that gained independence as a result of post–World War II decolonization. The sheer diversity in shape, size, and status of this group prevented member states from ever coming together as a coherent whole (or geopolitical force). Moreover, while many such states affirmed the principle of nonalignment, joining the "non-aligned movement" founded in 1961, they did so largely as a means of keeping their options open. In practice, they often seemed to lean toward one bloc or the other, typically in return for arms sales and diplomatic support.

Both Washington and Moscow assumed that the newly independent states would need to make their ideological choices, for either liberal capitalism or state socialism, and that their political allegiances would follow. In a number of cases, the superpowers were drawn into civil wars on the assumption (often mistaken) that the local contest had real links with their global ideological confrontation. The shifting allegiances in the Horn of Africa in the 1970s and 1980s, as Ethiopia and Somalia swapped camps, illustrate the point.

Even before the end of the Cold War, it had become apparent that while conflicts in the third world might be reshaped as a result of superpower interference, they were ignited by distinctive local factors. Ideological affinity did not seem to produce political harmony. In Asia, shared Marxism-Leninism did not prevent the Soviet Union, China, Cambodia, and Vietnam from clashing with each other. Moreover, the general appeal of state socialism declined as a result of its evident failure in the Soviet bloc. A number of the former leaders of the nonaligned camp that had once exhibited socialist inclinations—such as Indonesia and Egypt—ultimately moved into the Western camp, though they were not exactly liberal in their internal practices. After the implosion of European communism, a general continental realignment formed on the basis of the core Western institutions of NATO and the EU.

This was the moment when liberal capitalism peaked. As an ideology, liberalism had always contained many strands and was often contradictory, yet its core themes—with regard to free markets and human rights—had been continually influential for more than two centuries. The collapse of state socialism meant that capitalism emerged from the Cold War a clear winner. In this narrative, the West's victory was not simply a matter of deterrence and political cohesion but also a result of intellectual vitality and entrepreneurial drive. After the Cold War, liberal capitalism was promoted as the model to emulate if states wanted to get ahead in a globalized world. The idea of "globalization" stressed the breaking down of boundaries, particularly with regard to capital, goods, and services, but also ideas and people.

For a while this vision suggested that under the influence of free markets, countries around the word—including former adversaries—would adopt first the economic and then the political forms of liberal capitalism. The embrace of democracy was considered particularly important, not only because it meant that a larger proportion of the world's population would enjoy political rights, but also because of the assumption that democracies do not fight one another. Those with regimes resistant to this path, and likely to pose threats to their neighbors, were described as "rogue." Iraq, Iran, and North Korea fell into this category. Those unable to cope, often because they were torn apart by internal violence, such as Somalia, Congo, and Yugoslavia, were described as "failing." It was always likely that many states would go their own way, rather than follow a liberal democratic model, without becoming evidently roguish or failing. The main problem was the uncertain relationship between relatively free economies, with active participation in global trade and financial markets, and relatively free polities, with support for human rights and democratic elections. As the example of China vividly illustrates, it is possible, at least for a substantial period of time, to combine a strong capitalist ethos with an authoritarian political system. Even governments responsive to public opinion and subject to democratic accountability would not always wish to align themselves with the United States, especially as the American brand became more toxic during the 2000s. Liberalism, capitalism, and alignment with the United States turned out not to be inextricably linked. Furthermore, the particular capitalist model practiced by the West suffered a loss of credibility as a result of the financial crisis that began in 2008. As a more practical consequence, the crisis ushered in a more austere age, thereby reducing the appetite for expensive military interventions and possibly causing greater reluctance in the provision of economic assistance.

The U.S. appetite for military operations and foreign economic aid was already declining as a result of the cost and disappointing results of the interventions of the past two decades. Humanitarian intervention developed as a response to failing states, providing a methodology for the assertion of liberal values in areas marked by severe strife. Bosnia, Kosovo, and Sierra Leone were cited as evidence of how harm could be mitigated by timely intervention; Rwanda was the prime example of the consequences of abandoning a country in crisis. Intervention on humanitarian grounds implied a direct challenge to the post-Westphalian norms of international behavior by threatening to subvert sovereignty through the expressed readiness to interfere in the internal affairs of others. Challenges to sovereignty were always controversial, especially with states, including Russia and China, that wanted no interference in their more dissident and troublesome regions.

Humanitarian interventions also generated long-term and expensive responsibilities to those places where intervention took place. Initially, the action might have been prompted by evidence of acute but short-term humanitarian distress, but once engaged, the intervenors felt obliged to undertake wholesale reconstruction of the target countries by setting them on the road to democracy. The same impulse was evident in Iraq and Afghanistan. But as the United States became bogged down in Iraq, it let its own liberal standards drop in the conduct of interrogations and counterinsurgency operations. At the same time it demonstrated an inability to reshape local political structures according to its own preferences. Unless a functioning democracy was created, it was argued, there could be no guarantee that the conditions that created the problem in the first place would not recur. Why costly military exertions should be used to reestablish an authoritarian regime was hard to explain. The only way out was to work with the local political grain, which was not necessarily a natural support for the practices and norms on which liberal democracy depends and which would be under additional strain as a result of the internal violence that had prompted the intervention. On the one hand, walking away from a country still in recovery would have been difficult; on the other, an extended stay risked creating a local dependency culture and increasing resistance and hostility toward the United States and its allies.

This shifting political context moved U.S. military strategy a long way from the promise of the RMA. At the start of the 2000s, hope had been very much alive. Secretary of Defense Donald Rumsfeld's "transformation" agenda was intended to demonstrate the potential of forces that were high on quality and relatively low on quantity. Iraq, at least in its first stage, was taken as proof of those precepts. This new "dominant" form of combat involved moving with greater speed and precision, and over longer ranges, than was possible for the enemy; disorienting as much as destroying; attacking only what was necessary; and avoiding unnecessary collateral damage to civilian life and property. In the more enthusiastic versions, the prospect was to lift the fog of war. On land, where the fog was always the greatest, the RMA promised to dispel the inherent confusion caused by fighting in and around uneven terrain—woods, rivers, towns, and cities—day and night, in all weather, with the location of friends as much a mystery as that of enemies.

This form of warfare suited the United States because it played to U.S. strengths: it could be capital rather than labor intensive; it reflected a preference for outsmarting opponents; it avoided excessive casualties both received and inflicted; and it conveyed an aura of almost effortless superiority.

Those ideas were deeply comforting, and not entirely wrong. Information and communication technologies were bound to make a difference in military practice. Perhaps the RMA agenda understated the extent to which American predominance was dependent on not only the sophistication of its technology but also the sheer amount of firepower—particularly air-delivered—it had at its disposal. Nonetheless, the formidable cumulative impact was impressive. Furthermore, while the United States' evident military superiority in a particular type of war was likely to encourage others to fight in different ways, that military capacity would also constrain opponents' ambitions. As a regular conventional war against the United States appeared to be an increasingly foolish proposition, especially after the convincing U.S. performance in the 1991 Persian Gulf War, one form of potential challenge to American predominance was removed, just as the prospect of mutual assured destruction (MAD) had earlier removed nuclear war as a serious policy option.

But there was an important difference. With MAD, everybody would lose once nuclear exchanges began, which meant that, in principle, the side stronger in conventional forces could incur an advantage. The Warsaw Pact countries were believed to be in this position during the Cold War, thus putting the onus on NATO to escalate to nuclear use if its members were losing the battle. Once the NATO countries gained conventional superiority, deterrence was complete—at least against other great powers. If an aspirant superpower could in no way expect to fight and win (in any meaningful sense) a massive conflict along the lines of the two world wars, then not only was America's position more secure, but the risk of another catastrophic global conflagration was diminished. As with nuclear forces (whose midcentury arrival had also been described at the time as a "revolution in military affairs"), the RMA agenda required maintaining substantial conventional forces designed for a form of conflict that the very existence of those forces rendered unlikely. The challenge was to explain the need to pay for expensive forces that might never be used.

Yet the RMA model was deeply flawed. Far from representing a real revolution in military affairs, it harked back to an earlier, idealized prototype of modern warfare in which a decisive military victory could settle the fate of nations and, indeed, of whole civilizations. Once its forces have been defeated, an enemy government will have no choice but to hand over sovereignty to the victor. If war is accepted as the arbiter, politicians can set objectives and hold the commanders accountable, but the military must be allowed to conduct the campaign according to its professional judgment with a minimum role for civilians—preferably not as victims and certainly not as strategists. Under the most idealized version of this model, the victory comes quickly. The longer the war drags on, the more uncertain the situation becomes, as both sides increasingly depend on the performance of allies; the test becomes one of social and economic endurance more than military skill; morale suffers; and politicians become impatient. Thus, for military innovators, the acme of success is a new route to a swift and politically decisive military victory. This was the claim made for the RMA.

However, the lack of a political context was problematic. The new doctrine fixed on trends in military capabilities and neglected the types of conflict that might need to be addressed through force of arms. It recognized that armed force could have a range of purposes other than regular war but tended to set these possibilities to one side, imagining such cases either would be smaller in scale and easily supported by capabilities designed for regular war or would involve goals that could be picked up by lesser powers, such as peacekeeping duties.

A further problem was the assumption that because the new technologies fitted so well with American strategic preferences, they would not serve different and opposed objectives. This issue only became apparent when these capabilities were viewed not only as means to win a regular battle but also a way of defining the boundaries between the civilian and military spheres.

High-quality surveillance and intelligence communications and navigation became widely available, as consumer gadgets could be exploited by otherwise crude, small organizations with limited budgets. Precision intelligence, instantaneously communicated and combined with precision guidance, made it possible to concentrate fire accurately on solely military targets in order to cause maximum disruption to the enemy military effort. But it did not mandate such attacks. It could support concepts less dependent on discriminate targeting. Indeed, cruder versions of these same systems that made it possible to limit damage to civil society could also be used to ensure that attacks on civil society were more effective. Even in the American model there were always dual-use facilities that served both military and civilian purposes—for example, power and transportation. They might be targeted as part of a military purpose but still led to the disruption of civilian life.

By the end of the 1990s, the challenge to the RMA was recognized to lie in what was described as "asymmetrical warfare." Enemies would refuse to fight on America's terms, attempting to turn warfare toward civil society rather than away. The approach most feared was the direct targeting of large population centers with chemical, biological, or nuclear weapons (of which nuclear are in a category all their own, although they are lumped together with other weapons of mass destruction, or WMD). The approach that was actually largely followed was to adopt the various forms of irregular warfare: that is, to rely on the support of a section of the civilian population as well as on guerrilla and terrorist tactics. A degree of overlap between the two approaches manifested itself when terrorists found ways of causing mass casualties, particularly using vulnerabilities in transport. The 9/11 attacks, the most spectacular example of this type of warfare, raised the specter of terrorist access to WMD, perhaps aided by "rogue" states. The event significantly affected U.S. priorities in the subsequent decade, shaping the two main U.S. military operations in Afghanistan and Iraq.

In both these operations, enemy regular forces were unable to offer much resistance to U.S. strength. (The Taliban was already battling the Northern Alliance, and U.S. airpower and special forces tipped the balance.) Both conventional campaigns could be considered a vindication of RMA-type concepts in that quality defeated quantity with remarkable speed. Thereafter, however, the United States was stuck dealing with resourceful and determined irregular opponents while it desperately sought to construct sustainable indigenous state structures and forces. The experience underlined the danger of operating against the local political grain.

To say that, during the course of the 2000s, the United States mastered counterinsurgency operations would be an overstatement, yet after the severe initial setbacks in Iraq, the United States adapted. The group associated with General David Petraeus took some of the technologies associated with the RMA, accepted that numbers still made a difference, and then brought in a more streetwise grasp of the political circumstances in which the military was operating. The strategy emphasized that military actions must be evaluated by reference to their political effects, not simply by traditional metrics geared toward eliminating enemy forces, and stressed the importance of reinforcing these effects through what are now called "information operations." This approach has required not only tenacity but also a commitment of resources and a tolerance of casualties that would have been considered excessive, even prohibitive, as the campaigns were first planned in the aftermath of 9/11. The experience has demonstrated how much worse it is to lose a fight than to walk away from a fight before it has begun. Doctrine and tactics have been changed to deal with novel, and in some respects unique, situations. The enemy might not win in either Afghanistan or Iraq in the sense of not being able to seize the state. But it is also true that in neither case could it be said that the United States clearly achieved its objectives. Both countries remained unstable and suffered very high costs in lives and depressed social and economic development. In both cases their long-term political prospects were unclear, although with one naturally centralized and oil-rich and the other fragmented and poor, their circumstances were very different. In their own ways, both provided telling reminders that defeating insurgencies depended on the quality of government as much as, if not more than, military technique.

Can we assume that recent military engagements will set the pattern for the future? The military history of the 2000s was nothing like that of the 1990s, which in turn was quite different from the 1980s. Why should we expect to be able to predict the 2010s? Indeed, this decade began with a reluctant intervention in Libya. The combination of high ambition and self-imposed restraints that characterized the Libyan engagement was unlike any that had come before.

The main continuity in the post–Cold War period, in addition to the reduced risk of a great-power confrontation, was a shift of focus from preparing to deal with challenges from strong states to engaging with weak and failed states, at first under the guise of peacekeeping and humanitarian intervention and then under the capacious umbrella of the "war on terror."

Unlike the large-scale great-power wars of the past, in which the stakes were clear and the consequences of defeat grim, involving the mobilization of whole societies and international alliances, the strategic imperatives behind the operations of the past two decades were more controversial. The reason, however, was not the level of casualties. Those who fought were largely volunteer regulars. Losses did not approach the industrial scale of the great wars, though in some respects that difference made individual sacrifices more personal and poignant. Politically, the main issue was whether these lives were being sacrificed to any good purpose. Questions were constantly asked about why and how a war was being fought and the probability of success.

An attempt was made, notably by the George W. Bush administration, to distinguish the "wars of choice" of the 1990s from the "wars of necessity" of the 2000s. This distinction, for which I take some responsibility, was misleading. There was always a choice, even if it was a terrible one. Undoubtedly different was how the stakes were perceived. The term "war of necessity" implied the presence of an existential security threat, the handling of which would determine a state's future position. In these cases, indifference was not an option. But with the humanitarian interventions of the 1990s, the choice was first about whether to pay attention, and only then to decide what to do. If the issues that might have prompted, and in some cases did prompt, these interventions were ignored, the consequences for those directly involved might have been dire, but others could have carried on as before. Indifference was an option.

In that context, it was difficult both before and after 9/11 to measure the threat posed by Al Qaeda. The rhetoric of leaders such as Osama bin Laden was extravagant in its incitement to violence, yet their followers had only occasional successes. They made an appeal to an underlying ideology that ran deep and wide in certain countries but was patchy in others. The resulting violence was largely localized and sporadic.

For the moment, at least, the spectacular attacks on the World Trade Center and the Pentagon remain unique. At the same time, the insurgencies in both Iraq and Afghanistan, and countries where the United States and its allies have not made the same military commitments, were persistent, intensive, and troublesome. Strategy became preoccupied with issues such as the relationship between military technique and political legitimacy, the radicalization of populations, the management of intercommunal violence, governance and corruption, and the role of international opinion.

The belief that a period had been entered when conflicts would be dominated by irregular forms of warfare encouraged talk of a "fourth generation of warfare." This notion suffered from a historicist fallacy similar to the one affecting the RMA concept: namely, that forms of warfare pass through a natural progression. The difference is that the rhetoric behind the RMA was buoyed by a technological optimism, while the gloom surrounding the notion of the fourth generation reflects cultural and political pessimism. Irregular warfare, however, is hardly a novel phenomenon. It was used in the fight against colonialism to circumvent the evident superiority of the metropolitan states in military organization and firepower. During the course of major regular wars, there were often irregular elements. The two forms are not exclusive and can coexist. One of the textbooks of irregular warfare, Lawrence of Arabia's *Seven Pillars of Wisdom*, was based on his role in Arab harassment of Turkish forces during World War I. In World War II, German forces in Europe had to defend their territorial gains from irregular partisan attacks as well as from regular Allied forces. Regular war supposes that political disputes can be settled through battle with a military surrender followed by a transfer of sovereignty. But if a sufficient portion of a population refuses to accept the result, popular militias, along with other forms of resistance, may challenge the apparent victor. At this stage, the conflict is no longer a regular war. One such popular uprising occurred in France after the 1871 war with Prussia, eventually leading to the Paris Commune. It also happened in 2001 in Afghanistan and in 2003 in Iraq.

Regular warfare is perceived to be in decline. This view can be attributed to the likely destructiveness of war between great powers, especially those armed with nuclear weapons; a consequential readiness to solve great-power disputes by means other than war; and the superiority of Western states in the conduct of regular war. The increased focus on irregular war emerged from the apparent invincibility of U.S. forces, with or without their allies, in conventional battle. To the extent that states, not necessarily great powers, remain ready to resolve disputes through force of arms, regular war remains a possibility, as Egypt and Israel, and India and Pakistan, have shown over the years. For the moment, these particular conflicts are being carried out largely through irregular means, although Israel and India have indicated they are prepared to use regular forces if irregular attacks are pushed too far. The 2011 conflict in Libya saw regular forces taking on a cobbled-together militia that could survive only with support from NATO airpower.

Future regular wars that do not involve the United States and its allies directly are possible, even if they take on a cataclysmic form (for example, a confrontation between China and India or China and Japan).

For the United States, the issue is not the war the country is most likely to fight but the war for which its military should prepare. Preparedness is a form of deterrence; it should mean that the war does not have to be fought, which inevitably leaves open the question of whether the expenditure and effort were necessary in the first place. This is especially the case because a defensive preparedness must involve a substantial capability for major war. Thankfully, America's strength is only one of a number of reasons why such a war remains highly unlikely. Regardless, we can assume that the ability to fight and prevail in a war with another great power will continue to be the top priority for U.S. defense.

The key question is whether the United States will feel a need to maintain a substantial capacity to fight an irregular war. Over the past few years it has added a much more sophisticated counterinsurgency capability to its repertoire. In the 1970s, the U.S. Army considered Vietnam to be exactly the sort of war it never wished to fight again; thus it turned away from counterinsurgency in order to concentrate on its core task of preparing for great-power conflict, at that time against the Warsaw Pact in the center of Europe. In this setting, the RMA emerged: indeed, the embrace of the relevant technologies can be traced back to the rediscovery of maneuver warfare and the Army's adoption of "air-land battle" as core doctrine.

As Iraq and Afghanistan became more demanding in the 2000s, this comfort zone was no longer so available. A growing sense of a global conflict against a resourceful and ideologically driven opponent suggested another pattern. The messy, prolonged fights in which the United States was directly involved, as well as those in which the United States had an interest, if a less central role—such as Pakistan, Yemen, Somalia, Lebanon, Gaza, and Mali—appeared to be part of the picture. Instead of an occasional decisive campaign to ward off a challenge from an aspirant great power, the future would likely be marked by a succession of struggles against Islamist opponents operating in and out of broken, weak states. In most cases where states facing a serious Islamist threat looked to the United States for help, support took the form of intelligence and training as well as specific capabilities such as special forces and unmanned aerial vehicles. Indeed "drone warfare" emerged as the preferred response to the threat posed by militant enclaves. It raised important legal and moral issues related to sovereignty, and led to claims that accumulating numbers of innocent deaths accentuated anti-American feeling, which in turn could result in the multiplication of militants. From the administration's point of view, however, it offered a means of maintaining the pressures on terrorists without putting U.S. troops at risk.

Iraq, to say the least, was hardly an inevitable response to 9/11. The intervention in Afghanistan had a greater logic in that regard. Al Qaeda, residing brazenly in Afghanistan, could be targeted by means of a reasonably regular military campaign. An available conventional response was an unusual feature of this case, but it encouraged the perception of the utility of conventional military force in the "war on terror." However seriously we take the Islamist threat, it is important to emphasize that this response was the exception rather than the norm.

Irregular forms of warfare are favored by underdogs who know that they have little chance against superior conventional forces. By itself, irregular warfare cannot lead to a decisive victory. Some, of course, may acknowledge this point while insisting that it is irrelevant. The objectives of irregulars may be no more than to express anger, exact retribution, or promote a particular cause, such as animal rights. If, however, the objective involves an attempt to liberate some territory or seize political control, then at some point a direct challenge to other regular or militia-type forces will be required, possibly leading to open battle rather than to raids, harassment, and ambushes.

This scenario might come about as follows: persistent attacks try the patience and resilience of the ruling elite and its external supporters; their authority and confidence are undermined while an audience is created for a rival political creed; and eventually, there is sufficient support to topple the regime and put a new, popular government in its place. The crucial moment arrives when the irregulars gain recruits and support, and the enemy suffers from desertion and popular disaffection. As the balance of power shifts, the irregulars will be able to act in a more regular fashion.

This aspiration was explicit in Asian guerrilla theory, including in the campaigns of Mao in China or Giap in Vietnam. Irregular warfare—for example, in the form of guerrilla tactics—was not a preferred way of fighting: it was for want of something better. By itself, it could not produce victory, because it did not allow power to be wrested directly from the state. At some point, even if only during the endgame, the irregulars had to gain the strength to ensure a decisive victory over the state or, if the enemy collapsed, assert their authority as the armed forces of a state-in-waiting. In this way, Fidel Castro and his hitherto ragged bunch of guerrilla fighters marked their victory over the regular forces of Batista in Cuba in January 1959. Once state power is seized, even if relatively little effort is required, it must be secured against internal and external enemies. Defending state rule requires organizational and operational forms quite different from those required to wage guerrilla war, let alone mount random acts of terror.

Regardless of how successful they have been in mounting individual attacks and embarrassing enemies, irregular campaigns rarely lead to power. For example, even if successive terroristic attacks on U.S. targets persuaded the United States to disengage entirely from the Middle East, the responsible group would still be left fighting local opponents and rivals for actual power. Note what happened in Afghanistan after the Soviet Union withdrew. In this respect, the Libyan conflict was almost back-to-front. An anti-Gaddafi mass movement developed quickly, asserted itself in the capital, Tripoli, and soon seized other population centers—notably, the eastern city of Benghazi. Using superior firepower, crudely applied, the regime was able to regain control of Tripoli and would then have rolled up the rebels had it not been for the UN-authorized intervention. Ironically, it was the beleaguered regime claiming that the rebels were really Islamist terrorists masquerading as democrats, while NATO countries accepted the rebels more or less at face value, as a loose and largely uncoordinated collection of anti-regime elements. In the end a combination of Gaddafi's weak base and the superior, NATO-provided firepower available to the rebels made the difference.

The point here is that the great dramas of regime change differ significantly; further, they often involve substantial armed components as well as terrorist plots. It is not that every two-bit terror group must imagine itself as a great army-in-waiting, although many do. For most, the first priority is survival, perhaps through advertising their presence with a conspicuous act, which may be geared to recruitment and fund-raising as much as to the pursuit of long-term political objectives. They may have intense and contentious debates about long-term strategy—indeed, some do little else—but these are often exercises in futility. Nonetheless, even small and simple groups try to present themselves as regular forces in development, distinct from a political wing yet with military-type command structures and designations.

This is why it was unusual to be able to respond to Al Qaeda in 2001 by means of a regular operation. In general, terrorism is the most primitive form of irregular warfare. It might be defined as succeeding if the *only* intention is to cause hurt; if there is a wider political intention, the effort normally fails. Al Qaeda's Afghan base made it unusual for terrorist groups because it was not operating against the host state and, in fact, was afforded a degree of state protection as it mounted attacks elsewhere. When terrorist groups operate within hostile societies, the best option is to consider them to be criminals: that is, offenders to be dealt with through the methods of law enforcement, such as domestic intelligence, the police, and the judiciary. Terrorists involved in robbery, extortion, and even kidnapping to obtain finance may fit this description literally. Defining them in this way has benefits in terms of propaganda as well as in the choice of countermeasures. It is also likely to be appropriate as long as the terrorists consist of small cells of militants hiding within the host population. The most basic counterterrorist work in the West, therefore, involves intelligence gathering, arrests, and protecting key targets. If these groups reach the point where they are best dealt with by military means, then they have outgrown the terrorist label and have become something altogether more serious.

Groups with the size and persistence to challenge state power are usually described in terms of *resistance* or *insurgency*. Here, the intent is less to attack civil society than to use civil society as a base from which to attack the regular forces of the enemy, either demonstrating the weakness of the state or inviting the state to reveal its oppressive nature. Terrorist acts may play a role in such campaigns as part of a more integrated strategy involving various types of operations. Strategic *resistance*, which is essentially defensive, refers to the methods used to prevent an occupying force from establishing itself; a strategic *insurgency*, which is essentially offensive, refers to the methods used to expel a purportedly illegitimate force from a defined territory.

At either level, the attitude of the local population is crucial. Success for a resistance movement typically depends on a supportive population. The task for an insurgency is to create support where, at the outset, it is scarce. To do so, the insurgents must find a point of political contact with the target community. Support leads to sanctuaries, supply lines, recruits, and intelligence, without which either type of warfare risks defeat and suffers from a constant fear of informers and a lack of supplies and new recruits.

Relations with the community may be forged on the basis of a shared patriotism or kinship, but they may also be based on intimidation and fear—for example, the consequences of known collaboration with the enemy, or the expectation that even when the insurgents disappear, they may return ready for revenge if they ever feel betrayed.

As with any type of warfare, successful terrorism depends on strong and intelligent leadership and internal discipline and organization. The clandestine circumstances in which terrorists operate make these qualities much harder to achieve than in other forms of warfare. In practice, terrorism tends to rely on barely coordinated and fragmented attacks by independent cells. It risks alienating likely sources of support without denting state power. These groups, in part because of their radical, ideological nature, are often prone to fragmentation and intense arguments about political narratives, strategy, and tactics. Organizational survival may lead to operations undertaken to demonstrate leadership of the struggle and maintain activist morale as much as to hurt the enemy. There is always the potential for internecine warfare, as different groups vie with each other to control a struggle to which they all are notionally committed.

If a terrorist group makes progress, it does so by creating an aura of irresistibility, suggesting the state's inability to cope. This process generally depends on regular, incessant attacks. Regularity may be more important than scale, because the aim is to demonstrate an ability to operate at will—to outsmart the authorities at every turn—which is possible only with a degree of popular support. In this regard, terrorism as a strategy can be defined by its objective to create the conditions for resistance or insurgency. By extension, the objective of resistance or insurgency is to create the conditions for regular war. And regular warfare, in turn, seeks to create the conditions for a transfer of sovereignty.

The basic requirement for countering opponents who adopt irregular warfare is to take the progression described above and push it in the other direction: that is, force the enemy to take the backward step from an insurgency to terrorism. This task entails denying the credibility of irregulars' claims to be acting on behalf of whole communities. Front-line countering forces must ensure they are recognizably local and can play the patriotic card as effectively as the enemy. Further, they must acquire critical intelligence in order to identify and isolate the militants from their potential sources of support. These measures take time and put a premium on patience. They require sensitivity to grievances and fears and attention to culture and anthropology as much as technology and tactics. Their boundaries are blurred; there is no confined military space and time to be set apart from civilian space and time. On the one hand, heavy-handed tactics may confirm enemy propaganda and help the adversary gain recruits; on the other, an overly light touch might allow opponents to establish unencumbered their political authority—as in no-go areas where state forces dare not enter and where a parallel government may be established.

To fight an irregular war outside one's own territory is inherently difficult. Indeed, foreign armies can soon appear as an alien force of occupation. This perception will grow if they adopt harsh methods. Compared with colonial times, overt coercion of civilians is now out of bounds. Damage to civilian infrastructure or civilian casualties that result from attacks on military-related targets are explained as unintended and regrettable "collateral damage"; such consequences are not justified as a means of persuading the enemy to give up. When an enemy is engaged in irregular methods, however, following the precepts of regular warfare in distinguishing at all times between combatants and noncombatants becomes difficult. An enemy militant may well look like an innocent civilian. Frightened soldiers are apt to take few risks when they fear attack. For them, it can be frustrating to be forbidden to chase enemy fighters into their towns and villages, or to allow open supply lines to avoid creating a sense of civilian siege.

The need to win over "hearts and minds" is a frequent theme in discussions of strategies for irregular wars. It is referred to whenever tough methods used by one's own side are questioned and whenever there is a need to convince people, through good works and sensitivity to their concerns, that the government and the security forces really are on their side. The term captures the idea of wars being won in the cognitive (intellectual and emotional) rather than the physical domain. Practices that diminish support are not hard to discern: arbitrary arrests, displays of brute force, rudeness, and disrespectful behavior are likely to generate alienation and hostility. Winning support is harder: the real concerns and grievances of the local people must be addressed, even if attending to this task means upsetting local power structures. In part, it may be a matter of civic action—repairing roads and building schools, or securing power and sanitation infrastructures—but at some point, issues of official repression, land reform, or ethnic mix may become germane.

There is a chicken-and-egg problem. These strategies can be too dangerous to follow without local security, but until local security is established, they cannot be followed. Without security, foreign troops and local people will be unable to interact closely and develop mutual trust. Security is not just a matter of immediate safety. It also requires looking forward to assess the likely future power structure that will emerge as the conflict develops. As the irregulars and the counter-irregulars compete for local support, impressions of strength may be as important as those of kindness and concern. Support is as likely to be based on convincing people that you will win as it is on promises of future goods and services.

Thus, unlike regular warfare, irregular conflicts are unlikely to turn on having the most advanced technology or overwhelming force. In these conflicts, politics does far more than set the terms for the fight: it infuses every move. Incentives for authorities typically point toward minimizing the fighting and appearing not to rely on shows of force. The military role may therefore be quite limited; key tasks are instead in the hands of intelligence agencies, the police, and even political leaders and intellectuals who frame and describe the core issues at the heart of the struggle. The challenge for external forces intervening in such struggles, especially if their role is prominent, is not only to win local support but also to retain the public's favor back home. In both respects, a military strategy must be integrated with a political one.

This judgment does not change in the two most difficult scenarios. In the first, groups are able to develop forms of unconventional attack that could rock the foundations of society. The main concern in this category has been the possibility of chemical, biological, radiological, and—most frightening but least likely—nuclear weapons campaigns. Alternatively, irregulars might be able to attack the information networks that sustain core infrastructure. Other than in the particular case where terrorists are acting as agents of, or with substantial support from, another state, these threats are still best addressed through intelligence agencies and the police. There may be specialized military capabilities of potential value: intelligence support, specialist sensors, and the forms of assistance that may be required after any catastrophic incident. The military tends to play a role in the aftermath of any disaster because it can offer fit and disciplined troops as well as organizational capacity, including managing logistical problems, gathering information, and maintaining complex communication networks over time and in adverse conditions.

In the second difficult scenario, which is already common, a weak state that is unable to cope with a developing challenge requests support. There may be good reasons for its weakness. Supposed counterterrorism operations may just be part of an attempt to impose political order from the center, as a rationale for wider repression. Given that the parallel political processes necessary for a "hearts and minds" approach may be absent, there is little prospect that grievances will be addressed. The police may be unable to cope, or, if they are corrupt, incompetent, sectarian in nature, or distrusted by the target population, they may be part of the problem. If the supported regime is weak for these reasons, the situation is unlikely to be improved by the insertion of large numbers of foreign forces. The commitments in Iraq and Afghanistan were the result of the direct role the United States played in toppling the previous regime and its responsibility for what followed. Without that responsibility, the more likely inclination will be to limit liabilities and confine support to specialist capabilities.

Attitudes toward the use of force after the Cold War have been shaped from the start by Iraq. When Iraq invaded Kuwait in August 1990, the crudity of the aggression and the importance of the region led to a strong collective response. Desert Storm was a regular war as Kuwait was liberated by battle; but the vicious repression that followed the postwar insurrection led coalition forces to set up safe havens for the Kurds in northern Iraq. This engagement set the precedent for subsequent humanitarian interventions. As Saddam Hussein played games with UN inspectors, the United States used coercive means to force him back into line. Those efforts culminated in the December 1998 air strikes of Desert Fox. Frustration at the leader's continued defiance and survival led to the 2003 invasion, illustrating just how strong the United States is when fighting on its own terms. The subsequent irregular warfare, however, demonstrated just how difficult it finds fighting on another's terms.

Recent experience has illustrated both the potential and the limitations of irregular forms of fighting, from terrorism to insurgency. Unconventional methods can create contests of endurance, especially for external powers trying to assert control in places where they are not entirely welcome and where their strategic interests are uncertain. This scenario creates a paradox. In conventional warfare, the United States and its allies are unbeatable against countries lacking advanced military capabilities. At the same time, all powers struggle when facing resistance from a population, or from segments of that population. In the end, the United States and its allies can avoid defeat because such a loss would require irregular forces to undergo transformation into a regular force capable of seizing power. To win, however, the United States itself depends on the regimes it supports, or in the anomalous case of Libya, the rebels it supports, who lacked the wherewithal to take on the enemy effectively on the ground. There is no reason to doubt that Western forces would have faced far less difficulty in taking out pro-Gaddafi forces, but even the anti-Gaddafi forces, in addition to the relevant Western governments, felt that such a response would send the wrong political messages.

This analysis suggests four propositions. The first, to be blunt, is that after two decades of high-tempo and controversial operations, absent any further 9/11-type shocks, the United States will be increasingly wary about entering into any more long-term commitments involving direct combat. In Libya the Obama administration was prepared to accept the risks of an inconclusive outcome, and it framed U.S. involvement as participation in a coalition led from elsewhere, rather than as taking responsibility for another major operation.

The second proposition is that there are inherent limitations on what can be achieved through external intervention. It can have an important negative role in preventing humanitarian tragedies, but any positive role of economic, social, and political reconstruction depends on being able to work with a local government displaying genuine legitimacy and competence. Foreign powers will be unable to "mend" failed states by themselves, and the best that they can hope for if they try is a prolonged, costly, and frustrating stalemate.

Third, if external powers struggle to get a grip on weak states, then it is even more unrealistic to expect any single country, however large and resourceful, to achieve the sort of "global domination" that features in the excited imaginations of geopolitical dramatists. A new international political configuration has begun to take shape with a number of "emerging" powers making great strides economically, even as established liberal capitalist states have faltered.

These emerging powers are unlikely to coalesce into a new bloc—at least, no more than was ever the case with the "third world." Two of them, India and China, are the most populous countries on earth, and each is wary of the other. India, to some extent, has moved much closer to the West over the past decade, in part because of a shared concern over Islamism. China, which is now asserting itself, is considered a rising superpower and clearly has great economic clout, but it remains hampered by a lack of obvious allies (other than North Korea) and wide ideological appeal. Its foreign policy could be described as realist and mercantilist. Russia, which recovered (largely on the back of energy prices) from the shambles of the 1990s, is sometimes classed with these emergent powers; but its economy is narrowly based, and Moscow has uneasy relations with most of its neighbors.

The problems the United States has faced may help explain why others are wary of trying to compete for full great-power status, although they may well act forcefully around their own borders and, in a number of cases, have already done so. Great-power status implies a responsibility and a right to intervene at a distance from border areas. Any cost-benefit analysis would encourage caution. For this reason, the rising economic powers might turn out to be circumspect when claiming such a position for themselves. Brazil, Russia, India, and China, the supposedly ascendant powers, all voted against UN Resolution 1973, which authorized the Libyan intervention, when the decision came before the Security Council. Indeed, being a great power is severely overrated. The duties and responsibilities associated with the status are as likely to turn candidate great powers away as they are to inspire pursuit of the title. A wiser policy may be less about bossing everyone around and more about helping other peoples sort out their quarrels. The fourth proposition, therefore, is that while the United States is suffering from the financial crisis and the cumulative effects of its more recent interventions, both of which have diminished its standing, it will remain the world's predominant power. The European coalition of countries that acted in Libya still needed vital American "enablers." The United States has security arrangements of one sort or another with some seventy states. With cuts of half a billion dollars and possibly twice that amount in the pipeline, it may soon account for less than a half of world military expenditure, but it still has a considerable margin over countries such as China, especially in combination with allies.

The "rebalancing" in U.S. grand strategy, reflecting confidence in the ability of European states to look after themselves (somewhat belied by the Euro-zone crisis) and the urging of Asian-Pacific states to show more presence in their region to help impose restraint on China, may also be a rebalancing in that it sees a return of the United States back to its comfort zone preparing only for proper wars against other great powers. The hope must be that a higher American profile will have a deterrent effect. The Asian-Pacific region in particular is a part of the world where underlying animosities and tensions between major powers can be severe, and where there are a number of disputed boundaries, mostly at sea rather than on land. Here and elsewhere, if the United States engages with lesser states, it will be to prevent them from acquiring nuclear weapons or harboring militants, and this will be on the basis of economic sanctions and embargoes and direct strikes rather than invasion and occupation. For example, any action against Iran to prevent it from becoming a nuclear power will most likely involve strikes against the offending facilities without any attempt to promote regime change.

The cumulative impact of these conclusions points to a unique situation. For the first time since decolonization, no evident strategic imperatives draw Western countries directly into the affairs of the developing world. Oil continues to make some parts of the world more important to the West than others; it becomes a factor when tensions rise, but not to the extent where supply issues mandate certain forms of intervention. There is a view that scarce resources and other problems aggravated by climate change, such as population movements, may result in much more international conflict. It would certainly be unwise to argue that no larger circumstances exist that would lead to direct military engagement, let alone less-demanding forms of political or technical assistance. Yet for the moment, the incentives for involvement are much weaker than before, a situation that carries risks of a political vacuum.

Another view is that this reluctance to intervene will be all to the good; that past Western actions have inflicted more harm than benefit, stirring up discontent and anti-Western feeling; and that individual countries should take responsibility for their own regional discontents. Even NGOs, which have decades of development experience, are now far more realistic than sentimental, emphasizing long-term capacity building rather than financial subsidies or loans from rich countries. For a variety of reasons having to do with resources, practicality, prudence, and changing attitudes, we may now be entering a period in which international crisis management will become progressively less energetic and more dependent on local attitudes and efforts.

Libya appears as an exception, yet the intervention occurred only because of considerable provocation by a regime whose behavior had already been denounced. Further, a massacre in Benghazi appeared imminent; the Arab League was urging action; and even with strong UN support, numerous provisos were designed to limit the liabilities of the outside actors and ensure that the final struggle was between Libyans. Nothing in this episode suggests a lack of caution. The subsequent pressures to do something similar in Syria, with a compelling case being found as the regime killed large numbers of its own people, came up against the lack of limited options. Any intervention was likely to lead to serious and difficult fighting and long-term commitments. Syria also illustrated the risks of passivity, with the conflict not settling down to a lower level of violence and showing potential for drawing in neighboring states. In Mali, where instability was to some extent a consequence of the turbulence in Libya, the Americans were content for the French to take the initiative.

In the future we can expect more buck-passing, or looking to others to take the lead, only to blame them when things go wrong. In addition, there will be a greater stress on diplomatic efforts to encourage "common sense" among disputants and help mediate settlements. This will replace a readiness to actively knock heads together and impose settlements. In the face of defiance, the priority will be to explore political solutions, and force will be very much a last resort. Major reconstruction efforts will be desultory.

There is already evidence for this shifting outlook. It can be seen in the uncertainties over what to do about North Korea, Iran, and the Israel-Palestine dispute, or the popular uprisings in Iran, Egypt, and Bahrain. It is expressed in the frustration over Afghanistan and the lackluster or belated responses to the tragedies of Sudan, Congo, and the Ivory Coast, as well as of Syria. The Micawberish hope appears to be that something will turn up, perhaps the overthrow of an odious regime or an economic upturn, that will ease problems by creating a shared interest in prosperity. If this is the case, and sometimes it is, then international order will increasingly depend on good luck rather than good management.

Attempting to predict the future confronts the general problem that prospects depend on choices yet to be made. Nonetheless, in describing matters of degree, tendencies, shifting emphases, and declining capabilities and will, rather than their complete absence, the new norm is one of less activity rather than total passivity. It is no longer possible to think of international politics in terms of simple hierarchies of great powers. Certainly, particular events can change perceptions. The expectations about the George W. Bush administration, which was forecast to follow a cautious "realist" strategy along the lines implied here, were overturned by 9/11. A terrible humanitarian catastrophe, a set of terrorist outrages, or an old-fashioned border dispute may prompt surges of diplomatic, developmental, and military activity. If countries are used as sanctuaries for terrorism, or attempt to manipulate energy supplies or maritime trade, defensive measures may not be enough. There will still be arguments to address threats emanating from dangerous parts of the world at the source; in these cases, the prevailing view will be that it is best to nip dangers in the bud before they become critical. Crude forms of oppression will prompt calls to revive the "responsibility to protect" and the discretionary interventionism with which it came to be associated. But these claims, and the evidence on which they are based, will have to look extremely strong before they are taken as seriously as they were in 2002–2003. The question of the future of armed force lies in politics rather than technology, and of the two, politics is by far the murkiest. Nonetheless, the ambition of the 2000s is likely to be followed by the caution of the 2010s.

2 :: The U.S. Armed Forces' View of War

Brian McAllister Linn

Abstract: Many military analysts now argue that the challenges of Iraq and Afghanistan have prompted a paradigm shift within the U.S. armed forces. They believe that technocentric formulaic concepts of warfare, such as effects-based operations, have been replaced by more complex, human-centered approaches such as those laid out in the 2007 *Counterinsurgency Manual*. This chapter details the evolution of U.S. military thought about warfare. It discusses how lessons from the past shaped current policy, the impact of a technologically inspired revolution in military affairs (RMA), and the subsequent conviction that properly equipped U.S. armed forces could rapidly and decisively defeat any and all opponents. The inability of U.S. forces to achieve national objectives in either Iraq or Afghanistan despite their success on the battlefield has caused war intellectuals to seek new lessons from history, question the existence of an RMA, and formulate a new vision of war that stresses uncertainty, adaptation, and innovation.

Despite the continual issuance of buzzwords emphasizing service unity and harmony—such as "jointness," "An Army of One," or "The Few, the Proud"—the armed forces' internal divisions have been vividly displayed during the last decade. A number of important books detail the disagreements between civilian and military leaders and the long struggle to implement the "surge" and the counterinsurgency strategy.[1] Some argue that the wars in Iraq and Afghanistan generated a radical transformation in military thought: that is, a paradigm shift from idealized, techno-centric, scientific formulas—such as "network-centric warfare" (NCW) or "effects-based operations" (EBO)—to more complex, ambiguous, and human-centered visions of war, which were encapsulated in 2007 by *The U.S. Army/Marine Corps Counterinsurgency Field Manual*.[2] This intellectual renaissance has led, according to some, to military victory in Iraq and a path to eventual success in Afghanistan. This interpretation is attractive because it implies that the U.S. armed forces are adaptive, learning organizations that will develop new concepts to replace failed ones. But it begs a number of central questions, not least of which is how the armed forces and their war intellectuals—broadly defined in this chapter as officers who write on the theory and practice of war—could have been so wrong about the nature of warfare going into Iraq and Afghanistan. Answering this larger question requires looking beyond the immediate debate over Iraq-Afghanistan to examine how the U.S. armed forces arrive at their understanding, or vision, of warfare, particularly in their use of history and the role of war intellectuals.

Interpretations of the past, perceptions of the present military situation, and predictions for the future combine to shape the U.S. armed forces' vision of war. All three variables are the subjects of intense debate. War intellectuals argue over such basic questions as whether the preferable strategy is to employ primarily land, sea, or air power; to attack the enemy's physical resources or his morale; or to pursue a battle of annihilation or grind away in a long war of attrition. One Air Force officer identified no fewer than seventeen different theories of airpower, noting that the service had made little effort to reconcile them.[3] In a recent issue of *Joint Forces Quarterly*, two articles by Army officers, "Let's Win the Wars We're In" and "Let's Build an Army to Win *All* Wars," simultaneously provided commentaries on Iraq-Afghanistan and engaged in the latest round of almost two centuries of intra-service debate.[4] Few of these internal disputes are ever resolved, despite recurrent top-down efforts to impose conformity through "capstone" and "vision" statements, doctrine, and other official pronouncements.[5] Perhaps as a result,

American military thought tends to be cyclical, with concepts (often little more than buzzwords) being heralded as revolutionary or "transformational," then quickly going out of fashion, only to reemerge under a new rubric a decade or so later.

For many war intellectuals, the past is prologue to the future. But it is a past that has been carefully edited to display the correct lessons, most notably the importance of military preparedness in peace and military autonomy in wartime. There is a tendency to interpret the nation's martial history as a dismal cyclical narrative, or as one Army general staff described it in 1916: "a startling picture of faulty leadership, needless waste of lives and property, costly overhead charges ... due entirely to a lack of adequate preparation for war in time of peace. But we have not yet learned our lesson."[6] The critique of American society goes far beyond civilians' unwillingness to fund adequate military budgets. War intellectuals have attributed the nation's physical and moral decline to a variety of factors: immigration and urbanization prior to World War I; pacifism in the interwar period; permissive teachers and parents after World War II; the media, politicians, academics, and pot-smoking hedonists after Vietnam; and, in recent years, the physical, moral, and educational deficiencies that may render 75 percent of American youth unfit for military service. In many narratives, civilian fecklessness is only redeemed by the dedication, patriotism, courage, and skill of professional officers. Senior commanders' memoirs often detail the protagonist's struggle against inept or corrupt political masters, a tradition spanning more than a century, from the Civil War's General George B. McClellan, to World War II's General Douglas MacArthur, to the conqueror of Baghdad, General Tommy Franks.

The armed forces' ambivalence toward American society and its political representatives has helped shape military intellectuals' understanding of the present as well as their perceptions of future war. Since the 1820s, military scenarios dealing with foreign attacks have all assumed that the public would be essentially helpless to defend itself. In the view of many war intellectuals, civilians are to set policy, ensure the armed forces have sufficient resources, and let military leaders conduct the battles and campaigns that secure victory. Civilian leaders who violate this division, who dare to disregard the advice of military professionals—or worse, interfere in combat operations—are held in special disdain. One of the services' most bitter historical memories is that of President Lyndon B. Johnson and Secretary of Defense Robert McNamara micromanaging the war against North Vietnam, even to the extent of charting the daily bombing sorties, while the supine commanders in the theater and the Joint Chiefs of Staff abrogated their military responsibilities. General Franks asserted that this lesson from Vietnam taught him to insist on maintaining his operational independence against political and military superiors who sought to interfere in his conduct of the invasions of Iraq and Afghanistan.[7]

History also influences the U.S. armed forces' conception of war by providing examples to support or criticize current policies, organizations, equipment, or weapons. In the late nineteenth century, naval officer and historian Alfred Thayer Mahan, who all but invented maritime history, interpreted the past as demonstrating the need for the United States to acquire global markets and a new steel battle fleet. Following World War I, cavalry advocates looked particularly to the Civil War for evidence to repudiate those who said the horse had no place on the modern battlefield. For decades, Marine Corps war intellectuals have invoked the Gallipoli debacle to highlight their own service's superior conduct of amphibious warfare. The authors of a 1989 article on "fourth-generation warfare" postulated that war had passed through three successive generations and was entering a new one. Consistent with many other writings of the 1980s, the article warned of the threat from guerrillas and terrorists but also rhapsodized about futuristic technologies, such as directed-energy weapons and robotics, which few would argue have been the decisive factors in recent insurgencies.[8] Drawing on the lessons of the past as a means to anticipate the future, military intellectuals often claim to be prophets when some of their predictions are realized.

The dangers of what the services call "lessons learned" from history are evidenced in the use of "blitzkrieg." For decades, the term has been synonymous not only with a type of warfare characterized by speed, flanking, encircling movements, and psychological paralysis of the opponent, but also with institutional innovation and transformation. According to some American war intellectuals, after defeat in World War I, Germany learned the correct lessons and recognized the opportunities of a "revolution in military affairs" (RMA) defined by new technologies (tanks, airplanes), new concepts (infiltration, maneuver, close air support), and new organizations (mechanized forces). In contrast, France, which had access to the same lessons, the same technologies, and the same concepts, hid behind the Maginot Line. In 1940, Germany launched a whirlwind campaign that shattered France in six weeks, thereby demonstrating the consequences of the RMA. At this point, the narrative ends; rarely mentioned are the Wehrmacht's failure against the Soviet Union or its complicity in the Nazi state's atrocities. Indeed, the blitzkriegers were, and are, less interested in history than in proving that military organizations that seize the opportunities offered by an RMA achieve victory, and those that do not are defeated.

This sanitized, didactic, almost mythological blitzkrieg/RMA/ transformation narrative has been interjected into virtually every military reform debate in the last four decades, from discussions of Marine Corps doctrine to which fighters the Air Force should purchase. It has caused numerous unanticipated consequences, not least the fact that it may have led some U.S. senior commanders unknowingly to repeat what historians have identified as a major mistake in the "German way of war": that is, fixating on tactics and operations while failing to consider how individually successful battles and campaigns will achieve the nation's war aims (or strategy).[9] This fascination with rapid maneuvers, tactics, and battles was compounded when the blitzkrieg of 1940 was apparently replayed in the Gulf War of 1990 to 1991. The latter victory led many to conclude that "today, and in the future, armed conflict is expected to be short, decisive, and accompanied with a minimum of casualties."[10] That assumption, in turn, validated the belief that defeating the enemy's military forces on the battlefield defined victory, while everything else—including occupation, reconstruction, and pacification—was not in the dominion of war.

In the 1990s, many war intellectuals postulated that an "information RMA" was either about to occur or already had. They pondered its significance in a flood of diffuse and often self-contradictory writing, some of which now appears prescient, but much of which, in fact, was wrong. Supporters of both NCW (primarily in the Navy) and EBO (primarily in the Air Force) came to agree that by networking the technology of the information age—computers, sensors, satellites, the Internet, and so on—geographically dispersed military forces could synchronize their movements and firepower, deploy quickly, and just as quickly overwhelm their opponents. New weapons—stealth bombers, lasers, and precision-guided munitions—would allow a few aircraft to achieve effects that previously required hundreds of aircraft flying thousands of sorties and dropping several tons of bombs. In the words of one proponent, EBO allowed U.S. armed forces to "dominate an adversary's influence on strategic events" without having to "destroy an enemy's ability to act." Further, overtaking its "operational level systems" would induce systemic paralysis and force the enemy to "acquiesce to the will of the controlling force or face ever increasing degrees of loss of control."[11]

Supporters of this "new American way of war" alleged that rapid blows on carefully selected centers of gravity would create cascading effects, leading to psychological paralysis and loss of control, collapsing the will of military and political leaders, and resulting in a quick and bloodless victory. They even claimed the ability to predict the increments of violence that would achieve certain results. Yet for all their claims of being "outside-the-box" visionaries and futurists, the EBO/NCW prophets were, in retrospect, remarkably unimaginative in forecasting the consequences of their counsel. Indeed, the central fallacy of the EBO/NCW vision of war—that U.S. war objectives would be restricted to destroying the armed forces of a centralized nation-state—is readily apparent. Its advocates only considered "effects" in the most immediate military terms. They did not ponder the intermediate and long-term impacts of "loss of control" in states that were coercive theocracies, dictatorships, or fragile tribal alliances—the very "failed states" the national security strategy consistently identified as the most likely areas of conflict. Nor did they foresee the consequence of creating, under the mantra of "jointness," U.S. armed forces that were organized, equipped, and trained *only* for rapid, decisive operations. Most reprehensible, they did not consider that if EBO/NCW failed to deliver as promised, the most likely result would be the very long, bloody, frustrating attritional struggles they claimed their approach would avoid. In short, EBO/NCW were tactics in search of a strategy.

Unfortunately, ideological imperatives, such as imperialism, neoconservatism, and even apocalypticism, too often filled this strategic vacuum.[12] For instance, military strategist Thomas Barnett, who assisted Admiral Arthur Cebrowski in the development of NCW, maintained that Cebrowski's "vision was a fundamentally *American* way of war, one that promised not just better wars, and not just shorter wars, but perhaps the end of war itself." Barnett envisioned NCW as providing more than an efficient means to kill enemies; he further explained: "I wanted to see it used to short-circuit wars and warfare in general. I want wars to be obsolete because America becomes so powerful that no one is willing to take it on, and thus America is willing to take on anyone—a self-reinforcing deterrence."[13] In another example, commentator William Lind claimed that his earlier writings on fourth-generation warfare anticipated a clash of cultures between the West and the rest of the world. In his view, Islamic radicals were perhaps less dangerous than domestic "cultural radicals...who hate our Judeo-Christian culture" and promote "multiculturalism." He predicted that "the next real war we fight is likely to be on American soil."[14] According to these perspectives, military transformation was (and perhaps still is) less a plan for reforming the services than either a means to achieve American global hegemony or the West's last hope for survival.

In 1998, the operational (and perhaps ideological) rationale for military transformation received official sanction in the Department of Defense's blueprint for the future, *Vision 2010*. The document states: "Today, the world is in the midst of an RMA sparked by leap-ahead advances in information technologies.... [The] advent of the RMA provides the Department with a unique opportunity to transform the way in which it conducts the full range of military operations" by using "information superiority" to "leverage" the "capabilities" of other technologies and assert "dominant awareness of the battlespace."[15] *Vision 2010* assumed that the U.S. armed forces' superior access to information would disperse nineteenth-century theorist Carl von Clausewitz's "fog of war." Information superiority would allow commanders at all levels—from the four-star general at his desk in Tampa, to the infantry captain on the battlefield, to the pilot in his stealth bomber—to have "perfect real-time situational knowledge." By exploiting the potential of experimental technology, one cannon could achieve tactical results that previously required hundreds of shells, thus allowing the United States to use far smaller forces, which in turn would allow far more rapid movement at all levels. Ideally, each bomb or shell not only resolved a specific operational task (such as the destruction of an enemy tank), but also contributed to a cumulative series of "effects." In short order, these "massed effects" would both physically and psychologically shatter (or shock and awe) the enemy's command and control organization.

For America's opponents, *Vision 2010* promised only rapid and decisive defeat. Even before the battle began, their communications would be jammed and their access to accurate information disrupted. Precision attacks on command centers would cause further confusion and delay, so that even if an enemy commander were able to issue orders to subordinates, those instructions would have little relevance to the situation. Deprived of its guiding brain, the enemy army would be unable to coordinate its own firepower or maneuver forces effectively. Even if its troops survived and its equipment escaped destruction, the army would be little more than an armed mob incapable of coherent resistance. Unable to control its military forces, the enemy government would lose its will and submit to American dictates. In short, victory on the battlefield or in the air campaign alone was sufficient to secure U.S. national objectives.

For America's armed forces, and especially its senior leadership, *Vision 2010*'s implications were initially intoxicating yet ultimately stupefying. Proponents boasted that commanders would have real-time battle-space awareness to track both their own and enemy forces, recognize threats and opportunities, communicate their decisions, and have them executed instantly. But precisely because all future wars would be short and decisive—with success measured entirely in the destruction of enemy military forces—the services placed little value on strategic thinkers. Officers skilled at anticipating long-term implications and consequences were unnecessary for wars that would last a few weeks and had only one objective. Instead, the services selected and promoted officers who were skilled at managing the complicated control systems of EBO/NCW: commanders who defined themselves as "operators." Epitomized by Tommy Franks, such officers proved adept at assembling matrices to destroy enemy military forces but were intellectually unprepared to deal with the unforeseen consequences of battlefield victory.

Historians will continue to debate the degree to which the U.S. armed forces' embrace of high-tech warfare, applied with scientific precision, and rapid, decisive, and almost casualty-free victory contributed to two interminable, indecisive wars of attrition in Iraq and Afghanistan. Within the war intellectual community, there is little consensus. Some remain convinced that their prewar concepts and technologies were sound; they blame politicians (particularly Donald Rumsfeld) and the media. Others believe that although EBO/NCW was fundamentally flawed, innovative and adaptive leaders fought against the RMA/Rumsfeld "establishment," reinvented counterinsurgency, and gave the United States the means to victory in the war on terror. In keeping with a long tradition of American military historiography—most clearly seen in treatments of Korea and Vietnam—both interpretations, however much they differ on details, exculpate the armed forces and throw the burden of victory or defeat on the will of the American public and its political leaders.

Have the conflicts in Iraq and Afghanistan changed the armed forces' perception of war? The document credited with breaking the RMA stranglehold on military thought, and perhaps providing a path to victory in Iraq and Afghanistan, was *The U.S. Army / Marine Corps Counterinsurgency Field Manual* of 2007. A project directed by General David H. Petraeus and current U.S. Marine Corps commandant James F. Amos, the manual was in many ways an anti-doctrine. It even included such "paradoxes" as "sometimes doing nothing is the best action," and "sometimes the more you protect your force, the less secure you will be."[16] In contrast to doctrines of the 1990s—which emphasized technology and treated opponents as passive recipients of U.S. dominance—the *Counterinsurgency Field Manual* included an extensive and respectful analysis of the nature of insurgencies: who leads and who participates, how they are sustained, how they use intelligence and media, and what their capacity is to adapt and innovate. This complex and flexible approach to warfare appeared throughout the manual. The chapter on intelligence discussed culture, another covers leadership and ethics, and detailed appendices provide information on social networking and legal guidance. Not surprisingly, both military officers and civilians termed this doctrine revolutionary.

The two services most affected by the manual took different approaches to the lessons learned from Iraq and Afghanistan. The Marine Corps asserted that it has *always* engaged in counterinsurgency and stability operations—and has done so better than anyone. To add historical justification, Marine intellectuals noted that in the 1990s, when the other services were leaping onto the RMA/EBO/NCW bandwagon, Commandant Charles Krulak postulated that the future would be characterized by the "three-block war"—a scenario in which military forces would have to deal with a spectrum of challenges simultaneously, ranging from conventional war to humanitarian aid. The Marines' two-decade-old capstone statement, *Warfighting*, is unique both for its longevity and because it presents a theory of war that emphasizes combat as merely a means to a political end; indeed, it maintains that the application of violence must be consonant with strategic objectives.[17] Given the Marine Corps' conceptual foundation, the freedom of inquiry at such elite programs as the School of Advanced Warfighting, and the willingness to empower its commanders at all levels—what Krulak termed "the strategic corporal"—the corps was (and is) far better positioned, at least intellectually, to adapt and innovate in response to the challenges of the post–Cold War security environment. For the Marines, the challenge in Iraq and Afghanistan was in the execution of a war-fighting philosophy they believed was inherently sound.

The U.S. Army has been the service most influenced by the experiences of Iraq and Afghanistan. This was not the case at the beginning, when the first Army "historic" team to reach Iraq after the fall of Baghdad reportedly asked participants only one question: "What was your role in the greatest military victory ever won?" But the collapse of Iraq into chaos, the criticism directed at General Franks and General Ricardo Sanchez, the scandals of Abu Ghraib, and other irrefutable evidence led many Army officers to acknowledge just how poorly their service had trained for operations beyond the battlefield.

The resulting transformation in the Army's vision of war goes far beyond the counterinsurgency manual. The service's 2008 capstone combat doctrine, *FM-3: Operations*, repudiated many of the central ideas of its 1993 predecessor, *FM 100–5: Operations*. The 1993 operational manual was evolutionary, emphasizing its connection with earlier operational doctrines that (from the Army's perspective) had led to victory in the Cold War and the Gulf War. In the context of war intellectual tradition, *FM 100–5* was Jominian, conflating the methods of war—particularly the preparation and conduct of campaigns (or operations)—with war itself. Like its predecessors, the doctrine aimed to achieve a "quick, decisive victory on and off the battlefield anywhere in the world";[18] it assumed that "modern warfare" consisted of large-unit conventional combat between nation-states; and it used *battle* and *victory* almost synonymously with *war*. The few exceptions to the 1993 manual's intense battlefield focus—such as the comment that "military forces must be prepared to support strategic objectives after the termination of hostilities," and the few sentences devoted to counterinsurgency and peacekeeping—provided little preparation for Somalia, much less Iraq.[19]

FM-3 was, in its own words, "a revolutionary departure from past doctrine," a set of guidelines intended for a volatile era of "protracted confrontation among states, non-states, and individual actors increasingly willing to use violence to achieve their political and ideological ends."[20] The manual was consciously Clausewitzian, not only in its numerous quotations from *On War*, but also in its inclusion of sections on "uncertainty, chance, and friction" and its admonitions that officers must understand the nature of the war they are fighting. Whereas the 1993 doctrine was predicated on teaching officers essential skills to master complex technology, the 2008 doctrine emphasized "how to think—not what to think," because doctrine must be "consistent with human nature and broad enough to provide a guide for unexpected situations."[21] Almost heretically, it states that "winning battles and engagements is important but alone is not sufficient. Shaping the civil situation is just as important to success."[22]

Providing further evidence of the Army's transformation, *The Army Capstone Concept* of 2009 dismissed many previously held convictions—for example, the inevitability of the RMA, the potential of "leap ahead" technology, and the ideal of "full-spectrum dominance"—as no more than "labels." Equally revealing, whereas prewar vision statements portrayed military opponents as hapless victims of American might, the *Capstone Concept* cited numerous recent examples to illustrate their adaptability, dedication, and effectiveness. To defeat them, the Army must create military leaders who have a "tolerance for ambiguity, and possess the ability and willingness to make rapid adjustments according to the situation."[23]

Joint Operating Environment 2010 (*JOE 2010*) shows evidence of both the transformation and the congruence of Army–Marine Corps thought. Its prewar predecessor was essentially an engineering manual for the next decades, a self-described "conceptual template ... to leverage technological opportunities to achieve new levels of effectiveness in joint warfighting" and to allow the U.S. armed forces to achieve "dominance," which was an end unto itself.[24] *JOE 2010* rejects such determinism; indeed, one of its goals is "guarding against any single preclusive view of future war."[25] Whereas the prewar vision statement focused on future weaponry, *JOE 2010* begins with an extensive, rich examination of both the nature of war and the nature of change. And whereas the prewar joint vision was relentlessly optimistic about the capability of the U.S. armed forces to dominate any opponent, *JOE 2010* warns: "No one should harbor the illusion that the developed world can win this conflict in the near future. As is true with most insurgencies, victory will not appear decisive or complete. It will certainly not rest on military successes. The treatment of political, social, and economic ills can help, but in the end will not be decisive."[26]

Although the last decade of unconventional warfare had the most influence on the Marine Corps and the Army, there is considerable internal resistance to both counterinsurgency as a mission and to the methods prescribed in the *Counterinsurgency Field Manual*. War intellectual Gian Gentile is among the more vocal critics, arguing that the guidebook draws too heavily from the Iraq and Afghanistan examples, and that many of its proponents repeat the conceptual errors they attribute to conventional warfare advocates.[27] Even among those who argue that the armed forces developed the concepts and means to secure military—if not strategic—success in Iraq and Afghanistan, there are some who believe that neither the United States nor its armed forces can afford such Pyrrhic "victories." More discouraging yet, throughout much of the Iraq-Afghanistan conflicts the Army senior leadership insisted that the service's future was bound to its prewar, RMA-influenced Future Combat System that seemed ideally designed to refight the Gulf War of 1991.

The Air Force and Navy visions of war have been even less changed by Iraq and Afghanistan. Though adamant that their contributions to the current conflicts be acknowledged, they remain committed to their prewar concepts. Central to both services is the same assumption held in the 1990s—that is, if they achieve the means (capabilities), then the ends (strategy) will sort themselves out. From this assumption, both services look first to technology, then to concepts that will allow its application. Recent U.S. Navy vision statements emphasize sea power's ability to deter conflict, to control the littorals, to support expeditions, to protect the homeland, and to adapt to a variety of threats.[28] The foreword to the U.S. Air Force's 2003 basic doctrine acknowledged the danger posed by asymmetric adversaries who threaten the nation with weapons of mass destruction, terrorism, and information attacks. But for the most part, it reiterated earlier concepts, such as EBO and precision strike, viewing the experiences of Iraq and Afghanistan as further vindication of these approaches. While the doctrine recognized the importance of cooperation, it still maintained "the new view of conflict" in which "the prompt continued, aggressive application of airpower" could win wars without a land campaign. This statement, like the assertion that airpower changes the character of the "American way of war," dated back to one of the earliest proponents of airpower, General Billy Mitchell.[29] One senior Air Force officer who has engaged in counterinsurgency debate, Major General Charles J. Dunlap Jr., views the Army-Marine counterinsurgency manual as flawed by its "infatuation with the individual soldier, an affinity for the close fight, skepticism toward new technology, and an over-reliance on historical case studies."[30] Dunlap maintains that prewar concepts, particularly information RMA and Air Force doctrine, proved themselves in Iraq; thus, he criticizes his service for failing either to articulate its own contribution to the current conflicts or to confront the intellectual challenge of insurgency.

Has this long debate among war intellectuals in any way changed the current political rhetoric on American defense? Judging from the recent presidential election, the answer can be summed up in two words: not much. President Obama's January 2012 strategic guidance reportedly was the product of a prolonged dialogue with senior service chiefs and combat commanders. In keeping with war intellectual canons, it cited the "lessons of history." In contrast to the Bush administration's open-ended commitments, strident rhetoric, and unbridled faith in military force to achieve national aims, Obama's stated strategic imperatives were relatively modest. Conspicuously absent were any "silver bullet" doctrinal or technological panaceas, such as EBO, NCW, the RMA, or other concepts that had so dominated the pre–"Global War on Terrorism" (GWOT) national security discourse. The president reaffirmed his commitment to increasing the U.S. military presence in the Asia-Pacific region, and suggested that in the near future the withdrawal from Afghanistan would mark the "end of long-term nation-building with large military footprints."[31] In the ensuing press Q&A, both Secretary of Defense Leon Panetta and Chairman of the Joint Chiefs of Staff Martin Dempsey essentially dismissed the long-held planning paradigm that the nation's military force structure should be based on the contingency of fighting two major theater wars. Instead, they emphasized smaller, more efficient, more deployable joint forces that could deal with a wide variety of contingencies and still defend the nation.

Obama's strategic defense guidance provided only the broadest direction. Indeed, it scarcely qualified as a strategy at all, in the traditional military sense of balancing ends, ways, and means. The president and his subordinates did not stipulate their criteria for determining risks or benefits with respect to this strategy. They postulated no ultimate objective or "end" to the strategy, but did lay out at least three potentially irreconcilable goals: "global responsibilities that demand our leadership," "keeping America strong and secure in the 21st century," and "keeping our armed forces the very best in the world."[32] Somewhat contradictorily, the president first asserted that strategy would drive military force structure and budgets, but then argued that the primary indicator of both U.S. security and the excellence of its armed forces would be a defense budget exceeding that of the next ten nations combined. Equally reminiscent of pre-GWOT strategic thinking was his assertion that U.S. armed forces must be "agile, flexible, and ready for the full range of contingencies and threats."[33] But despite so much evidence of past, present, and future U.S. opponents applying "asymmetric" warfare—which is predicated on outthinking a stronger opponent—and despite considerable evidence dating back to Vietnam that the nation's armed forces have a propensity to select senior officers who turn tactical victory into strategic defeat, there does not seem to be much interest in creating a smarter military.[34]

It is too soon to determine whether this last decade of persistent conflict will result in a major transformation in the American armed forces' vision of war. Perhaps the interest in counterinsurgency was no more than a reaction to the unique challenges of Iraq and Afghanistan. In this respect, it is well worth remembering that the initial campaigns in both countries were hailed as vindicating the armed forces' commitment to the RMA and EBO/NCW. They are now cited as proof of the fallacies in these visions—in some cases by the same pundits.[35] Beyond the specific issues raised by the Iraq-Afghanistan conflicts lies a host of more general questions. Is there an American way of war that predisposes the nation and its armed forces to certain strategies or methods? Is military transformation the result of new ideas or new technology? Are concepts such as the RMA, transformation, or fourth-generation warfare the intellectual sparks that will ignite true change in the nation's armed forces? Or are they little more than dangerously simplistic buzzwords that promote the military's traditional agendas? How will strategic thinkers assimilate the lessons of the past decade into their new visions of war? If nothing else, this last decade has shown that the armed forces' vision of war matters, and that war intellectuals have more impact, and deserve far more study, than they have received.

Notes

1 David Cloud and Greg Jaffe, *The Fourth Star: Four Generals and the Epic Struggle for the Future of the U.S. Army* (New York: Three Rivers Press, 2009); Thomas E. Ricks, *Fiasco: The American Military Adventure in Iraq* (New York: Penguin Books, 2006); Thomas E. Ricks, *The Gamble: General David Petraeus and the American Military Adventure in Iraq, 2006–2008* (New York: Penguin, 2009); Linda Robinson, *Tell Me How This Ends: General David Petraeus and the Search for a Way Out in Iraq* (New York: Public Affairs, 2008). For an overview of the development of post-Vietnam U.S. concepts of war, see Fred Kagan, *Finding the Target: The Transformation of American Military Policy* (New York: Encounter Books, 2006). I thank Gian Gentile, Bryon Greenwald, Joe Cerami, Jeff Engel, and Richard Muller for their insight on the service perspectives and the current defense debate.

2 David A. Deptula, *Effects-Based Operations: Change in the Nature of Warfare* (Arlington, VA: Aerospace Education Foundation, 2001); James N. Mattis, "USJFCOM Commander's Guidance on Effects-Based Operations," *Joint Forces Quarterly* 51 (2008): 105–8; Edward A. Smith, *Effects Based Operations: Applying Network Centric Warfare in Peace, Crisis, and War* (Washington, DC: DOD Command and Control Research Program, 2002); David H. Petraeus and James F. Amos, *The U.S. Army / Marine Corps Counterinsurgency Field Manual* (Chicago: University of Chicago Press, 2007).

3 James M. Smith, "Air Force Culture and Cohesion," *Airpower Journal* 12 (Fall 1998): 40–53; William C. Thomas, "The Cultural Identity of the United States Air Force," *Air & Space Power Journal* 18 (January 2004), http://www.air-power.au.af.mil/airchronicles/cc/thomas.html (accessed October 14, 2010); Peter Faber, "Competing Theories of Airpower: A Language for Analysis," *Aerospace Power Chronicles*, http://www.au.af.mil/au/awc/awcgate/au/faber.htm (accessed October 14, 2010). For further information on airpower and military thought, see Air University, "Military Theory, Theorists, and Strategy," http://www.au.af.mil/au/awc/awcgate/awc-thry.htm.

4 John Nagl, "Let's Win the Wars We're In," *Joint Forces Quarterly* 52 (January 2009): 20–26; Gian Gentile, "Let's Build an Army to Win All Wars," *Joint Forces Quarterly* 52 (January 2009): 27–33.

5 Peter M. Swartz with Karin Duggan, *U.S. Navy Capstone Strategies and Concepts (1970–2009)* (Alexandria, VA: Center of Naval Analysis, February 2009), http://www.cna.org/documents/D0019819.A1.pdf.

6 "A Proper Military Policy for the United States," *Journal of the Military Service Institute* 59 (July–August 1916): 29.

7 Tommy Franks with Malcolm McConnell, *American Soldier* (New York: Regan Books, 2004), 441. Brian McAllister Linn, *The Echo of Battle: The Army's Way of War* (Cambridge, MA: Harvard University Press, 2007), 79–80, 109–10, 236–37; Peter Maslowski, "Army Values and American Values," *Military Review* 70 (April 1990): 10–23; H. R. McMaster, *Dereliction of Duty: Lyndon Johnson, Robert McNamara, the Joint Chiefs of Staff, and the Lies That Led to Vietnam* (New York: HarperCollins, 1997).

8 William S. Lind, Keith Nightingale, John F. Schmidt, Joseph W. Sutton, and Gary I. Wilson, "The Changing Face of War: Into the Fourth Generation," *Marine Corps Gazette*, October 1989, 22–26, http://globalguerrillas.type-pad.com/lind/the-changing-face-of-war-into-the-fourth-generation.html (accessed November 13, 2010); Antulio J. Echevarria II, *Fourth-Generation War and Other Myths* (Carlisle, PA: Strategic Studies Institute, 2005); William F. Owen, "The War of New Words: Why Military History Trumps Buzzwords," *Armed Forces Journal* (November 2009): 34–35.

9 Robert M. Citino, *The German Way of War: From the Thirty Years' War to the Third Reich* (Lawrence: University Press of Kansas, 2005); Echevarria, *Fourth-Generation War and Other Myths*, 14–16; Rolf Hobson, "Blitzkrieg, the Revolution in Military Affairs and Defense Intellectuals," *Journal of Strategic Studies* 33 (August 2010): 625–43.

10 Deptula, *Effects-Based Operations*, foreword.

11 Ibid., 5–6.

12 For a provocative interpretation of this confluence of military reformers, militarism, and imperialism, see Andrew J. Bacevich, *The New American Militarism: How Americans Are Seduced by War* (New York: Oxford University Press, 2005).

13 Thomas P. M. Barnett, *The Pentagon's New Map: War and Peace in the Twenty-First Century* (New York: G. P. Putnam's Sons, 2004), 328. Arthur K. Cebrowski and John H. Garska, "Network-Centric Warfare: Its Origin and Future," *Proceedings*, January 1998, http://www.kinection.com/ncoic/ncw_origin_future.pdf.

14 William S. Lind, "Fourth-Generation Warfare: Another Look," *Marine Corps Gazette*, November 2001, http://www.mca-marines.org/gazette/fourth-generation-warfare-another-look.

15 Secretary of Defense William S. Cohen, *Annual Report to the President and the Congress* (1998), chap. 13, "The Revolution in Military Affairs and Joint Vision 2010," http://www.dod.gov/execsec/adr98/index.html (accessed September 23, 2010).

16 Petraeus and Amos, *U.S. Army / Marine Corps Counterinsurgency Field Manual*, 48–49.

17 U.S. Marine Corps, *Warfighting* (Washington, DC: Department of the Navy Headquarters, 1989).

18 Department of the Army, *FM 100–5: Operations* (Washington, DC: Department of the Army Headquarters, June 14, 1993), preface. Antoine-Henri Jomini was a nineteenth-century military historian and strategist who has been criticized for his allegedly geometric approach to warfare.

19 Ibid., 1–4. For the treatment of counterinsurgency, see 13–18.

20 Department of the Army, *FM 3: Operations* (Washington, DC: Department of the Army Headquarters, February 27, 2008), foreword.

21 Ibid., D-1.

22 Ibid., introduction.

23 U.S. Army Training and Doctrine Command, *The Army Capstone Concept: Operational Adaptability: Operating under Conditions of Uncertainty and Complexity in an Era of Persistent Conflict, 2016–2028*, TRADOC Pam 525-3-0 (Fort Monroe, VA: Department of the Army Headquarters, December 21, 2009).

24 Joint Chiefs of Staff, *Joint Vision 2010* (Washington, DC: Joint Chiefs of Staff, 1995).

25 General James N. Mattis, foreword, in U.S. Joint Forces Command, *Joint Operating Environment 2010* (Norfolk, VA: USJFCOM, February 18, 2010).

26 U.S. Joint Forces Command, *Joint Operating Environment 2010*, 53.

27 Gian Gentile, "A Strategy of Tactics," *Parameters* 39 (August 2009): 5–17.

28 U.S. Navy, U.S. Marine Corps, and U.S. Coast Guard, *Naval Operations Concept 2010: Implementing the Maritime Strategy* (2010); U.S. Navy, U.S. Marine Corps, and U.S. Coast Guard, *A Cooperative Strategy for 21st Century Seapower* (2007); Swartz with Duggan, *U.S. Navy Capstone Strategies and Concepts*, slides 1481–84.

29 U.S. Air Force, *Air Force Basic Doctrine* (November 17, 2003), 17; U.S. Air Force, *The U.S. Air Force Transformation Flight Plan* (2003).

30 Charles J. Dunlap Jr., *Shortchanging the Joint Fight? An Airman's Assessment of FM 3-24 and the Case of Developing Truly Joint COIN Doctrine* (Maxwell Air Force Base, AL: Airpower Research Institute, 2008), 18.

31 Department of Defense, "Defense Strategic Guidance Briefing from the Pentagon," January 5, 2012, http://www.defense.gov/transcripts/transcript.aspx?transcriptid=4953.

32 Ibid.

33 Ibid.

34 Cloud and Jaffe, *Fourth Star*; Ricks, *Fiasco*; Paul Yingling, "A Failure in Generalship," *Armed Forces Journal* (May 2007), at http://www.armedforces-journal.com/2007/05/2635198.

35 Max Boot, "The New American Way of War," *Foreign Affairs* 82 (July–August 2003): 41–58.

3 :: Weapons

THE GROWTH AND SPREAD OF THE PRECISION-STRIKE REGIME

Thomas G. Mahnken

Abstract: For two decades, scholars and practitioners have argued that the world is experiencing a revolution in military affairs (RMA) brought on by the development and diffusion of precision-strike and related capabilities, such as intelligence, surveillance, and reconnaissance; precision navigation and tracking; and robustly improved command and control. The United States took an early lead in exploiting the promise of precision-strike systems, and the use of precision weaponry has given the United States a battlefield edge for some twenty years. However, precision-strike systems are now spreading: other countries, and non-state actors, are acquiring them and developing countermeasures against them. As the precision-strike regime matures, the United States will see its edge erode. The ability of the United States to project power will diminish considerably. In addition, U.S. forces, and eventually the United States itself, will be increasingly vulnerable to precision weapons in the hands of our adversaries.

This chapter begins by exploring the concept of an RMA, as well as the general structure of military revolutions. Using this model, the chapter then describes the growth of the precision-strike regime to date, speculates on the features of a mature precision-strike regime, and concludes with some implications for the United States.

The evolution of military technology and doctrine has redefined the conduct of war throughout history.[1] Defense policy analyst Andrew F. Krepinevich, for example, has identified ten military revolutions stretching back to the fourteenth century.[2] These include the Napoleonic revolution of the late eighteenth and early nineteenth centuries, which saw the advent of the mass army; the adoption of the railroad, rifle, and telegraph in the mid–nineteenth century, which marked the industrialization of warfare; and the development of nuclear weapons in the twentieth century. Although each revolution was unique in its origin, trajectory, and content, all had common features. In each case, new combat methods arose that displaced previously dominant forms of warfare by shifting the balance between offense and defense, space and time, and fire and maneuver.[3] The states that first adopted these innovations gained a significant advantage, forcing competitors to match or counter them to have any chance of prevailing on the battlefield. Those who adapted, prospered, while those who did not, declined, often precipitously.

Military revolutions display a common structure: a cycle of innovation, diffusion, and refinement. Their development is driven not just by changes in the character and conduct of war, but also by the perceptions of both participants and observers that change is afoot and drastic action is required. Indeed, the perception of dramatic change and the urgent need to respond to it is a defining feature of a military revolution. For example, although scholars debate whether something called "blitzkrieg" actually existed in German military doctrine, the demonstrated effectiveness of combined-arms armored warfare against France and the Low Countries in May and June 1940 convinced participant and observer alike that the character of warfare had shifted and compelled them to respond by changing their force structure and doctrine.[4]

The Embryonic Phase. The first phase of a new revolution builds on the achievements of the preceding cycle, while the last phase forms the foundation of the next transformation. During the first, or embryonic, phase, military organizations refine old combat methods and experiment with new ones in an effort to gain or maintain advantage against potential adversaries.[5] Most major military innovations have, in fact, come about because of the perception of an operational or strategic problem that defied a conventional solution.

New weaponry alone is insufficient to transform warfare.[6] Those practices that have changed the character and conduct of warfare have combined weapon systems with innovative operational concepts and the organizations necessary to carry them out.[7] Yet determining how new weapons and concepts will perform without the test of war is exceedingly difficult. In peacetime, military organizations operate, in the words of military historian Sir Michael Howard, in "a fog of peace."[8] They must place bets about the effectiveness of new and unproven ways of war, but combat is the only, and final, arbiter. In addition, past experience serves as a cognitive anchor that limits the ability of military organizations to comprehend the magnitude of change that is under way and constrains the ability of intelligence organizations to understand foreign military developments.[9] As a result, periods of change in the character and conduct of warfare frequently witness a growing gap between perception and reality. The magnitude of this divergence depends on the amount of time that passes between wars and the amount of technological and doctrinal dynamism in the interwar period.

The Immature Phase. The second, or immature, phase of a military revolution begins with the successful use of new military practices in a major war. Success often takes the form of a decisive battle or campaign in which forces that have mastered new combat methods defeat those who remain wedded to traditional approaches. The demonstrated effectiveness of these methods realigns perception and reality, convinces belligerent and observer alike of a change in the character of warfare, and forces both friend and foe to adjust their force structure and doctrine. For example, revolutionary France's adoption of the *levée en masse* not only allowed it to survive, but also permitted Napoleon to win a series of decisive battles against his foes at Ulm, Austerlitz, Jena, and Auerstadt. Prussia's embrace of the railroad, rifle, and telegraph helped it, the least of Europe's great powers, defeat Austria at Königgrätz and France at Sedan and unify the German state. And Germany's use of combined-arms armored warfare delivered a series of quick, decisive victories in the opening campaigns of World War II.

One way military organizations adjust to new combat methods is by emulating successful practices. Indeed, the spread of new capabilities offers the central mechanism by which one military regime supplants another. Military organizations may attempt to import foreign practices wholesale; more often, however, they modify them somewhat in the process.[10]

Adversaries may also attempt to develop countermeasures to new combat methods, particularly when the barriers to emulation are prohibitively high. As British army officer and military historian J. F. C. Fuller put it, "Every improvement in armament is eventually met by a counter-improvement which gradually or rapidly whittles down its power."[11] Although technical and operational countermeasures rarely succeed in nullifying the effectiveness of new military practices, they do, over time, erode it somewhat.[12] The competition between measure and countermeasure becomes a defining feature of the ensuing military regime.

The process of emulation is typically neither rapid (let alone automatic) nor complete.[13] First, the process of change in military organizations is wrenching and painful, reducing their effectiveness in the short term even if it promises to increase it in the long term. As a result, military leaders tend to delay difficult change unless and until it is starkly apparent that it is necessary. Second, leaders may disagree in their perception of the threat environment, including debates over which contingencies are most serious and when they might arise. Third, the path to success is rarely obvious. Military organizations may have difficulty perceiving that a military revolution is under way even after new practices have appeared on the battlefield. Because new combat methods often have their roots in the past, contemporary observers may fail to discern what is new and different about them. Fourth, the organizational culture of the military can constrain both how it perceives the environment and how it responds.[14] Organizations may emphasize those events that are in accord with doctrine and discard those that contradict it.

The Mature Phase. The spread of successful practices creates a new style of warfare that supplants the existing paradigm. The inauguration of a new military regime marks the third, or mature, phase of a revolution. The basis for competition in a mature regime is different from that in a developing one. In the latter, advantage accrues to the military that is best able to exploit an emerging innovation; in the former, advantage accrues to those powers that are able to replicate an innovation on a large scale. Whereas a developing regime often witnesses wars of maneuver and quick, decisive victories, a mature regime is characterized by wars of attrition. For example, Germany used its early lead in developing combined-arms armored warfare to defeat Poland, France, and the Low Countries in the early phases of World War II. However, in an example of successful emulation, Germany was ultimately defeated by a coalition that was able to field far more tanks than the Germans were, and to use them reasonably well.[15]

The structure of military revolutions is easiest to discern in retrospect, with the benefit of hindsight once history has rendered its verdict. It is far more difficult to comprehend contemporary developments, not least because we are immersed in them. Nonetheless, we can cast our gaze backward to the origins of the precision-strike revolution, and we should look ahead to predict, albeit with a sense of modesty, its future course.

The embryonic phase of the precision-strike revolution stretched from World War II to the end of the Cold War. Guided weapons, including the V-1 cruise missile and V-2 ballistic missile, but also the Fritz X air-to-surface weapon, were first used in combat by Germany during World War II. However, the United States took the lead in developing precision weapons in the decades that followed.[16] Indeed, many of the weapon systems associated with the information revolution—precision-guided munitions (PGMs), unmanned air vehicles (UAVs), and sensors—date back to the 1960s and 1970s, and many saw their debut in the Vietnam War. Between 1968 and 1973, for example, the Air Force and Navy expended more than twenty-eight thousand laser-guided bombs (LGBs) in Southeast Asia, mainly against bridges and transportation choke points.[17]

The seeming ease with which the U.S.-led coalition defeated Iraq during the 1991 Gulf War caused many observers in the United States and elsewhere to conclude that the information revolution was bringing about a new RMA.[18] In their view, the lopsided battles in the deserts of Kuwait and southern Iraq and the seemingly effortless domination of the Iraqi air force signaled that warfare had indeed changed. The contrast between prewar expectations of a bloody fight and the wartime reality of Iraqi collapse struck many as indicating a transformation in warfare.

The 1991 Gulf War thus marked the transition between the embryonic and immature phases of the precision-strike revolution. The combination of the stealthy F-117 Nighthawk aircraft and PGMs gave U.S. forces extremely high effectiveness. A typical non-stealth strike formation in the Gulf War required thirty-eight aircraft, including electronic warfare and defense-suppression aircraft, to allow eight planes to deliver bombs on three targets. By contrast, only twenty F-117s armed with 2,000-pound LGBs were able simultaneously to attack thirty-seven targets in the face of more challenging defenses. As a result, although F-117s flew only 2 percent of the total attack sorties in the war, they struck nearly 40 percent of strategic targets, such as leadership and command-and-control facilities. In addition, the war witnessed the innovative use of PGMs to strike not only fixed strategic targets and hardened aircraft shelters, but also Iraqi tanks in revetments. On one night alone, 46 F-111F attack aircraft dropped 184 LGBs, which destroyed 132 Iraqi armored vehicles.[19] Despite the fact that PGMs accounted for only 8 percent of the bombs dropped over Kuwait and Iraq, televised scenes of U.S. aircraft bombing targets with precision, broadcast worldwide, became the most evocative images of the war.

In the years that followed, the war became a central reference point in debates over the hypothesis that an RMA was under way.[20] Some of the more breathless RMA advocates argued that the information revolution marked a complete break with the past. One 1993 report predicted: "The Military Technical Revolution has the potential fundamentally to reshape the nature of warfare. Basic principles of strategy since the time of Machiavelli... may lose their relevance in the face of emerging technologies and doctrines."[21] The authors of the Air Force's official study of the Gulf War were closer to the mark when they concluded, "The ingredients for a transformation of war may well have become visible in the Gulf War, but if a revolution is to occur someone will have to make it."[22]

The United States embraced precision weaponry in the decade that followed the Gulf War. Throughout the 1990s, the combination of stealth and precision-guided munitions gave U.S. air forces the ability to strike adversaries from the air with near impunity. In addition, airpower seemed uniquely suited to the types of conflicts in which the United States was involved: wars for limited aims, fought with partial means, for marginal interests. Airpower coupled with PGMs appeared to offer the ability to coerce Iraq, intervene in the Balkans, and retaliate against terrorist groups while avoiding the difficult decisions associated with a sustained commitment of ground forces.

The congressionally mandated 1997 Quadrennial Defense Review acknowledged the existence of an RMA and committed the department to transforming the U.S. armed forces. As Secretary of Defense William Cohen put it: "The information revolution is creating a Revolution in Military Affairs that will fundamentally change the way U.S. forces fight. We must exploit these and other technologies to dominate in battle."[23] That same year, the congressionally mandated National Defense Panel argued even more strongly in favor of the need to transform U.S. forces. The panel's report suggested that an RMA was under way and urged the Defense Department leadership to "undertake a broad transformation of its military and national security structures, operational concepts and equipment, and...key business processes." The report stated:

> We are on the cusp of a military revolution stimulated by rapid advances in information and information-related technologies. This implies a growing potential to detect, identify, and track far greater numbers of targets over a larger area for a longer time than ever before, and to provide this information much more quickly and effectively than heretofore possible. Those who can exploit these advantages— and thereby dissipate the fog of war—stand to gain significant advantages.... [The Defense Department] should accord the highest priority to executing a transformation of the U.S. military, starting now.[24]

Much of the discussion of the RMA in the 1990s was predicated on opportunity: the United States should pursue new ways of war because they would allow it to win wars faster, cheaper, and more decisively. Characteristic of this view was defense analyst James Blaker's statement: "The potency of the American RMA stems from new military systems that will create, through their interaction, an enormous military disparity between the United States and any opponent. Baldly stated, U.S. military forces will be able to apply military force with dramatically greater efficiency than an opponent, and do so with little risk to U.S. forces."[25]

The confidence, even hubris, of the 1990s permeated the U.S. officer corps. Officers in the late 1990s perceived the benefits of transformation, but refused to believe that adversaries could acquire precision-strike capabilities themselves. A survey of 1,900 U.S. officers attending professional military education institutions conducted in 2000 found that most tended to believe that the emerging RMA would make it easier for the United States to use force in order to achieve decisive battlefield victories. Most also believed that it would allow the United States to engage in high-intensity operations with substantially reduced risk of casualties and that it would greatly reduce the duration of future conflicts. They also tended to believe that the United States would have a greatly enhanced ability to locate, track, and destroy enemy forces in limited geographic areas.[26] By contrast, these same officers were skeptical of the ability of potential adversaries to exploit the precision-strike revolution to harm the United States. For example, only 9 percent of officers surveyed in 2000 believed that future adversaries would be able to use long-range precision-strike weapons such as ballistic and cruise missiles to destroy fixed military infrastructure, including ports, airfields, and logistical sites; only 12 percent believed that adversaries would be able to use such weapons to attack carrier battle groups at sea.[27]

The 1999 war over Kosovo saw the introduction of a new generation of PGMs guided by data from the Global Positioning System (GPS) satellite constellation, most notably the GBU-31 Joint Direct Attack Munition (JDAM). The weapon consists of a $20,000 kit, including a GPS receiver, sensors, and tailfins, that converts an unguided bomb into a guided weapon. In contrast with the laser-guided bombs used in Vietnam and the Gulf War, such weapons allow aircraft to strike at night and through inclement weather. The Kosovo war also saw the use of unmanned aerial vehicles (UAVs), such as the Air Force RQ-1A Predator, for reconnaissance and surveillance.

At the dawn of the new millennium, however, concern mounted that the precision-strike revolution, once an American monopoly, was on the verge of spreading. Of particular concern was China's development of so-called anti-access/area-denial capabilities. Reflecting this concern, the 2001 *Quadrennial Defense Review*, issued in the wake of the September 11, 2001, terrorist attacks, argued that the Defense Department's transformation efforts should focus on overcoming six emerging strategic and operational challenges:

- Protecting critical bases of operations, including the U.S. homeland, forces abroad, allies, and friends, and defeating weapons of mass destruction and their means of delivery
- Assuring information systems in the face of attack and conducting effective information operations
- Projecting and sustaining U.S. forces in distant anti-access or area-denial environments and defeating anti-access and area-denial threats
- Denying enemies sanctuary by providing persistent surveillance, tracking, and rapid engagement with high-volume precision strike against critical mobile and fixed targets
- Enhancing the capability and survivability of space systems and supporting infrastructure
- Leveraging information technology and innovative concepts to develop an interoperable, joint C4ISR architecture and capability that includes a joint operational picture that can be tailored to user needs[28]

This shift was reflected in officer attitudes. In 2000, the vast majority of officers had been unconcerned about the full spectrum of threats; those surveyed in 2002 and 2006 expressed obvious concern about a range of threats over the next two decades. Officers now worried about the threat from long-range precision-strike missiles with respect to current platforms and deployment schemes, with 69 percent of officers surveyed in 2002 and 2006 predicting that within a decade, adversaries would be able to use ballistic and cruise missiles to deny the United States the use of ports, airfields, and logistical sites. Similarly, 73 percent of officers surveyed in 2002 and 68 percent in 2006 believed that within a decade, adversaries would be able to use such weapons to attack carrier battle groups at sea.[29]

Between 1991 and 2003, PGMs grew from a niche capability to represent a new standard of warfare. Whereas 8 percent of the munitions employed during the Gulf War were guided, 29 percent of those used over Kosovo eight years later, 60 percent of those used in Afghanistan ten years later, and 68 percent of those used in Iraq twelve years later were guided. In Afghanistan, the JDAM became the weapon of choice for U.S. forces. Between October 2001 and February 2002, U.S. forces dropped 6,600 of the munitions; during just one ten-minute period on October 18, 2001, the Air Force dropped a hundred of the bombs. Two years later in Iraq, U.S. forces dropped more than 6,500 JDAMs in the march on Baghdad.[30]

Precision weaponry has also assumed an important role in the panoply of weapons to combat terrorism. The decision to arm the Predator UAV and use it against Al Qaeda came in 2000, and the weapon was quickly pressed into use after the September 11, 2001, terrorist attacks. In November 2002, an AGM-114A Hellfire air-to-surface missile launched by a Predator destroyed a car carrying six terrorists, including Salim Sinan al-Harethi, Al Qaeda's chief operative in Yemen and a suspect in the October 2000 bombing of the destroyer USS *Cole*. Most of the strikes that followed targeted Pakistan's lawless border region. Begun by the George W. Bush administration, the program has reportedly been expanded by the Obama administration. According to one estimate, U.S. drones, including the Predator and the more powerful MQ-9 Reaper, have reportedly carried out nearly three hundred strikes in northwest Pakistan, killing between 1,500 and 2,310 militants, including a number of senior Al Qaeda leaders as well as Baitullah Meshud, the head of the Pakistani Taliban.[31] More controversial has been the death toll among innocents resulting from the attacks, but these deaths appear to be declining dramatically even as the number of strikes has increased, in part because of the deployment of new munitions with an even smaller warhead than that on the Hellfire.[32]

Despite—or, in fact, because of—America's success in embracing the precision-strike revolution, the United States is losing its military edge. Adversaries are acquiring PGMs, as well as the vital supporting capabilities needed to wage precision warfare, including commercial sources of imagery, precision navigation and timing, and upgraded command and control. Moreover, states are developing the ability to counter U.S. precision-strike capabilities by hardening, concealing, and dispersing their forces and infrastructure. We are, in other words, currently experiencing the maturation of the precision-strike revolution and the emergence of the precision-strike regime.

A growing number of actors are acquiring PGMs. These include not only U.S. allies, but also competitors such as China, which has become a leading player in the precision-strike regime. Unconstrained by the Intermediate-Range Nuclear Forces Treaty, which prevents the United States and Russia from deploying land-based intermediate-range missiles, China has become the world leader in precision-guided ballistic missiles. According to unclassified Defense Department estimates, China has deployed more than one thousand precision-guided conventional ballistic missiles opposite Taiwan. Moreover, it is fielding an antiship ballistic missile capable of striking ships at sea up to 1,500 kilometers from China and may in the future field a precision-strike system with intercontinental range.[33] Nor are states any longer the only actors in the precision-strike revolution. For example, Lebanese Hezbollah used antitank guided missiles against Israeli forces in its 2006 war with Israel.[34] More recently, Hamas employed such a weapon against an Israeli school bus.

We should not be surprised by the spread of precision-strike capabilities. It was historically inevitable, even if the process has been accelerated by the commercial availability of key supporting capabilities, such as imagery and command and control. Of greatest significance, however, is the universal free access to precision navigation and timing data, such as that from the U.S. GPS satellite constellation. Whereas the development of precision guidance cost the United States billions of dollars over the course of decades, both states and non-state actors can now strike accurately with a minimum investment.

As other states are increasing their precision-strike capabilities, the United States has devoted less attention to precision strike than it has in the past. Rather, for the last decade the Defense Department focused on countering insurgency in Iraq and Afghanistan—conflicts where precision strike has played a role, to be sure, but not a central one. Although the Defense Department has indicated its desire to shift its focus to the Pacific and the challenge posed by a rising China, it is unclear whether it will have the resources to make rhetoric a reality.

Meanwhile, both states and non-state actors, such as insurgents and terrorists, are seeking to counter U.S. precision-strike capabilities. Insurgents in Afghanistan and Pakistan, for example, have sought to camouflage themselves and hide among the local population. They have also sought to constrain the ability of the United States to bring airpower to bear by falsifying the number of innocents that have been killed in air strikes.[35]

If history is a guide, the future scope and spread of the precision-strike regime will be uneven. The ability of states and non-state actors to deploy an effective precision-strike capability will depend on their ability not only to field weapons, but also to develop or buy the command and control and intelligence, surveillance, and reconnaissance capabilities that are needed to strike with precision as well as to develop appropriate doctrine and operational concepts for their use. They will also seek ways to circumvent our precision-strike capability.

The most capable states are likely to possess an intercontinental precision-strike capability. The United States is pursuing a Conventional Prompt Global Strike system, and analysts believe that China may be seeking a similar capability. By contrast, short-range precision-strike systems, such as guided rockets, artillery shells, and mortar rounds, are likely to proliferate faster and more widely.

At the strategic level, states and non-state actors alike will be driven to adopt some combination of precision-strike and adaptive countermeasures. At the operational level, the interaction between the development of precision-strike systems, on the one hand, and attempts to protect against them, on the other, will drive the maturation of the precision-strike regime. Precision-guided weapons are putting an expanding range of targets at risk. It is already possible to strike effectively targets that were previously invulnerable. Indeed, precision-guided munitions are increasingly seen as substitutes for nuclear weapons. These trends are likely to continue. At the same time, the emergence of precision-strike systems is already leading adversaries to try to protect targets by making them mobile, as well as hardening, burying, defending, camouflaging, or concealing them.

Over time, this offense-defense interaction will render some targets difficult, if not impossible, to strike. Mobile weapons based deep in a nation's territory, deployed in the deep oceans or underwater, and located at great distances from attackers may remain for all intents and purposes invulnerable. More broadly, military forces will adopt measures to reduce their vulnerability. However, some targets cannot be buried or made mobile and will thus remain vulnerable. These will include civilian infrastructure such as electrical power distribution and oil refineries, but also military infrastructure, such as ports, bases, and logistical depots. Because of the enduring asymmetry between strike and protection, long-range precision-strike campaigns could increasingly come to target an adversary's vulnerable homeland infrastructure rather than his less vulnerable armed forces. Indeed, the twenty-first century may witness the resurrection, or transfiguration, of doctrines of strategic bombing, such as those that Italian army general Giulio Douhet espoused at the beginning of the twentieth century, and theories of coercion, such as those economist and strategist Thomas Schelling advanced during the Cold War.

In a world where many states possess precision-strike systems, traditional conquest and occupation will become much more difficult. They may, in fact, become prohibitively expensive in some cases. Imagine, for example, if the Iraqi insurgents had been equipped with precision-guided mortars and rockets and had reliably been able to target points within Baghdad's Green Zone. Or imagine that the Taliban were similarly armed and were thus able to strike routinely the U.S. and Afghan forward operating bases that dot the Afghan countryside. U.S. casualties could have amounted to many times what they have been in either theater.

Because invasion and conquest are becoming increasingly difficult, wars in a mature precision-strike regime will likely focus on coercion and limited political objectives. In this world, the ability to punish an adversary to force him to concede—what Thomas Schelling dubbed the "power to hurt"—is likely to become an increasingly popular theory of victory.[36] One potential result of this strategic interaction would be conflicts that involve campaigns whereby each side uses precision-strike weapons to hold the other's economic and industrial infrastructure at risk. In such a situation, stability would depend on each side possessing an assured survivable retaliatory capability. Unlike the condition of mutual assured destruction that obtained during the Cold War, however, this retaliatory capability could be based on precision-strike systems rather than nuclear weapons.

A mature precision-strike regime would feature a new set of "haves" and "have-nots," with an actor's status determined by the robustness of its precision-strike capability rather than other attributes, such as the possession of nuclear weapons. The precision-strike haves will be those countries that possess both geographic depth as well as the resources to invest in survivable, effective precision-strike systems and large stockpiles of munitions. They will likely include the United States, China, India, and potentially Russia. The precision-strike have-nots will be those countries that are threatened by precision-strike systems but that lack the geographic depth or resources to invest in a survivable, effective precision-strike capability, such as Japan and Taiwan. These states will have incentives to invest in other forms of warfare, such as nuclear weapons.

The growth and diffusion of precision-strike systems could also affect international relations more broadly. To the extent that U.S. military power in general, and power projection in particular, has underpinned global norms, the emergence of anti-access capabilities could undercut world order. For example, the development and diffusion of anti-access systems could undermine the principle of freedom of navigation. In other cases, actors could seek to limit precision-strike capabilities. It is not inconceivable, for example, that states or non-state actors could seek to curb precision-strike systems through an international treaty, much as land mines have been limited. Amnesty International has already decried the U.S. drone campaign over Pakistan, and the United Nations special rapporteur on extrajudicial killings, Philip Alston, has condemned the U.S. drone campaign over Pakistan and called for greater "accountability" to prevent what he called a "slippery slope" of killing.[37] Future attempts to proscribe the use of such unmanned systems are not beyond the realm of possibility.

Precision-strike systems are already affecting expectations regarding the use of force, and that trend is likely to continue. The ability of weapons to destroy targets reliably and accurately has fostered the notion in many countries that war is a bloodless and error-free undertaking. In such an environment, targeting errors—the U.S. strike on the Chinese embassy in Belgrade in 1999, for instance—are likely to be perceived as deliberate acts.

The advent of precision strike and UAVs has separated warriors mentally and physically from the act of killing. Dropping unguided weapons required considerable skill to ensure that the bomb struck near (let alone on) the target in the face of enemy ground fire. Delivering LGBs similarly required the operator to designate the target with a laser and keep it illuminated throughout the bomb's flight, a process that took long seconds as the aircraft sough to avoid enemy air defenses. Delivering a GPS-guided bomb merely requires the operator to input the target's coordinates into a computer. Similarly, UAV operators are physically removed from combat. The pilots who operate Predators and Reapers launching missiles over Pakistan are as far distant from the battlefield as Creech Air Force Base in Nevada. They report for work and routinely locate, identify, and track terrorists; sometimes they fire missiles and kill them. They then leave work and return home to their families at the end of every shift. Although they see their targets, often more vividly than combat aircraft crews would, they do not face imminent death. The advent of precision strike weaponry has transformed air combat from among the most casualty-intensive forms of warfare in World War II to one whose practitioners face no physical danger.

This arrangement represents a profound change in the relationship between the warrior and warfare, one whose implications are only now beginning to play out. In the future, adversaries will likely possess UAVs of their own, including armed variants. They will also seek to deny the United States the ability to operate in their skies with impunity, either by shooting down UAVs or jamming communication links between the vehicles and their controllers.

Despite the changes brought on by armed UAVs, they are still "manned" in the sense that an operator remains in control of the aircraft and decides when to release munitions. In the future, however, we are likely to see the emergence of truly autonomous weapon systems, where key decisions are made not by men but machines. A move to autonomous weaponry is attractive for a number of reasons, including potentially lower cost and reduced susceptibility to enemy jamming of communication links and sensors. However, truly autonomous weapons would move human intervention to an earlier phase in the vehicle's flight. Moreover, the experience of past autonomous weapon programs, such as the Low-Cost Autonomous Attack System, or LOCAAS, shows that such weapons will have to surmount high organizational barriers before they are accepted. Soldiers, sailors, airmen, and Marines are still learning to trust UAV operators; it will be a long time before they trust machines.

The emergence of a mature precision-strike regime is likely to have dramatic consequences for the United States. Since the end of World War II, the United States has based its defense strategy on a combination of forward-based forces to deter adversaries and reassure allies and friends and the projection of power from those bases and the continental United States to defeat foes in wartime. The spread of precision-strike systems will call that formula into question.

U.S. bases are increasingly under threat of precision-strike systems. For example, some U.S. bases in the western Pacific are now within range of Chinese precision-guided conventional ballistic missiles; others will come in range as China deploys longer-range weapons. Over time, the vulnerability of these bases will undermine the deterrence of aggressors and reassurance of allies.

The threat to U.S. forward bases, in turn, calls into question the model that the United States has relied on for power projection in recent decades. Without access to ports and airfields in Saudi Arabia and across the Persian Gulf region, for example, it would have become considerably more difficult for the U.S.-led coalition to eject Iraqi forces from Kuwait in 1991. A future campaign against an adversary armed with precision-guided missiles, rockets, and mortars may more closely resemble the Normandy invasion and Iwo Jima than the relatively unopposed attacks on Iraq and Afghanistan.

Finally, over time it is likely that states will be able to strike the U.S. homeland with precision-strike systems, offering them a way to attack the United States directly. This threat could further increase the cost of U.S. intervention overseas and potentially offer adversaries a way to coerce the United States without resorting to the use of nuclear weapons.

However it manifests itself, the emergence of a mature precision-strike regime is likely to result in a pattern of conflict that will differ considerably from that of recent decades. The United States will no longer be able to rely on its absolute superiority in precision strike for battlefield advantage. To compete, the United States will have to seek new sources of comparative advantage. Ironically, it may also have to revert increasingly to its nuclear arsenal to deter not only nuclear attacks but also strikes from precision-guided nonnuclear weapons. Here as in other areas, old ideas may reappear in new form as the revolution matures.

Notes

1 See Bernard Brodie, "Technological Change, Strategic Doctrine, and Political Outcomes," in *Historical Dimensions of National Security Problems*, ed. Klaus Knorr (Lawrence: University Press of Kansas, 1976); J. F. C. Fuller, *Armament and History: A Study of the Influence of Armament on History from the Dawn of Classical Warfare to the Second World War* (London: Eyre & Spottiswoode, 1946); Karl Lautenschäger, "Technology and the Evolution of Naval Warfare," *International Security* 8, no. 2 (Fall 1983); William H. McNeill, *The Pursuit of Power: Technology, Armed Force, and Society since AD 1000* (Chicago: University of Chicago Press, 1982); Jeremy Black,

A Military Revolution? Military Change and European Society, 1550–1800 (London: Macmillan, 1991); Geoffrey Parker, *The Military Revolution*, 2nd ed. (Cambridge: Cambridge University Press, 1996); Clifford J. Rogers, ed., *The Military Revolution Debate: Readings on the Military Transformation of Early Modern Europe* (Boulder, CO: Westview Press, 1995); Keith L. Shimko, *The Iraq Wars and America's Military Revolution* (Cambridge: Cambridge University Press, 2010), chap. 1.

2 Andrew F. Krepinevich identifies the following military revolutions: (1) the infantry revolution of the first half of the fourteenth century; (2) the artillery revolution of the early to mid–fifteenth century; (3) the revolution of sail and shot that stretched from the sixteenth century to the mid–seventeenth century; (4) the fortress revolution of the sixteenth century; (5) the gunpowder revolution of the seventeenth century; (6) the Napoleonic revolution of the late eighteenth and early nineteenth centuries; (7) the land warfare revolution that stretched from the mid–nineteenth century to the early twentieth century; (8) the naval revolution that stretched from the mid–nineteenth century to the early twentieth century; (9) the interwar revolutions in mechanization, aviation, and information of the early twentieth century; and (10) the nuclear revolution of the mid–twentieth century. Andrew F. Krepinevich, "Cavalry to Computer: The Pattern of Military Revolutions," *National Interest* 37 (Fall 1994): 31–36.

3 Eliot A. Cohen, "A Revolution in Warfare," *Foreign Affairs* 75, no. 2 (March/April 1996): 43–44.

4 See, for example, Rolf Hobson, "Blitzkrieg, the Revolution in Military Affairs and Defense Intellectuals," *Journal of Strategic Studies* 33, no. 4 (August 2010): 625–43.

5 There is a considerable literature on the issue of military innovation. See Adam Grissom, "The Future of Military Innovation Studies," *Journal of Strategic Studies* 29, no. 5 (October 2006): 905–34; Barry R. Posen, *The Sources of Military Doctrine: France, Britain, and Germany between the World Wars* (Ithaca, NY: Cornell University Press, 1984); Stephen Peter Rosen, "New Ways of War: Understanding Military Innovation," *International Security* 13, no. 1 (Summer 1988): 134–68; Stephen Peter Rosen, *Winning the Next War: Innovation and the Modern Military* (Ithaca, NY: Cornell University Press, 1991); Kimberly Marten Zisk, *Engaging the Enemy: Organizational Theory and Soviet Military Innovation, 1955–1991* (Princeton, NJ: Princeton University Press, 1993).

6 The Napoleonic revolution, for example, was not brought about by technological innovation, nor did it involve new weaponry. See Peter Paret, "Revolutions in Warfare: An Earlier Generation of Interpreters," in *National Security and International Stability*, ed. Bernard Brodie, Michael D. Intriligator, and Roman Kolkowicz (Cambridge: Oelgeschlager, Gunn, and Hain, 1983), 158.

7 See, for example, the cases in Williamson Murray and Allan R. Millett, eds., *Military Innovation in the Interwar Period* (New York: Cambridge University Press, 1996).

8 Michael Howard, "Military Science in an Age of Peace," *Journal of the Royal United Services Institute for Defence Studies* 119, no. 1 (March 1974): 4.

9 Anchoring occurs when the mind uses a natural starting point as a first approximation to a judgment. It modifies this starting point as it receives additional information. Typically, however, the starting point serves as an anchor that reduces the amount of adjustment, so that the final estimate remains closer to the starting point than it ought to be. Amos Tversky and Daniel Kahneman, "Anchoring and Calibration in the Assessment of Uncertain Quantities," *Oregon Research Institute Research Bulletin* 12 (1972).

10 Everett M. Rogers, *Diffusion of Innovations*, 3rd ed. (New York: Free Press, 1983), 175.

11 Fuller, *Armament and History*, 143.

12 *Jeune école* tactics did not, for example, displace the battleship as the centerpiece of naval warfare. Nor have antitank weapons made the tank obsolete. Instead, in each case the development of countermeasures triggered responses that restored the effectiveness of the practice that was being countered. See Edward N. Luttwak, *Strategy: The Logic of War and Peace* (Cambridge, MA: Belknap Press of Harvard University Press, 1987), 27–39; Robert L. O'Connell, *Of Arms and Men: A History of War, Weapons, and Aggression* (New York: Oxford University Press, 1989), 7–9; Michael Vlahos, "A Crack in the Shield: The Capital Ship under Attack," *Journal of Strategic Studies* 2, no. 1 (May 1979): 47–82.

13 Emily O. Goldman and Leslie C. Eliason, eds., *Adaptive Enemies, Reluctant Friends: The Impact of Diffusion on Military Practice* (Stanford, CA: Stanford University Press, 2003).

14 See, for example, Thomas G. Mahnken, *Technology and the American Way of War since 1945* (New York: Columbia University Press, 2008); Thomas G. Mahnken, *Uncovering Ways of War: U.S. Military Intelligence and Foreign Military Innovation, 1918–1941* (Ithaca, NY: Cornell University Press, 2002).

15 Thomas G. Mahnken, "Beyond Blitzkrieg: Allied Responses to Combined-Arms Armored Warfare during World War II," in Goldman and Eliason, *Adaptive Enemies, Reluctant Friend*.

16 Barry D. Watts, *Six Decades of Guided Munitions and Battle Networks: Progress and Prospects* (Washington, DC: Center for Strategic and Budgetary Assessments, 2007).

17 Mahnken, *Technology and the American Way of War*, 115.

18 See, for example, William J. Perry, "Desert Storm and Deterrence," *Foreign Affairs* 70, no. 4 (Fall 1991): 66–82; Krepinevich, "Cavalry to Computer"; and Cohen, "Revolution in Warfare."

19 Mahnken, *Technology and the American Way of War*, 169, 171.

20 Shimko, *Iraq Wars and America's Military Revolution*, 23.

21 Michael J. Mazarr et al., *The Military Technical Revolution: A Structural Framework* (Washington, DC: Center for Strategic and International Studies, 1993), 28.

22 Thomas A. Keaney and Eliot A. Cohen, *Gulf War Air Power Survey Summary Report* (Washington, DC: Department of the Air Force, 1993), 251.

23 William S. Cohen, *Report of the Quadrennial Defense Review* (Washington, DC: Department of Defense, 1997), iv.

24 *Transforming Defense: National Security in the 21st Century* (Arlington, VA: National Defense Panel, December 1997).

25 James R. Blaker, "The American RMA Force: An Alternative to the QDR," *Strategic Review* 25, no. 3 (Summer 1997): 22.

26 Thomas G. Mahnken and James R. FitzSimonds, *The Limits of Transformation: Officer Attitudes toward the Revolution in Military Affairs* (Newport, RI: Naval War College Press, 2003), chap. 6.

27 Ibid., chap. 7.

28 *2001 Quadrennial Defense Review Report* (Washington, DC: Department of Defense, 2001), 30.

29 James R. FitzSimonds and Thomas G. Mahnken, "Officer Attitudes toward Transformation, 2000–2006," paper presented at the annual meeting of the International Studies Association, March 24, 2006, San Diego.

30 Mahnken, *Technology and the American Way of War*, 200, 209.

31 "The Year of the Drone: An Analysis of U.S. Drone Strikes in Pakistan, 2004–2012," at http://counterterrorism.newamerica.net/drones (accessed May 17, 2012).

32 Brian Glyn Williams, "The CIA's Covert Predator Drone War in Pakistan, 2004–2010: The History of an Assassination Campaign," *Studies in Conflict and Terrorism* 33, no. 10 (October 2010): 871–92; "A New Weapon in the War on Terror," *Newsweek* blog, http://www.newsweek.com/blogs/declassified/2010/09/10/a-new-weapon-in-the-war-on-terror.html (accessed December 9, 2010).

33 Mark Stokes, *China's Evolving Conventional Strategic Strike Capability* (Washington, DC: Project 2049 Institute, 2009).

34 Lieutenant Colonel Scott C. Farquar, *Back to Basics: A Study of the Second Lebanon War and Operation CAST LEAD* (Fort Leavenworth, KS: Combat Studies Institute Press, 2009).

35 Williams, "CIA's Covert Predator Drone War," 880–82.

36 Thomas C. Schelling, *Arms and Influence* (New Haven, CT: Yale University Press, 1966), 2.

37 Williams, "CIA's Covert Predator Drone War," 881–82.

4 :: American Military Culture from Colony to Empire

Robert L. Goldich

Abstract: Until World War II, the primary peacetime job of the U.S. Army was not to be ready to fight instantly, but to provide a core of military expertise that would enable a wartime force of citizen-soldiers to be built up after war began. Wars were infrequent. Since the end of the Cold War, the Army has become a force that deploys and fights on a regular basis. The true citizen-soldier who serves only for a few years, usually in wartime and often involuntarily, and remains, at heart, a civilian, is no longer with us and is not likely to return in the foreseeable future, despite nostalgia for his passing. In the midst of a civilian society that is increasingly pacifistic, easygoing, and well adjusted, the Army (career and noncareer soldiers alike) remains flinty, harshly results-oriented, and emotionally extreme. The inevitable and necessary civil-military gap has become a chasm.

In 1963, Theodore R. Fehrenbach published a magisterial and in many places poetic history of the Korean War. Almost fifty years later, his book remains the seminal treatise on limited frontier wars and the American national psyche. Fehrenbach addressed the incompatibility of America's changed strategic circumstances after World War II with the traditional American view of the purpose of an army and how it should be manned. For such limited wars, he maintained, the United States needed "legions."

> However repugnant the idea is to liberal societies, the man who will willingly defend the free world in the fringe areas is not the responsible citizen-soldier. The man who will go where his colors go, without asking, who will fight a phantom foe in jungle and mountain range, without counting, and who will suffer and die in the midst of incredible hardship, without complaint, is still what he always has been, from Imperial Rome to sceptered Britain to democratic America. He is the stuff of which legions are made.
>
> His pride is in his colors and his regiment, his training hard and thorough and coldly realistic, to fit him for what he must face, and his obedience to his orders. As a legionary, he held the gates of civilization for the classical world; as a blue-coated horseman, he swept the Indians from the Plains; he has been called United States Marine. He does the jobs—the utterly necessary jobs—no militia is willing to do. His task is moral or immoral according to the orders that send him forth.[1]

In this chapter, I argue that the United States has finally created Fehrenbach's legions,[2] and that in doing so we have transformed American military culture to a degree unprecedented in American history.

The United States' geostrategic situation and the military practices and capabilities associated with it have determined American military culture to a much greater extent than have our political institutions and social attitudes. For the purposes of this analysis, I define "culture" as the most significant internal attitudes and mind-set of the collective membership of the armed forces. It can be argued that one should differentiate between officers and enlisted, or career and noncareer, personnel; in fact, a recent convergence of the two is one of the central points of this chapter. I posit that there has been only one decisive change in the country's geostrategic situation since American independence from Britain, gained during the Revolutionary War, was ratified by the War of 1812; that our political institutions have been fundamentally constant since the adoption of the Constitution in 1788; and that the actual effects

of changing American social attitudes on the nation's military culture, particularly respecting the inclusiveness of hitherto excluded
groups, have been remarkably small.

The Army, at the fore of American military culture and its relationship to the larger society, receives the greatest emphasis in this
chapter. The Navy, attached to the shorelines of North America or at
sea, has had comparatively little cultural interaction with the general population on a sustained basis. The Marine Corps is small and
did not establish its current image among Americans until, at the
earliest, during and after World War I. The Corps' image is vivid,
but its culture has, arguably, changed little if at all since the turn of
the twentieth century. The Air Force is new, and its culture blends
that of the Army from which it sprang in 1947 and the technological circumstances that lead to comparatively few Air Force personnel training and preparing for, or engaging in, direct combat. The
Army expands the most in time of major mobilizations, sustains by
far the heaviest casualties, and always comprises the vast majority of
forces deployed for war. In both public and private discussions since
the Revolution, it is the Army infantry soldier who has instinctively
come to the mind of the American people whenever "the military"
has been under consideration.

From 1815 through 1989, the professional outlook and doctrine
of the Army involved preparation for periodic conventional wars,
although Indian wars of course occupied much of the time and
energy of the Army throughout the nineteenth century. The actual
need to wage conventional wars, however, did not occur very often.
The Mexican War of 1846 to 1848, the Civil War of 1861 to 1865, the
Spanish-American War and subsequent Philippine Insurrection of
1898 to 1902, World War I (1917–1918), World War II (1941–1945), the
Korean War (1950–1953), the Vietnam War (1965–1973, in terms of
major American involvement): all involved an intake of vast numbers of citizen-soldiers into a tiny peacetime all-volunteer Army.
When the country was not at war, the Army had minimal contact
with Americans because so few soldiers were on active duty. During
the century or so that preceded the nation's breakout into competi-
tive international politics between 1898 and 1917, most soldiers were
stationed in the thinly populated frontier as it steadily moved west.

The contrast with European armies—and others on the European model, such as the post–Meiji Restoration Japanese army[3]—is striking. In countries with large armies manned almost entirely by conscripts in peacetime as well as during war, tactical units were dispersed throughout their territory. Large numbers of "garrison towns," with constant contact between soldiers and civilians, was the norm.[4] In general, this has not been the case in the United States. Throughout American history, the average American civilian has lived his or her life with minimal to nonexistent interaction with soldiers, and soldiers, whether in the service for a few years or a career, have had comparatively little day-to-day contact with civilians other than those in small, isolated towns adjacent to bases.[5] This civilian-Army separation existed both before and after brief periods of peacetime conscription: namely, from 1940 to 1941; from 1948 to 1950; and the twelve-year period from the end of the Korean War in 1953 to the beginning of major U.S. ground combat in Vietnam in 1965. The American enlistee and draftee have, in most cases, trained and served in remote areas, far from the major population, economic, and cultural hubs of American life. The small size of the American military also contributed to this isolation. Not until the post-1945 era was the U.S. Army more than an insignificant fraction of the total U.S. population, except in times of total mobilization such as the Civil War and both world wars.

But it was the psychology of a cadre-mobilization model that affected the fundamental self-image of the Army probably more than anything else. Certainly, the Army at times had ongoing missions—principally, the Indian wars—other than training and preparing for conventional conflict. The Army's consistent view of itself as a conventional force preparing for battle against a comparable foe was integral to the development of military professionalism in the United States.[6] However, the Army was so small that for *any* sustained conflict against an organized state-based force, huge numbers of volunteers and/or conscripts had to be enlisted or inducted.

Even the Mexican War and the Spanish-American War (and subsequent Philippine Insurrection / Philippine-American War) required large numbers of wartime volunteers to augment the tiny regular Army. Such mobilizations, especially in an egalitarian democracy, required that these conflicts be cast in terms of ideological crusades. Such campaigns included "manifest destiny" in 1846 to 1848; preserving the Union and ending slavery in 1861 to 1865; freeing Cuba and "remembering the *Maine*" in 1898 and its aftermath;[7] making the world safe for democracy against the Central Powers in 1917 to 1918; and crushing Axis totalitarianism in 1941 to 1945. Until the aftermath of World War II, after each spasmodic mobilization the citizen forces were demobilized en masse. The Army reverted to a small cadre force and a prolonged period of peace ensued.

The results were twofold. First, the Army was not only physically isolated from the citizenry in terms of basing structure and domestic deployment, but was functionally isolated as well. In peacetime, the Army needed little from the citizenry. It did not conscript or require many volunteers. Second, the Army learned to think of itself as a force with the primary mission of training itself for infrequent mobilizations for ideological crusades based on popular interpretations of democratic principles. Its primary peacetime job was *not* to be ready to fight instantly, whether on North American soil or overseas, but to provide a core of professional military expertise that would enable a large wartime force of citizen-soldiers to be built up after wars—fairly infrequent events—began. Under this rubric, the Army career force, officers and noncommissioned officers (NCOs), developed a culture of austere professionalism, cultural introversion, and preparation for war rather than frequently going to war.[8] Men commonly joined the career force, either as officers or NCOs, and retired without ever serving in combat. This was particularly true during the long peace between 1918 and 1941, when the Army was engaged in no combat whatsoever.[9] Wartime service was expected to occupy only a small portion of a military career.

The first major change in this culture began to appear immediately after the end of World War II. For the first time in American history, the United States maintained a large force in peacetime. Millions of Americans served in the armed forces, primarily the Army, based on the first true peacetime draft in American history.[10] With its public profile raised enormously, the military became a much more salient institution in the minds of the American people.

Nonetheless, the cadre-mobilization model still governed the military, in general, and the Army, in particular. After World War II, the traditional American concepts of "peace" and "war," sharply differentiated, continued to govern how the Army thought of itself. Notably, this attitude did not change after the abolition of conscription in 1973. Between 1945 and the end of the Cold War in 1989, the Army fought two major wars: Korea, between mid-1950 and mid-1953, and Vietnam, which involved major U.S. combat participation from 1965 through early 1973.

When the Army was not involved in a major conflict, it was almost entirely at peace, and its mission was to train for a major, worldwide conflict with the Soviet Union and its client states and surrogates—that is, a third world war. The number of minor contingency operations involving Army combat forces (as distinct from advisory functions in Vietnam from 1961 to 1965) between VJ Day and the fall of the Berlin Wall in 1989 was actually remarkably low. The actions in Lebanon (1958), the Dominican Republic (1965–1966), and Grenada (1983) were brief and involved only light casualties. Between 1973 and the end of the Cold War, the Army remained a training-oriented force rather than one organized for ongoing or immediate operations.

Nonetheless, transition to the all-volunteer force had significant effects on Army culture.[11] First, it tended to diminish—but by no means end—the diametrically opposed views and outlooks of the career force on one hand and junior officers / junior enlisted personnel on the other. There will always be a large gap between those who command and those who obey. What has changed is that those who obey at the bottom of both the officer and enlisted chains of command have freely opted into the institution and its characteristics. While most do not plan on a military career, they are not unwilling participants, who seek to accommodate rather than succeed. The junior officer and enlisted ranks are no longer composed primarily of draftees or draft-motivated volunteers who, more or less, did not want to be in uniform, even if they accepted their lot and tried to do their best.[12] As Andrew J. Bacevich has noted in his sadly underused study of the Army of the 1950s, the nature of the Cold War Army, "far larger than any previous peacetime force, composed largely of short-service draftees, and dependent on frequent rotations to man large overseas garrisons—virtually ensured that its ethos would be centralized, bureaucratic, and impersonal."[13] Under the volunteer force, the average length of service in the Army rose considerably, decreasing the rapid turnover in the ranks. The emphasis on rebuilding the Army after Vietnam greatly increased the opportunity and emphasis on systematic professional education and training for NCOs. Pay, benefits, and housing quality went up.[14]

Finally, while scarcely the intimate organization that it was before World War II, the post-1973 Army was nonetheless much smaller than that which gave rise to the conditions Bacevich describes. Massive and bureaucratic it may have been compared to just about any other American organization, public or private, but it was less so than the pre-Vietnam force. The pre-Vietnam Army of about a million soldiers remained at about 780,000 between 1973 and 1987; shrank slightly to about 750,000 at the end of the Cold War; contracted to 480,000 during most of the 1990s; currently stands at about 570,000 and is programmed to drop to 490,000 by 2017, reflecting the withdrawal of U.S. forces from Iraq and the planned end of large U.S. ground-force commitments in Afghanistan. All these developments have contributed to decreasing the width of the officer-enlisted gap in terms of common motivations.

Furthermore, the end of conscription, combined with an acceleration of long-term social trends, meant that the moral, ethical, and philosophical outlook of everyone in the armed forces—not just career personnel—tended to be more sharply differentiated from that of civilians.[15] The armed forces, both in peace and in war, are now composed mostly, if not almost entirely, of people who accept the social legitimacy of violence and the infliction of pain, suffering, death, and anguish on other human beings. In contrast, civilian society increasingly takes the attitude that any form of physical coercion of, or even exertion of influence on, human beings by other human beings is morally wrong.[16] Even the open expression of remarks considered psychologically, as opposed to physically, harmful—such as verbal "bullying" in schools—is being subject to administrative and, in some cases, statutory penalties. The medicalization of, and requirement to forcibly change, personality characteristics that go beyond a fairly narrow range of acceptable behavior, such as Asperger's syndrome, is another example of the societal tendency to control behaviors deemed disruptive.

In addition, absolute pacifism has increased steadily in the West (albeit much less in the United States than in Western and Central Europe), an important component of this being a theological reassertion among Protestants and Catholics of the early Christian pacifist tradition (Judaism, symbolically but not demographically important, has tended to morally eschew violence throughout the two thousand years of the Diaspora).[17]

The military remains hierarchical and, ultimately, authoritarian (although there is much more give-and-take, especially in combat units and environments, than most civilians might believe). It emphasizes organizational and collective effectiveness, discipline, and commitment rather than individual rights, prerogatives, and liberties. With life tending to be infinitely less harsh in the industrialized world than it was in the past, the individual who joins the armed forces enters a lifestyle and environment that has become far removed from the civilian world. Before the nineteenth century, the average individual was much more used to having insufficient or inadequate food, living without adequate shelter and little temperature control, and inured to omnipresent death from disease, from infancy onward. He or she was commonly confronted with much greater day-to-day amounts of civil disorder and low-level interpersonal violence than is the case in the modern world.[18] With most of these premodern rigors of everyday life gone, comparatively unpleasant and rigorous physical environments in even peacetime military training and service—especially on the ground—heighten the contrast with civilian life. In combat, the variation from the civilian norm is enormous.[19] Furthermore, everyday speech in the services, particularly the ground combat arms, is extreme. Aggressive males are constantly testing one another through verbal altercations and insults. Disagreements are still sometimes resolved through barracks fights. This reinforces cohesion and, in fact, has been fairly normal among men, particularly young men, in groups. However, such physical and verbal aggression is increasingly not tolerated in gender-integrated civilian society, where harmony and agreement are accorded a higher priority than any other governing principle. This in turn relates to another difference between the military and civilian worlds. That is, despite the vastly increased proportion of women in uniform, the military remains an overwhelmingly masculine-defined institution, to which military women must, and do, adapt. Compare the military situation with the developed world in general, where gender segregation, social or occupational, has largely died out.

It is not clear what the recently announced policy of beginning to admit women to the ground combat arms will do to these attitudes and to the ground combat culture.[20] Importantly, the policy as announced involves progressive and sequential study and implementation, not to be completed until 2016, with opportunities for the military services to recommend continuation of all-male occupational specialties if they deem it militarily necessary. (Unlike the recently repealed "Don't Ask, Don't Tell" relating to the exclusion of openly gay men and lesbians from military service, the current restrictions on women in the ground combat arms are not based on statute, and therefore no congressional action is required to change them.) If the standards for physical endurance and strength are maintained, it is certain that very few women will qualify for the infantry, field artillery, armor, or special operations forces. If their numbers are few, they will simply have to adapt to being a member of a very small female minority in an overwhelmingly masculine culture. If there is any modification downward of these standards to admit more women to these branches of the Army and Marine Corps than would otherwise be the case, then the impact could be profound, and arguably negative on the cohesion of ground combat units, particularly if the United States becomes involved in a high-intensity war where casualties are much higher, the amount of artillery fire received much greater, and the living conditions substantially more arduous over longer periods than has been the case in the Iraq and Afghanistan wars. There is also the possibility of congressional and judicial action related to the policy change. All of this makes authoritative predictions very difficult to make as of this writing.

In passing, it should be noted that although members of the reserve components of the armed forces are, by definition, "citizen-soldiers," their very presence in the military implies their acceptance of the entire panoply of military-institutional characteristics just noted, making them, in psychological and moral outlook, more like active-duty military personnel than their fellow civilians in the communities in which they work and live.

The most profound change in American military culture, however, has taken place since 1989. The collapse of the Soviet Union and the Warsaw Pact; the drastic reduction in Soviet and Russian military power, particularly its conventional forces; and the removal of Russian borders to where they had been in approximately 1500, created the largest transformation in the American strategic situation since 1917. No longer did the U.S. armed forces have a primary mission of planning for war against peer adversaries.[21] At the same time, the end of the Cold War released forces inimical to American national interests and influence from the iron lock of U.S.-Soviet nuclear stalemate. The result? Over the past two decades, the paradigm of long periods of peace interspersed with apocalyptic mobilizations for war, involving the accession of huge numbers of draftees into the force, has been replaced by one of fairly continuous operational deployments. Though some engagements involve more casualties and forces than others, all place constant demands on the Army to provide units and soldiers for expeditionary warfare. It is impossible to overstate how much this has changed the entire set of expectations both officers and enlisted personnel bring to Army service. Continuous operations against current enemies have replaced training, planning, and education for periodic operations against future ones. Preparations for raising a citizen force and activating large numbers of new units, using the active Army as a cadre, are apparently not done at any level within the Army staff.[22] More broadly, although planning for both industrial and manpower mobilization beyond the existing force structure was an integral part of the George H. W. Bush administration's post–Cold War defense paradigm,[23] when the Clinton administration came to power in 1993, this component also vanished, and has remained officially buried ever since. Therefore, the true citizen-soldier—who serves only during the spasmodic, totalistic, ideological conflicts that last a few years and retains a fundamentally civilian outlook on life—no longer has any place in the Army's consideration of how it must prepare for future war.

Although nostalgia for the conscripted citizen-soldier persists, that soldier is gone—at least for the foreseeable future. We have indeed transitioned to Fehrenbach's legions. In my view, the Army's outlook is beginning to resemble that of the Marine Corps, whose ethos was best described in *Harper's* in 1914. Commenting on the American occupation of Veracruz, Mexico, the author observed: "Just an order issued ... and one regiment after another are on their way to Cuba, or Mexico, or the world's end. Where they are going isn't the Marine's concern. Their business is to be always ready to go."[24]

One might also say that American soldiers are becoming more like "soldiers of the Queen [or King]": that is, without immediate ideological concerns.[25] This development enables frustrating and lengthy counterinsurgency campaigns, or others without immediate gratification, to be conducted with much less regard for public opinion in the short term. As French international relations scholar Étienne de Durand put it, "Mobilizing the population generally comes with a heavy price tag attached to it; the nonnegotiable need to show quick results."[26]

A professional force that does not require situation-specific ideological mobilization is much more suited to these kinds of military operations. The difference from the popular conception of the American soldier that dominated the draft era of 1940 to 1973 is clear. The pre-1973 image of the American soldier at war, going all the way back, arguably, to the Revolution, and certainly to the Civil War, was perhaps best exemplified by cartoonist Bill Mauldin's Willie and Joe characters during World War II. They were infantrymen who were unshaven, possessed good combat discipline but uneven administrative discipline, were not overly obeisant to uniform regulations beyond what was required of them, and, in general, represented well what they were: men who would rather not be there, but either felt a call to serve or realized they had no choice and would therefore do their best. The last words in Mauldin's immortal collection *Up Front* superbly evoke the American draftee's attitude:

They are big men and honest men, with the inner warmth that comes from the generosity and simplicity you learn up there. Until the doc can go back to his chrome office and gallstones and the dogface can go back to his farm and I can go back to my wife and son, that is the closest to home we can ever get.[27]

While Mauldin's view of the infantryman at war is timeless,[28] the concept of the citizen-soldier who will serve only for the duration, then return home, is not. The same goes for the traditional U.S. Army combat uniform, which displayed far fewer insignia, decorations, and accoutrements compared to those of European armies from World War I through the Vietnam War, and which was draped without much tailoring on the Sad Sack, Beetle Bailey, and their fellow soldiers. The pre-hyperpower American military image of Willie and Joe has been replaced by combat uniforms with unit insignia and American flags, close-cropped haircuts, the variety of equipment on load-bearing packs and vests, the goggles and flip-down night-vision devices on angled helmets, all of which betoken a tough, hard, cold, isolate professionalism.

Although the Army's career force always maintained a rigid professional image and an accompanying set of attitudes, its citizen-soldier enlisted ranks did not. Draftees typically did not internalize the norms and psychology of the career force; rather, they accepted them, externally and reluctantly, and adapted as best they could. Today, broadly uniform attitudes permeate the entire force, from private to full general, although naturally they are stronger in those who have been in service longer. The enlistee and junior officer, as well as the career force member, voluntarily subjects himself or herself to military values, which vary considerably from those of the civilian culture, rather than accommodating those values because of events beyond his or her control. This shift is particularly telling for enlisted men in the ground combat arms of the Army and Marine Corps. Like all enlistees, they choose their military occupational specialty upon enlistment; thus, they have volunteered not only for military service generally, and for their particular armed force, but for that part of the force that has the most arduous and dangerous tasks in peace and war.

What other effects has the ongoing transformation into a force of legions had on American military culture? It has created a force that has immense expertise in the conduct of combat operations and one that is well aware of this advantage. The high casualties due to simple inexperience, lack of rigorous training, and thinly spread professional military expertise that marked American military performance during much of the world wars and Korea, and to some extent Vietnam, no longer occur. Several factors account for much of this improvement: in the counterinsurgency wars we are now fighting, troops in combat are in smaller and more dispersed units; the enemy does not have artillery and other indirect-fire weapons with a high rate of fire; and the tactical expertise of the Germans, Japanese, North Koreans, Chinese, and Vietnamese Communists is not as prevalent in Iraqi and Afghan insurgents. We also have provided first-rate equipment to our troops. But the key factors are probably the high quality of the people and the unprecedented realism in unit training that have been enabled by investment in training facilities and courses and much lower personnel turnover.

The opportunities for disasters at the platoon and company levels, though present, have rarely materialized in Iraq and Afghanistan, in contrast to the carnage of past twentieth-century American wars, particularly in their initial stages.[29] The bumbling incompetence of commanders not used to wartime stresses, and equally superficial training of hastily conscripted soldiers taught in frenetic wartime situations by trainers with scarcely more practical experience than they,[30] has been greatly diminished. (I do not address the issue of bumbling incompetence among the high-level political leadership of the country, or the sluggish and reluctant adaptation of senior military leaders, accustomed to a long peace, to war in general and irregular warfare in particular.) The post-1973, post-Vietnam all-volunteer force is much less tolerant of tactical and operational failure than its predecessors, owing partly to vastly enhanced training, but also to a deepened ethos of physical and mental toughness.[31]

The downside, perhaps, is that if our legions are always deployed fighting the barbarians on the frontiers, there is less time for their officers to think, reflect, and educate themselves in their profession, particularly in higher-level strategy. The career officer corps, by all accounts, is a much less contemplative institution, largely (although not entirely) because the constant press of deployments and operations has left much less time in a military career for not only civilian graduate education, but increasingly even for the professional military education that has always been an outstanding part of the American military system. The inevitable decrease in the tempo of operations post-Iraq, and then post-Afghanistan, will certainly restore this situation somewhat, but its long-term consequences could be pernicious.

Notably, American military culture has moved sharply from a Cavalier to a Roundhead attitude in social mores. The hard-drinking, chain-smoking, womanizing "alpha male" has to a considerable degree—especially in the officer corps—been replaced by the tee-totaling, often very religious, nonsmoking, family-man paragon of virtue. (Indeed, a drunken driving arrest and conviction will ruin an officer's career.) Similarly, a retired general officer recently stated to me that current infantry NCOs "seem to be more independent, introverted, quietly professional...religious, and if they do associate and drink they do it well away from the flagpole," in contrast to the Vietnam era.[32] The decrease in drinking and smoking relates to the need for constant readiness to go to war and the associated need for physical health and endurance, which mirrors similar trends among the more educated classes in American society. The change in sexual mores seems to have more diffuse causes. The increased proportion of women in the force, with the exception of all-male ground combat arms units, is one. Another is the considerable rise, over the past several decades, of open religiosity in the force, especially but not limited to evangelical Protestant Christianity,[33] which has encouraged heterosexual monogamy.[34] Much of the latter development simply tracks the steady increase in the salience of religious commitment throughout most of American society over the past several decades. But it also reflects the split between, on the one hand, the increasingly antiwar and anti-coercion socially liberal mainline Protestant denominations, some Catholics with an affinity for (to use a Protestant term) the "social gospel," and Reform Judaism, and, on the other hand, the willingness to use force for patriotic American purposes and the social conservatism of evangelical Protestantism, conservative Catholicism, and Orthodox Judaism.[35]

The advent of the all-volunteer force has also created an attitude among military personnel that they are, in a variety of ways, better than, or superior to, civilians. To a considerable extent, soldiers have always had such an attitude. They contrast the courage and resolution their profession demands with a softer, less austere, and less rigorous civilian world—even if they are conscripts eager to return to it. This outlook can be traced back to ancient times. However, what is new is the extent to which military personnel think they are "superior" because of the intrinsic human qualities they bring with them to military service, in addition to those they acquire while serving. Although human motivations are difficult to pinpoint, there appear to be two reasons for these feelings of superiority.

First, service members are constantly made aware, through both internal communications and through media reportage, that most young Americans cannot meet enlistment standards. This understandably makes them feel that they are, in some ways, superior to peers who could not be accepted into military service regardless of their desire to serve. Certainly, the quantitative data support this belief. Most first-term enlistees (like most Americans) certainly do not come from the more affluent sectors of American society, but the conventional wisdom that military service is a last resort for the substandard, however dubious even in the past, is utterly wrong in the modern American military. Military personnel are much less likely to be ill-educated;[36] are more intelligent (or at least show more aptitude when measured on a standardized test);[37] generally come from higher-income households; and are infinitely more physically fit.[38] They are much less likely to have encounters with the criminal justice system, and much less likely to use illegal drugs than their civilian counterparts, both in general and when age, race, and gender are controlled.[39]

Second, there is an utterly unquantifiable set of attitudes that may be even more important in propelling young men and women who enlist, or seek appointments as junior officers, to view themselves as superior to their civilian peers (again, regardless of socioeconomic status). The young person who enlists knows that he or she is opting to leave behind the comfortable, perhaps complacent, environment of family, friends, and community. Even before young enlistees are sworn in, they believe that they have opted to enter a more dangerous and demanding institution, one that is held to higher standards than civilian society, well-regarded among civilians, and more exciting and realistic than the humdrum world of daily civil life they left behind. They are, in a sense, internal immigrants, emigrating from their familiar surroundings to find more opportunity (economic and psychological) in the new and in many ways utterly alien institutional land of the armed forces.

Whatever their socioeconomic status in civilian life, young men and women who choose military service believe that in doing so, they demonstrate that they are taking a harder, more arduous, and utterly different path from their contemporaries who lack the moral and physical courage to choose differently. This situation is compared to the image of soldiers who manned past professional armies. In A.D. 69, when for the first time in a century Roman soldiers tramped through Italy en masse because of the year-long civil war that marked the "year of the four emperors,"[40] the peaceable civilians remarked on how barbaric, unlettered, and savage they looked and acted.[41] Two thousand years later, American legionaries, while as capable on a modern battlefield as those who wielded the *gladius* (the Roman short sword), appear to march through a civilian population that in some ways is more barbaric, more ill-educated, less physically fit, and less disciplined than they are.[42]

Where this meritocratic isolation from civilian norms of conduct will lead is unclear; nonetheless, it is unprecedented, at least as far as the large noncareer force the United States now maintains is concerned. Secretary of Defense Robert Gates, in his last major policy speech before leaving office, addressed this issue squarely, and critically. He noted that the concept of both inherent and acquired moral and ethical superiority of military personnel compared to American civilians was widespread at present, and essentially flatly denied that such superiority existed:

> But when you think about it, it is rather peculiar to suggest that attributes such as integrity, respect, and courage are not valued in the

United States of America writ large. If you spend enough time getting around this country, especially in successful organizations or close-knit communities, you would find the seven Army values are considered pretty important and being practiced across our great country and by Americans across the world. Just ask a policeman, fireman, teacher, or volunteer working in the inner city. Or the families of aid workers, diplomats, journalists, or intelligence officers slogging away under dangerous or Spartan conditions overseas. Or even inside any well-run business.

Of course, we are constantly bombarded with news of people and institutions across the country who fall short of these standards, or ignore them altogether—on Wall Street, on Capitol Hill in Hollywood, in all walks of public and private life. But the military, like any large, proud organization filled with fallible human beings, is not immune from shortcomings—whether in terms of morality or competence. Just think of

- The reality of poor—or even toxic—leadership by some officers at all levels;
- The careerism and inertia that can infect the middle layers of any big bureaucracy;
- The disturbingly high rates of sexual harassment and assault that persist within the ranks; and
- The tendency to hide or deflect unflattering information from superiors or the news media.

The real difference is that those who serve in uniform are opening themselves up to physical danger and long separation from family. Nevertheless, it is off-putting to hear, albeit anecdotally, comments that suggest that the military is to some degree separate and even superior from the society, the country, it is sworn to protect.[43]

It is difficult to see the sentiments expressed by Secretary Gates gaining much traction. The quantitative data speak for themselves. To a certain extent the secretary set up a straw man. Few if any people in the military would deny the existence of the deficiencies he mentions. This component of the civil-military gap concerns not whether these failings are present among those in uniform—indeed, military personnel are not shy about expressing their dissatisfaction with things they think need fixing—but their frequency. Furthermore, the "real differences" Secretary Gates alludes to—physical danger and family separation (interestingly, he left out physical discomfort and hardship, which are common in much of military life)—are central to the self-perceptions of military moral superiority, and it is hard, if not virtually impossible, to find civilian analogies. It is unlikely, therefore, that comments such as those of Secretary Gates will have much effect on the general image of military personnel as "superior."

Some have suggested, understandably, that this sense of superiority could lead to a greater willingness among military personnel to challenge civilian control of the military.[44] Do these attitudes indeed presage a possible increased tendency toward "putsches and caudillos and the Freikorps and Fasci di Combattimento" in the United States?[45] Theoretically the answer is yes; practically, probably not. The much larger military we have maintained since 1945 has, without question, maintained a correspondingly higher profile in American life, and American politics, than ever before. This is unavoidable. Nonetheless, the conditions for such an extreme development are almost entirely absent from the United States. We have no lost wars in which huge proportions of the male population were killed or wounded, followed by mass economic depression (compare putsches and *Freikorps* and Italian *Fascisti*); we have no culture of intensive military involvement in partisan national politics (caudillos and putsches); and we do not face a major breakdown of civil order due to the previous two conditions.

Finally, occasional attempts by members of the career officer corps to justify a greater degree of military autonomy vis-à-vis political leadership in the United States are not new and have rarely, if ever, obtained a coherent following. American career military personnel may grumble—have always grumbled—about the alleged character deficiencies of the society on whose behalf they bear arms, but their very disdain for such shortcomings inclines them to recoil from involvement in broader political matters rather than press toward it.[46] Nor is there any indication of profound political factionalism within the Army career force, such as that which existed in the French army in the late nineteenth and early twentieth centuries, and which greatly demoralized the French officer corps and seems to have contributed markedly to French military-readiness problems in the two decades before World War I.[47] In addition, first-term enlisted personnel and junior officers may indeed have the same combination of aloofness and disdain for the broader society, but they do not guide the institution and are not, at least in the context of the developed world, fruitful ground for serious military repudiation of civilian authority. This is not sub-Saharan Africa where sergeants become presidents or prime ministers.

I have made almost no mention of how conventional wisdom defines *culture* in terms of today's identity-oriented intellectual discourse. I think of the distinctions of race, gender, sexual orientation, or ethnicity. Why? I think the more diverse identities of this type that are present in the U.S. armed forces have little or no effect on the more fundamental aspects of American military culture I have discussed. The admission of African Americans into a desegregated military fifty-five to sixty years ago, and the steady accretion of modern immigrant groups—such as Hispanics and Asians—have done nothing to change the austere, isolate, self-referential traditional masculinity of the force. Nor has the increased presence of women, who have had to adapt to these underlying characteristics to serve. For that matter, there is little indication that the recent repeal of the statute (it was not simply a "policy") banning open and admitted homosexuals from serving (known colloquially as "Don't Ask, Don't Tell") will cause a decisive shift in the psychological and emotional underpinnings of the military. Gay men and lesbians who are out of the closet will, as have gay men and lesbians in the closet, conform to the larger culture, and that will be that.

The changes in American military culture over the past few decades, in short, and the extension of the attributes of the career officer and NCO corps to the entire force, are caused not by matters of identity such as gender, race, or ethnicity, but by the adaptation of the American military, particularly the Army, to a changed American strategic situation. The exertions of largely drafted American military forces in peace and war during most of the twentieth century have provided a long period of extended internal peace and prosperity to American society.

Without an apparent immediate need to endure the burdens of compulsory military service, the American civilian population has been unwilling to enlist, and the public has begun to question the practical necessity and moral legitimacy of institutionalized violence. The U.S. military has become the shield behind which civilian society can hold fast to its pacific views about the absolute supremacy of kindness and compassion. The entire military, in turn, not just the career force, has become a refuge for those who question the basic orientation of civilian society and do not wish to live within many of its central boundaries. There appears to be a gap—if not a chasm—between an increasingly sensate, amiable, and emotionally circumscribed civilian world and a flinty, harshly results-oriented, and emotionally extreme military, career and noncareer personnel alike.

The chasm's increased depth is not physical. The armed forces remain physically isolated from the major metropolitan areas of the nation as they always have been, but that isolation has in no way increased over the past several decades. An active-duty military force (all four services) of 1.4 million personnel, and a Selected Reserve of 850,000, is still a considerable number of people, and the reserve components in particular are spread all over the country, albeit a larger number in the South and Plains states.[48] Active-duty personnel and their families are no more isolated from civilian communities in their vicinity than they ever have been. In fact, the rise in the proportion of married personnel has probably resulted in more military members "living on the economy" than before; almost all junior enlisted single personnel, who constituted a much higher proportion of the total force during the draft era, live on base in barracks. As of 2007, the most recent year for which I could obtain data, 63 percent of military personnel lived in civilian off-base housing, and 37 percent in military housing,[49] and the standard rule of thumb over the past forty years is that at any one time one-third of military personnel are living on base and the others off base. Comments by some, therefore, that the Army "resides in remote fortresses—the world's most exclusive gated communities" seem misplaced at best.[50] Given modern communications, the fortresses are, if anything, less remote than ever before, and the proportion of military personnel living in them, if it has changed, has gone down, not up.

The chasm is, therefore, intellectual and cultural, and it has grown because of the steadily increasing incompatibility of military with civilian values. The military has not changed its basic institutional outlook over the past several decades, even though that outlook is now ubiquitous throughout the force rather than being confined to career personnel. The central task of the American military remains—must remain—inflicting pain and suffering on other human beings who are enemies of the United States, and physical damage on the economic and social infrastructure of those human beings and their societies. It is civilian society that has shifted. The difference is so decisive that it is difficult to see how mere organizational or "strategic communications" efforts, no matter how well-intentioned, can compensate for it.[51]

Nonetheless, some historical perspective is in order. As British military historian John France has pointed out, the postmodern developed world's assumption that armies are, or should be, "integrated into society and obedient to its norms" is extraordinarily unusual and anomalous. "Throughout recorded history, with very rare exceptions, armies have been isolated from social culture: 'War is a special activity and separate from any other pursued by man.'"[52] What appears to be happening is that the increasingly nonviolent and anti-coercion civil society is unwilling to accord legitimacy to the continued existence of war, and therefore unwilling to confront its "special" and "separate" nature in any way other than an entirely negative one.

An infantry lieutenant in the Marines recently observed, "For better or worse, real or imagined, the military is one of the few organizations that still attract people looking for an alternative to the 'world of clerks and teachers, of co-education and zo-ophily, of "consumer's leagues" and "associated charities," of industrialism unlimited, and feminism unabashed,'" as William James described it in his classic essay "The Moral Equivalent of War."[53] However, if this alienated shield fails, the demilitarized civil society may have neither the means nor the psychological will to defend itself. The shield itself may turn directly or indirectly on those whom it is supposed to defend, out of disgust for their failure to step up and contribute, either directly or with moral support. This has been an eternal conundrum in large societies facing threats that are far away, since at least the days of the later Roman and Han Chinese Empires, and it is still with us today.

Notes

1 T. R. Fehrenbach, *This Kind of War: Korea, a Study in Unpreparedness* (New York: Macmillan, 1963), 658.

2 I emphasize that I refer here to Fehrenbach's "legions" as embodying the concept of a professional army primarily tasked to defend or extend a nation's interests on frontiers far from the nation's borders or core territory. This is opposed to a conscription-centered force whose major mission is to fight enemies on a nation's land borders. The Roman imperial army, of course, differed enormously from the contemporary U.S. Army in terms of its relationship to the state, its exact deployment patterns, and the details of its recruiting and career structure, let alone the obvious technological differences. Its organization, however, is strikingly modern. For more detail, see *A Companion to the Roman Army*, ed. Paul Erdkamp (Malden, MA: Blackwell, 2007); Adrian Goldsworthy, *The Complete Roman Army* (London: Thames & Hudson, 2003); Lawrence Keppie, *The Making of the Roman Army: From Republic to Empire* (1984; repr., New York: Barnes & Noble, 1994); and David J. Breeze and Brian Dobson, *Roman Officers and Frontiers*, Mavors Roman Army Researches, vol. 10 (Stuttgart: Franz Steiner Verlag, 1993), 11–70, 113–217.

3 See Edward J. Drea, *Japan's Imperial Army: Its Rise and Fall, 1853–1945* (Lawrence: University Press of Kansas, 2009); Naoko Shimizu, *Japanese Society at War: Death, Memory, and the Russo-Japanese War* (New York: Cambridge University Press, 2009); and Richard J. Smethurst, *A Social Basis for Prewar Japanese Militarism: The Army and the Rural Community* (Berkeley: University of California Press, 1974).

4 For an in-depth discussion of this interaction in one major European country, see David M. Hopkin, *Soldier and Peasant in French Popular Culture, 1766–1870* (Rochester, NY: Boydell Press and Royal Historical Society, 2003).

5 See Edward M. Coffman, *The Old Army: A Portrait of the American Army in Peacetime, 1784–1898* (New York: Oxford University Press, 1986), and idem, *The Regulars: The American Army, 1898–1941* (Cambridge, MA: Belknap Press of Harvard University Press, 2004).

6 The literature on this phenomenon is vast. See the still-unmatched Russell F. Weigley, *History of the United States Army* (New York: Macmillan, 1967),

144–292; and William B. Skelton, *An American Profession of Arms: The Army Officer Corps, 1784–1861* (Lawrence: University Press of Kansas, 1992).

7   Many men who in 1898 volunteered to free Cuba, avenge the *Maine*, and punish the supposedly brutal and dastardly Spaniards found themselves instead engaged in a very different war of colonial pacification in the Philippines, and the cognitive dissonance could be considerable. Rather than liberating (or after they liberated), they found themselves cast in the role of imperial conquerors. Not being regular soldiers whose military orientation was professional and organizational rather than situation-specific, they were often quite bitter, although throughout they performed well in combat. For a vivid example, see Kyle Roy Ward, *In the Shadow of Glory: The Thirteenth Minnesota in the Spanish-American and Philippine-American Wars, 1898 to 1899* (St. Cloud, MN: North Star Press of St. Cloud, 2000).

8   For a vivid example of this isolation, see John M. Collins, "Depression Army," *Army*, January 1972, 8–14, in particular, his telling remark that "Intercourse with civilians was just that."

9   The small irregular wars in Central America and the Caribbean to which American forces were committed between the world wars were waged entirely by the Marine Corps.

10 The peacetime draft was the first in substantive, not technical, terms. The draft law enacted in September 1940, fifteen months before Pearl Harbor was attacked, was clearly in response to, and designed to prepare for, possible American participation in World War II, which had erupted in Europe on September 1, 1939. The reenactment of Selective Service in mid-1948, after the armed forces had been unable to recruit sufficient personnel through voluntary enlistment after expiration of the World War II draft at the end of 1946, did not result in the induction of many draftees because the pre–Korean War military was relatively small. The measure was, in social and cultural terms, a seamless continuation of the World War II draft. See George Q. Flynn, *The Draft: 1940–1973* (Lawrence: University Press of Kansas, 1993), 88–109. This is an invaluable volume for those investigating American military recruiting and manpower from World War II to the present.

11 Three works are essential to a study of the shift from a draft-based Army to the AVF: Bernard D. Rostker, *I Want You! The Evolution of the All-Volunteer Force* (Santa Monica, CA: Rand Corp., 2006); Beth Bailey, *America's Army: Making the All-Volunteer Force* (Cambridge, MA: Belknap Press of Harvard University Press, 2009); and Robert K. Griffith Jr., *The U.S. Army's Transition to the All-Volunteer Force, 1968–1974* (Washington, DC: Center of Military History, United States Army, 1997). For a very insightful shorter analysis of the background and current status of the AVF, see Crispin Burke, "America's All-Volunteer Force: The Right Choice, Despite Stress of Two Wars," parts 1–3, http://www.printfriendly.com/print/new?url=http%3A%2F%2Fwww.offizier.ch%2F3Fp%3D5382;

http://www.printfriendly.com/print/new?url=http%3A%2F%2Fwww.offizier.ch%2F%3Fp%3D5444; and http://www.printfriendly.com/print/new?url=http%3A%2F%2Fwww.offizier.ch%2F%3Fp%3D5496 (accessed April 22, 2012).

12 I have never heard an Army or Marine officer with personal experience commanding/serving with both draftees and volunteers in combat in both Korea and Vietnam state anything other than the performance of men in the two categories was absolutely indistinguishable. Indeed, I have frequently heard it said that during the peacetime post-Korea, pre-Vietnam years officers found the quality of draftees to be higher than that of volunteers, although because many of the latter were draft-pressured into enlisting it is difficult to disaggregate the two groups. I am particularly indebted to the insights of the following now-retired officers on these particular subjects over the years: General Volney F. Warner, U.S. Army; Major General John A. Leide, U.S. Army; Brigadier General Thomas V. Draude, U.S. Marine Corps; Colonel John D. (Scot) Crerar, U.S. Army (an informal manuscript written by Colonel Crerar was particularly helpful); and Lieutenant Colonel Donald Bowman, U.S. Army. More recently I am obliged to Lieutenant General (ret.) Bernard (Mick) Trainor, U.S. Marine Corps, for his insights on this issue.

13 Andrew J. Bacevich, *The Pentomic Era: The U.S. Army between Korea and Vietnam* (Washington, DC: National Defense University Press, 1986), 119. Professor Brian McAllister Linn of Texas A&M University is currently preparing a study of the post-Korea, pre-Vietnam Army, titled *Elvis's Army: Transformation and the Atomic-Era Soldier, 1946–1965,* which will be a needed contribution to the literature on post-1945 American military history.

14 The best comprehensive discussion of the post-Vietnam reconstruction of the Army remains Robert H. Scales Jr., *Certain Victory: The United States Army in the Gulf War* (Washington, DC: Office of the Chief of Staff, United States Army, 1993), 1–39.

15 The essence of this divergence in attitudes is captured by Azar Gat, *Victorious and Vulnerable: Why Democracy Won in the 20th Century and How It Is Still Imperiled* (Lanham, MD: Rowman & Littlefield, 2010).

16 A discussion of the changing meaning of the word "imperialism" over time seems appropriate here. Scholar Mark Proudman observes in the term "a fastidiousness, even a squeamishness, about power or influence, however attenuated or even consensual." Mark F. Proudman, "Words for Scholars: The Semantics of 'Imperialism,'" *Journal of the Historical Society* 8, no. 3 (September 2008): 425. Another interesting example is a Stanford University course in management science and engineering titled "The Ethical Analyst," in which "questioning the desirability of physical coercion and deception as a means to reach any end" is mentioned in the course description. *Stanford University Bulletin, 2008–09,* 608–9.

17 For the Christian component, see *The New Conscientious Objection: From Sacred to Secular Resistance*, ed. Charles C. Moskos and John Whiteclay Chambers II (New York: Oxford University Press, 1993); and Peter Brock, *Against the Draft: Essays on Conscientious Objection from the Radical Reformation to the Second World War* (Toronto: University of Toronto Press, 2006). For insightful remarks on the complex relationship of Diaspora Judaism and sanctioned violence, see Martin van Creveld, *The Culture of War* (New York: Ballantine Books, 2008), 376–94. Modern Israel, of course, is a state, and harbors a culture, in which the military has extraordinary influence, probably more than in any other developed democratic society. However, this does not invalidate the overwhelmingly pacifistic and anti-interhuman violence attitude that has existed in Judaism worldwide since the Romans crushed the Bar Kochba revolt of A.D. 132–135. In addition, in recent decades a substantial reassertion of the pacifistic Jewish tradition within Israeli Jewish society has resulted from internal controversy about the Israeli occupation of the Palestinian territories since 1967.

18 A good summary of all these conditions is Patricia Crone, *Pre-Industrial Societies: Anatomy of the Pre-Modern World* (1989; Oxford: Oneworld Publications, 2003).

19 This distinction could not always be made. What Victor Davis Hanson has said about ancient Greek citizen-soldiers would apply to virtually any soldier, conscript or volunteer, before the Industrial Revolution removed a substantial part of the population of some countries from farming: "Bloodletting, the art of tearing apart flesh and breaking bone, was no strange sight to farmers who butchered their own meat and hunted game." *The Other Greeks: The Family Farm and the Agrarian Roots of Western Civilization*, 2nd ed. (Berkeley: University of California Press, 1999), 265.

20 Official documents related to this issue include "Defense.gov News Article: Defense Department Expands Women's Combat Role," January 24, 2013, at http://www.defense.gov/newsarticle.aspx?id=119098; United States Department of Defense, News Release No. 037-13, January 24, 2013, "Defense Department Rescinds Direct Combat Exclusion Rule; Services to Expand Integration of Women into Previously Restricted Occupations and Units," at http://www.defense.gov/releases. aspx?releaseid=15784; United States Department of Defense, Speech, January 24, 2013, "Statement on Women in Service as Delivered by Secretary of Defense Leon E. Panetta," at http://www.defense.gov/ speeches/speech.aspx?speechid=1746; and Memorandum from General Martin E. Dempsey, chairman of the Joint Chiefs of Staff, and Leon E. Panetta, secretary of defense, January 24, 2013, "Subject: Elimination of the 1994 Direct Ground Combat Definition and Assignment Rule," link available at http://www.defense.gov/newsarticle.aspx?id=119098.

21 This may be changing slowly owing to Sino-American strategic competition and the much-publicized increased attention to American military strength in Asia and the Pacific. However, the U.S.-China relationship has scarcely attained the centrality in American military and strategic planning that the U.S.-Soviet competition did during the Cold War. For a summary, see Catherine Dale and Pat Towell, *In Brief: Assessing DOD's New Strategic Guidance. Report R42146* (Washington, DC: Congressional Research Service, Library of Congress, January 12, 2012). For the defense strategic guidance itself, see Department of Defense, *Sustaining U.S. Global Leadership: Priorities for 21st Century Defense*, January 2012, available at http://www.defense.gov/news/Defense_Strategic_Guidance.pdf.

22 Recent high-level pronouncements by General Raymond T. Odierno, Army chief of staff, may signal the beginning of change in this regard. In a recent widely distributed document he issued shortly after taking office, he stated that "reversibility and expansibility of the force also contribute to strategic depth." It remains to be seen what, if any, concrete measures result from this general statement of policy. *Marching Orders: 38th Chief of Staff, U.S. Army: America's Force of Decisive Action*. January 2012. Available at http://usarmy.vo.llnwd.net/e2/c/downloads/232478.pdf.

23 See Robert L. Goldich, *Defense Reconstitution: Strategic Context and Implementation. Report no. 92–832 F* (Washington, DC: Congressional Research Service, Library of Congress, November 20, 1992).

24 Cited in Robert Debs Heinl Jr., *Soldiers of the Sea: The United States Marine Corps, 1775–1962* (1962; repr., Baltimore: Nautical and Aviation Publishing Co. of America, 1991), 164.

25 I am indebted to Australian army lieutenant colonel David Kilcullen for this observation, made in an unsaved e-mail ca. 2005. However, see British military historian Richard Holmes's telling observation regarding the Iraq War: "The British army goes on operations…. But the U.S. army is at war." Richard Holmes, *Dusty Warriors* (London: Harper Perennial, 2006), 111.

26 Octavian Manea, "Reflections on the French School of Counter-Rebellion: An Interview with Étienne de Durand," *Small Wars Journal*, March 3, 2011, http://smallwarsjournal.com.

27 Bill Mauldin, *Up Front* (1945; repr., New York: W. W. Norton, 1968), 228.

28 I sent my original copy of *Up Front* to my son during his first tour as a Marine infantryman in Iraq in 2006, and he said that he and his fellow Marines found it both hilarious and accurate.

29 References to this issue are scattered widely throughout operational histories, but some accounts zero in on it more than others. For Korea, see Fehrenbach, *This Kind of War*; Allan R. Millett, *The War for Korea, 1950–1951: They Came from the North* (Lawrence: University Press of Kansas, 2010); and Roy E. Appleman, *Disaster in Korea: The Chinese Confront MacArthur* (College Station: Texas A&M University Press, 1989). For World War II, see Henry G. Gole, *General*

William E. DePuy: Preparing the Army for Modern War (Lawrence: University Press of Kansas, 2008), 13–65; and Peter R. Mansoor, *The GI Offensive in Europe: The Triumph of American Infantry Divisions, 1941–1945* (Lawrence: University Press of Kansas, 1999), esp. 49–180. For World War I, see, above all, Richard S. Faulkner, *The School of Hard Knocks: Combat Leadership in the American Expeditionary Forces* (College Station: Texas A&M University Press, 2012); as well as Mark Ethan Grotelueschen, *The AEF Way of War: The American Army and Combat in World War I* (New York: Cambridge University Press, 2007); Edward G. Lengel, *To Conquer Hell: The Meuse-Argonne, 1918: The Battle That Ended the First World War* (New York: Henry Holt, 2008); William S. Triplet, *A Youth in the Meuse-Argonne: A Memoir, 1917–1918,* ed. Robert H. Ferrell (Columbia: University of Missouri Press), 2000. I am not aware of any monographs on U.S. tactical, as opposed to operational and strategic, effectiveness, in Vietnam.

30 How the minimal expertise of the trainers compared to the trained during the frenetic mobilization of 1917–1918 resulted in catastrophic American casualties is described in Faulkner, *School of Hard Knocks*, particularly 26–139.

31 It is difficult to overstate the extent of demoralization, incoherence, indiscipline, and lack of readiness brought on by the results and effects of the Vietnam War, and which in fact characterized the Army throughout most of the 1970s. For examples, see Larry H. Ingraham, *The Boys in the Barracks: Observations on American Military Life* (Philadelphia: Institute for the Study of Human Issues, 1984); and Michael Lee Lanning, *The Battles of Peace* (New York: Ivy Books, 1992). I am also indebted to conversations over the years with U.S. Army colonel (ret.) James C. Crinean on his initial post-commissioning service at Fort Hood, Texas, from 1972 to 1976.

32 E-mail dated March 14, 2012; I must preserve his confidentiality.

33 Consider this admittedly impressionistic but telling example of this growing religiosity: In the early 1980s, my class at the National War College included one student who was a fervent evangelical Christian. He was well liked, and did not proselytize, but his open and profound religious commitment was very unusual for the times. At one bull session, somebody mentioned this student's view of an issue, and another officer said, "Yeah, but he has the sword of righteousness on his side," and everybody laughed. My sense—and that of people in and out of uniform to whom I have related this anecdote—is that thirty or so years later, the remark would not be made, and if it were made, there would be as much criticism as laughter.

34 The ending of "Don't Ask, Don't Tell" and the consequent acceptance of open and admitted gay men and lesbians into the force will probably have little effect on this attitude. Given the larger military culture, most will have little if any outward manifestation of their sexual orientation, as has been the case with homosexuals who have been serving all along while in the closet.

35 Too little has been written about this phenomenon, and most of what has been written is both superficial and pejorative. Two invaluable exceptions are Anne C. Loveland, *American Evangelicals and the U.S. Military, 1942–1993* (Baton Rouge: LSU Press, 1996) [see also my review of this work in *Armed Forces and Society* 24, no. 1 (Fall 1997): 169–71], and Kim Philip Hansen, *Military Chaplains and Religious Diversity* (New York: Palgrave Macmillan, 2012). There are indications of differences among the services in the extent to which emphasis on observant religion shades into active religious intolerance, the latter arguably being more common in the Air Force than in the other services. I must admit that my views on the reasons for this are based entirely on impressionistic observations of officers of all four services. Given this caveat, I would argue that the greater degree of religious dogmatism among Air Force personnel is due to a hypertrophic military authoritarianism that derives from overcompensating for the small proportion of their service that is actually in contact with the enemy; a lack of broader social, political, and intellectual sophistication resulting from the highly technological and managerial orientation of their service; and—I have been told this by a surprising number of individuals—the co-location of the national headquarters of several evangelical Christian organizations in Colorado Springs, the location of the Air Force Academy. For an interesting contrast between the religious atmospheres in one Air Force and one Army institution of professional military education, see Daniel J. Hughes, "Professors in the Colonels' World," and Bradley L. Carter, "No 'Holidays from History': Adult Learning, Professional Military Education, and Teaching History," both in *Military Culture and Education*, ed. Douglas Higbee (Burlington, VT: Ashgate, 2010), 164–65, 176.

36 For instance, in 2006 and 2007, only 2 percent of nonprior service enlistees were non-high-school-diploma graduates (NHSDGs). Of the general American population ages eighteen to twenty-four, about 21 percent were NHSDGs. While recruits were much less likely to have had at least some college, or be a college graduate, compared to eighteen-to-twenty-four-year-old civilians (7 percent vs. about 39 percent), the difference is due to the fact that, by definition, if one is in the military between ages eighteen and twenty-four, one is not in college. See Shanea J. Watkins and James Sherk, *Who Serves in the U.S. Military? Demographic Characteristics of Enlisted Troops and Officers. Report CDA08–05* (Washington, DC: Center for Data Analysis, Heritage Foundation, August 21, 2008), 5; available online at http://www.heritage.org/Research/Reports/2008/08/Who-Serves-in-the-US-Military-The-Demographics-of-Enlisted-Troops-and-Officers. The key factor is that the bottom 20-odd percent who are high school dropouts are almost completely absent from the military. I have a personal impression that the proportion of new enlistees with at least some college may well be higher than 7 percent, perhaps because they are embarrassed to tell recruiters why they left

higher education. I have been told repeatedly that many young men (much more than young women) enter the military after a comparatively brief time in college, having flunked out because of emotional immaturity, and that they view the service as a way to attain both that maturity and the GI Bill benefits that will be available upon completion of service.

37 In 2007, only 2.3 percent of enlisted recruits scored in the bottom thirtieth percentile of the Armed Forces Qualification Test, the standardized aptitude test given to prospective enlistees—that is, only about 2 percent of those young men and women actually enlisted were in these lower categories, compared to 30 percent of those who took the test. Ibid.

38 For a scholarly examination of the relationship of obesity to military recruiting, see John Cawley and Johanna Catherine Maclean, *Unfit for Service: The Implications of Rising Obesity for U.S. Military Recruitment. NBER Working Paper No. 16408* (Washington, DC: National Bureau of Economic Research, September 2010). For numerous reports, some functional and some done by state, see www.MissionReadiness.org (accessed April 22, 2012); "Mission: Readiness is the organization of over 250 retired generals, admirals, and other senior military leaders who support policies and investments that will help young Americans succeed in school and later in life and will enable more young adults to join the military if they choose to do so."

39 See Adam B. Lowther, "The Post-9/11 American Serviceman," *Joint Force Quarterly* 58, no. 3, 75–81; for a plethora of detailed data, see the annual publication of the Department of Defense titled *Population Representation in the Military Services*, which is published on a fiscal-year basis, and Watkins and Sherk, *Who Serves in the U.S. Military?*

40 See Kenneth Wellesley, *The Year of the Four Emperors*, 3rd ed. (New York: Routledge, 2000).

41 Lawrence Keppie, "The Changing Face of the Roman Legions (49 BC–AD 69)," in *Legions and Veterans: Roman Army Papers, 1971–2000* (Stuttgart: Franz Steiner Verlag, 2000), 56.

42 Recent scholarship suggests that the level of literacy, education, social status, and culture among professional volunteer soldiers throughout history may have been substantially understated by historians and contemporary observers, who have mistaken toughness and hardness for intellectual and moral inferiority. Recruiters often looked for, and tried to enlist, men with some education who came from stable backgrounds, as these individuals made better soldiers and posed fewer disciplinary problems. For example, regarding Roman imperial soldiers, see Jean-Michel Carrie, "The Soldier," in *The Romans*, ed. Andrea Giardina, trans. Lydia G. Cochrane (Chicago: University of Chicago Press, 1993), 120–30; and Yann Le Bohec, *The Imperial Roman Army* (New York: Hippocrene Books, 1994), 88–89. A more recent and searching debunking of the volunteer infantryman as "scum of the earth" is in Edward J. Coss, *All for the King's Shilling: The British Soldier*

under Wellington, 1808–1814 (Norman: University of Oklahoma Press, 2010), 29–85. It is therefore possible that the American volunteer soldier is less unusual in history in this regard than has been thought to be the case.

43 West Point Association of Graduates. *Robert M. Gates Thayer Award Remarks.* U.S. Military Academy, West Point, NY, October 6, 2011, http://www.westpointaog.org/page.aspx?pid=4843 (accessed April 23, 2012).

44 See, for example, Andrew R. Milburn, "Breaking Ranks: Dissent and the Military Professional," *Joint Force Quarterly* 59, no. 4, 101–7; and discussion of the article, particularly the response of Richard Kohn and comments on his remarks, "Richard Kohn Fires a Warning Flare about a *Joint Force Quarterly* Article," Foreign Policy blog, September 29, 2010, at http://ricks.foreignpolicy.com. See also David Wood, "Military Officers Chafe for Bigger Role in Policy Decisions," *Politics Daily*, October 4, 2010, http://www.politicsdaily.com/2010/10/04/military-officers-chafe-for-bigger-role-in-policy-decisions/print/ (accessed October 29, 2010); and Anna Mulrine, "Can Troops Get Too Much Love? Military Struggles with a Dark Side on Veterans Day," *Christian Science Monitor*, November 10, 2010, http://www.csmonitor.com/layout/set/print/content/view/print/342309 (accessed November 11, 2010). For an earlier discussion of such possible tendencies, see the widely circulated and controversial Charles J. Dunlap Jr., "The Origins of the American Military Coup of 2012," *Parameters* 40 (Winter 1992/93): 2–20.

45 In an October 26, 2010, e-mail message containing comments on an initial draft of this paper, David Kennedy suggested this question as a framework for this discussion, though he did not endorse the concept.

46 For recent scholarship indicating that the conventional stereotype of the Army as being overwhelmingly politically conservative and Republican is overdrawn, and which suggests that members of the Army are in fact less politically engaged than their civilian counterparts, see Jason K. Dempsey, *Our Army: Soldiers, Politics, and American Civil-Military Relations* (Princeton, NJ: Princeton University Press, 2010).

47 For the pernicious effects of this politicization in fin de siècle France, see Douglas Porch, *The March to the Marne: The French Army, 1871–1914* (New York: Cambridge University Press, 1981); Paul-Marie de La Gorce, *The French Army: A Military-Political History*, trans. Kenneth Douglas (New York: George Braziller, 1963), 17–92.

48 This is entirely the result of the decision, made shortly after the United States entered World War I, to construct most training bases in parts of the country where the weather was milder. Training could thus be conducted year-round and barracks and other facilities did not have to be as well-heated and insulated, and hence were less expensive and could be built

more quickly. Contrary to conventional wisdom, the traditional stereotype of the pro-military South was not involved.

49 Office of the Deputy Under Secretary of Defense (Installations and Environment), *Military Housing Privatization. Overview: Military Housing*, http://www/acq.osd.mil/housing/housing101/htm (accessed April 21, 2012).

50 Lieutenant General David Barno, USA (Ret.), "Dave Barno's Top 10 Tasks for General Dempsey, the New Army Chief of Staff," *The Best Defense: Tom Ricks's Daily Take on National Security* blog, January 21, 2011, at http://ricks.foreignpolicy.com. I thank General Barno for providing me with this as an e-mail attachment on February 9, 2012.

51 For examples of the latter, see Ike Skelton, "The Civil-Military Gap Need Not Become a Chasm," *Joint Force Quarterly* 64, no. 1: 60–66.

52 John France, *Perilous Glory: The Rise of Western Military Power* (New Haven, CT: Yale University Press, 2011), 240, citing Carl von Clausewitz, *On War*, indexed ed., ed. and trans. Michael Howard and Peter Paret (Princeton, NJ: Princeton University Press, 1989), 187.

53 Sam Jacobson, "The Few, the Proud, the Chosen," *Commentary* online, September 2010, http://www.commentarymagazine.com/printarticle/cfm/the-few-the-proud-the-chosen-15507 (accessed September 30, 2010). William James's original essay can be found in many places; I obtained it at http://www.constitution.org./wj/meow.htm (accessed October 29, 2010).

5 :: Manning and Financing the Twenty-First-Century All-Volunteer Force

David R. Segal and Lawrence J. Korb

Abstract: The transition from a conscription-based to a volunteer force after 1973 required a force of reduced size that could compete financially with the civilian labor market. To compensate for these changes, the Department of Defense took three steps: developing the "Total Force," which integrated the reserve component with active duty; maintaining the Selective Service System, which could be activated in case of prolonged and manpower-intensive conflict; and civilianizing as many support functions as possible. Despite this original blueprint, political pressures prevented military and civilian leadership from activating the Selective Service after it became apparent that the Bush administration's national security strategy in Iraq and Afghanistan required prolonged, large-scale deployments. The result has been enormous physical and psychological strain on personnel, especially in the Army and reserve components; diminishing standards for the quality of recruits; and severe financial strain related to pay raises, retention bonuses, retirement, and health care benefits. Because personnel in the all-recruited force serve longer on average than did those who served under conscription, it is also an older force, supporting more family members— primarily spouses and children—than was the case in the years of the military draft. Reflecting an increasingly diverse American labor force, it includes more racial and ethnic minorities and more women than did the conscription-based force, although it under-represents women, some religious groups, and some regions of the country. And the replacement of the high personnel turnover of the conscription era with a smaller force of personnel who serve longer has raised questions about whether there is now a culture gap between the American military and the society it serves.

In 1973, in the wake of the Vietnam War, the United States transitioned from a conscription-based military to an all-volunteer force (AVF).[1] Faced with new challenges of cost and recruitment, the military substantially reduced the size of its active forces, particularly the Army. Previously, the Selective Service System had made accessing the required number of entry-level military personnel relatively easy. The system drafted young men, who frequently served simply to comply with the law, and motivated others to volunteer for service to avoid being drafted. Once the draft ended, attracting the requisite number of qualified recruits each year became much more difficult. Now subject to the dynamics of the labor market, the military confronted competition from other employers, especially in times of low unemployment, and from institutions of higher education, as increasing numbers of young men and women attended college. Thus, the force had to be downsized.

Except for brief periods during the twenty-five years of Cold War conscription, the Army was the only service that had to rely on the draft to fill its ranks. The other three services met their quotas with draft-induced volunteers; indeed, many men "volunteered" for the Air Force, Navy, or Marines to avoid being drafted into the Army. By volunteering, they gained some control over when they served, in what service, and, frequently, in what occupational specialty they would be trained. In the absence of conscription, the services lost both draftees and draft-motivated volunteers.

As the military began to downsize after the end of conscription and the Cold War in Europe, the demography of the force also
started to change, in both composition and patterns of utilization.
The young, predominantly unmarried male conscription force was
replaced by an older, more professional, more-likely-to-be-married
force. The mean age of enlisted personnel in 2009 was more than
two years older than it had been in 1973 (27.2 years vs. 25.0 years),
and the mean length of service of enlistees was almost a year longer (80.4 months vs. 69.8).[2] It became more diverse in terms of
race, ethnicity, gender, and sexual orientation.[3] President Nixon's
Commission on an All-Volunteer Force (the Gates Commission),
which drafted the initial blueprint for the volunteer force, had
assumed that the end of the draft would not alter racial composition and made virtually no mention of women in uniform.[4] In
fact, with the end of conscription, the military immediately began
to recruit disproportionately from the African American community. In the early years of the AVF, more than one-quarter of new
recruits and, in some years, as many as one-third of new recruits
in the Army, were black. Moreover, black service members have
been more likely than white soldiers to reenlist; thus, the proportion of African Americans in the force increased. In 2006, 12.6
percent of the civilian labor force ages eighteen to forty-four was
African American, compared to 19.3 percent of active-duty enlisted
personnel.[5] By 2009 this had dropped slightly, due to a decline in
African American enlistment, but continued high rates of African
American reenlistment still kept it at 18.5 percent, compared to 14
percent in 1973.[6]

Although Hispanics were too few to be regarded as a significant recruitment pool in 1973, making up less than 2 percent of the
enlisted force, changes in the past three decades in the percentage
of Hispanic men and women in the U.S. military have been dramatic. Not only is the Hispanic population larger, but the fraction
of Hispanics who meet entrance exam and education requirements
for military service has increased. In 1985, less than 4 percent of
the enlisted force was Hispanic, compared to almost 7 percent of
the civilian labor force, ages eighteen to forty-four, that identified
as Hispanic.

By 1994, less than 6 percent of enlisted personnel were Hispanic, while the civilian proportion of Hispanics had grown to more than 10 percent of the total U.S. population. As of fiscal year 2000, Hispanics made up 13 percent of the military-age civilian labor force but only 9 percent of enlisted personnel. In 2006, though the civilian labor force was 17.1 percent Hispanic, only 12.8 percent of the enlisted force identified as Hispanic. (Table 5.1 shows the shares of black and Hispanic military personnel in recent years.)[7]

Representation of Hispanics in the military has not kept pace with the rise in Hispanics eighteen to forty-four years old in the civilian labor force. However, the civilian figure includes men and women who do not meet requirements for enlistment based on education and immigration status. Until recently, enlistees had to have a high school degree; almost all enlisted personnel (99 percent) in fiscal 2001 were either high school graduates or had earned a comparable credential, such as a General Educational Development (GED) certificate, with the services considering graduation more favorable than a GED. Until recently, enlistment also required that immigrants be citizens or legal permanent residents. If these qualifications are used to determine the eligible Hispanic population, Hispanics may have actually been overrepresented among enlisted personnel. For instance, in 2006, the share of Hispanics in the civilian labor force ages eighteen to forty-four with at least a high school degree was 10.9 percent, compared to 11.2 percent of active-duty enlisted personnel. Given that not all high school graduates are citizens or even legal immigrants, Hispanics most likely are enlisting and remaining in the military at rates greater than their share of

Table 5.1 Percent of Black and Hispanic Representation among Non-Prior-Service Military Accessions, 2003 to 2010

	2003	2004	2005	2006	2007	2008	2009	2010
Black	15.0	13.5	13.1	13.0	13.6	15.0	15.2	15.8
Hispanic	11.5	13.2	13.9	13.3	13.5	14.3	17.0	16.9

Sources: David J. Armor and Curtis L. Gilroy, "Changing Minority Representation in the U.S. Military," *Armed Forces & Society* 36, no. 2 (2010): 242; Office of the Under Secretary of Defense for Personnel and Readiness, Population Representation in the Military Services.

those in the labor force who meet the minimum qualifications for service.

With regard to gender, military service in most countries and throughout much of history has been viewed as a masculine occupation. Women have been excluded entirely, or have served with an auxiliary status or in segregated branches. They have faced restrictions on the highest rank they can achieve and the military occupations they can pursue.[8] The culture of the American military is still predominantly masculine, and although women compose half of the American labor force, they remain a minority in the military. However, as has been the case in other countries that have substituted volunteer forces for conscription, as the size of the military has contracted, the proportion women represent has increased.[9] At the beginning of the current volunteer force, women composed about 2 percent of military personnel; they now make up 14 percent.

Legal and regulatory changes have also opened new occupations to women. In 1991, Congress repealed the provisions of a 1948 law that prohibited women from flying combat aircraft; since 1994, women have been allowed to serve on Navy surface combatant ships. Moreover, the Navy is now training the first cohort of women officers who will serve on submarines. Although occupations and positions that involve direct offensive ground combat have remained closed to women, military women have been attached (but not assigned) to ground combat units in both Iraq and Afghanistan. Given that male American soldiers cannot search or interrogate Muslim women without greatly offending cultural and religious sensitivities, U.S. military women have filled an important role in dealing with a population whose support we are trying to win. Department of Defense regulations have been changed to approve the assignment of women to ground combat units at the battalion level, and in January 2013 Defense Secretary Panetta announced that combat specialties and small combat units would be gender integrated in the near future.

Women are not the only underrepresented population in the armed forces. Recruits are drawn disproportionately from some regions of the country, particularly the South and the Rocky Mountain states, while a much smaller percentage of young people from the Northeast, north central states, and Midwest serve.[10] And while the Pew Research Center reports that military veterans are roughly comparable to the general population in terms of religious affiliation,[11] we find that Catholics are slightly underrepresented, and Christian churches other than those designated as Protestant or Catholic/Orthodox are somewhat overrepresented.[12] Jews and Muslims in the military reflect about their same proportions as in the military-age population.[13] Thus, the transition from conscription to a volunteer force shaped by the dynamics of the labor market led to a reduction in the size of the force and an aging of the force as well as increased recruitment among segments of the population that were relatively disadvantaged in the civilian market. The aging of the force, in turn, has produced a more married force, with more children in military families. About 40 percent of enlisted personnel in 1973 were married, compared with more than 50 percent in 2009. Family-friendly policies such as child-care centers led enlisted personnel to marry earlier, to have children earlier, and to have more children than their civilian counterparts. For example, 36 percent of junior enlisted men are married, compared to only 24 percent of their civilian peers ages eighteen to twenty-four with comparable earnings. By age thirty, 75 percent of active-duty men and 59 percent of active-duty women are married, compared to slightly more than 50 percent of men and women in the civilian workforce.[14]

To compensate for the smaller size of the active force, the Department of Defense (DOD) took three steps. First, it developed the "Total Force" concept to integrate the reserve component (the state-based National Guard and the federal reserves) with the active-duty component in those areas where the reserves had unique capabilities that were not needed on a full-time basis, such as civil affairs. During the draft period, reservists were only marginally involved in contingency planning and did not receive the equipment and training necessary to maintain the proper level of readiness for deployment. Thus, the reserve components played a very minor part in the Vietnam War.

This arrangement also minimized the role of Congress, which must authorize long-term or large-scale reserve mobilizations, in Vietnam. But when the DOD transitioned to the AVF, the reserves were fully integrated into the Pentagon's war plans and, for the most part, were given the training and equipment necessary to carry out their new responsibilities. Beginning in 1973, the DOD no longer planned for separate active-duty and reserve components. Instead, it stipulated that a Total Force would be maintained at an appropriate level of readiness so that its reserve component could be mobilized quickly and effectively. In the context of the Cold War, the AVF was intended to be a deterrent force, albeit one that was prepared to address small-scale military contingencies. During the first, relatively short Gulf War, for example, the Army had to mobilize some National Guard combat brigades and some reserve combat support units to carry out its mission, although none of these units served more than six months on active duty.

While some analysts have argued that having to mobilize some reserve components (as part of what is mistakenly called the Abrams Doctrine) would weaken the president's ability to engage in a large or extended conflict, this potential outcome was not the major impetus for the creators of the AVF or the Total Force. Moreover, once conscription was ended, men and women who joined the reserve component were also volunteers. Therefore, mobilizing the reserve has not had a significant impact on the willingness of Congress or the American people to raise the threshold for going to war, as was the case during Vietnam, when many men, including future leaders of the country, joined the reserves to avoid the draft.

Second, to prepare for a long war or an extended or major conflict, the country still required men to register with the Selective Service when they turned eighteen. Thus, if the Total Force could not handle a particular contingency by itself or without putting undue stress on the Total Force, the president and Congress could quickly activate the Selective Service. Put differently, in case of a significant conflict, the Guard and reserve would be a bridge to conscription. The reserve components would serve as pretrained citizen-soldiers, to be mobilized in order to buy time while the conscripts who would join the other components of the Total Force on the battlefield were being trained. Thus, if the nation became involved in a war resembling Korea or Vietnam, which would require maintaining a significant number of troops on the ground for a prolonged period in a war or combat zone, the Selective Service would be engaged so that the active-duty volunteers would be able to spend at least two months at home for every month they spent in a combat zone (as was the case during the ten-year war in Vietnam). Moreover, the National Guard and reserve personnel would not have to be mobilized more than one year out of every six. Not only would this arrangement ease the strain on the troops, but it would prevent the ground forces from having to lower their standards to meet recruiting and retention goals in prolonged conflicts—a necessary step, given that Americans tend to become impatient and less supportive when wars drag on.

The Joint Chiefs of Staff (JCS) made the point forcefully in 1981 when the Reagan administration was on the verge of reversing President Carter's action to reinstitute draft registration, which had been temporarily suspended between 1975 and 1980. In a memo to the secretary of defense, the JCS stated, "The AVF provides peacetime manpower." In their view, "Selective Service registration supports mobilization for war."[15]

Third, to allow the now more costly military personnel to focus on their core missions and competencies, the Pentagon would privatize, civilianize, or contract out as many support functions as possible. New recruits would no longer be required to perform such nonmilitary tasks as cooking and cleaning (KP, or "kitchen police," as it was then known). The use of civilians has been part of the American way of waging war since before the Civil War.[16] However, the downsizing of the military, coupled with the increase in the number of U.S. missions and deployments in the wake of the Cold War resolution in Europe, has resulted in an unprecedented number of civilians supporting the active-duty military, including in the battle space.[17]

After 1973, if the Pentagon had a task to be performed, it would look first to private contractors, as long as doing so did not compromise national security. If the job was an inherently governmental function, the DOD would assign it to a civilian government employee. If it required a military person, the DOD would recruit a member of the reserve component. Using active-duty military personnel would be a last resort; indeed, recruiting and retaining AVF members were much more costly and difficult than outsourcing tasks to members of the private sector, civilians, or the reserve component.

After a bumpy start that led many civilian and military leaders to call for a return to the draft, the AVF came into its own in the mid-1980s. The force performed so well in the first Persian Gulf War in 1991 that many who had been skeptical about ending the draft became convinced that the AVF was the best model for the United States. Moreover, when the Cold War ended in Europe in the early 1990s, the military was able to reduce the size of the active force from 2.2 million to 1.3 million, or by 40 percent, and thus meet its recruitment and retention goals at a comparatively low cost during a period of low unemployment and an economic boom in the private sector. Between fiscal years 1990 and 1999, the cost of maintaining military personnel declined by $31 billion, or 26 percent, in real dollars.

The second reason for the reduction in active-duty forces was that, in order to compete in the marketplace for personnel, the military had to substantially raise basic pay, particularly for new recruits. From 1948 to 1973, when the draft was in existence, the Pentagon could pay those individuals it compelled to serve only subsistence wages. In fiscal 1968, the average pay of an individual on active duty was $5,780. With 3.4 million people on active duty in that year (the peak year for the size of the force), the total cost of military personnel for military annual compensation (basic pay and benefits) was $19.9 billion. By 1974, the number of people on active duty had been slashed to 2.2 million, a 35 percent reduction. Yet military personnel costs had gone up. By 1974, expenses had risen to $24.2 billion, a 22 percent jump from 1968, and the personnel portion of the budget grew from 28 to 35 percent. The cost per individual had risen to $10,895, a 90 percent increase compared with the days of the draft. The services could not simply raise the pay of new service members to attract volunteers. To maintain pay equity and avoid pay compression among the ranks, basic pay was increased across the board.

However, the civilian leadership failed to use the period from the end of the Cold War to 9/11 to bring military pay and benefits under control. In fact, senior officials took steps or allowed policies to be adopted that made the force more expensive. One of the major military personnel expenses, the military retirement system, was designed in an era when active-duty pay was comparatively low, very few people served on active duty until retirement, and Social Security and Medicare did not exist. Nor was life expectancy very high. Until 1986, the system allowed a person who spent twenty years on active duty to receive an immediate annuity of 50 percent of his or her base pay, indexed to inflation, and free medical care (including for dependents) for life. A member who served for at least thirty years would receive 75 percent. Most military personnel did not serve long enough to earn retirement. In the 1980s and early 1990s, fewer than 10 percent of separations were retirements, with most people leaving because they had completed contractual periods of service, or for disciplinary, medical, or other reasons. However, in 1993, after twenty years of the AVF, the retirement figure reached 15 percent of separations, showing that while most people did not serve for a full career, the size of the career force had grown significantly. And with increased longevity, the people who served for a career were likely to draw retirement pay for more years than they served on active duty. Enlisted personnel who joined at age eighteen could start drawing retirement pay at thirty-eight, while officers, who were likely to have been commissioned upon graduation from college at age twenty-two, could draw retired pay at age forty-two. Moreover, retirements are not equally distributed among the services. The Marine Corps, which places a premium on youth, prefers the great majority of its personnel to serve for less than ten years. The Air Force, which invests heavily in technical training, seeks to retain personnel to realize a return on its investment. Between 20 percent and 30 percent of Air Force separations have been retirements since the 1980s, and fewer than 30 percent have been simply fulfillment of enlistment contracts.

Given that neither the Pentagon nor individual service members put money into a trust fund to pay for the cost of retirement, the DOD paid these benefits off the top of each year's budget. By the 1980s, the unfunded liability of the military retirement system had grown to almost $1 trillion, while retirement funds for civilian federal employees and Social Security were running surpluses because workers had to contribute to these plans. To bring this situation under control, Congress directed the DOD to switch to an accrual system and reduce benefits after twenty years of service to 40 percent, for those joining the military after August 1, 1986.

However, in 1999, under pressure from lobbyists for military retirees, the DOD reversed the decision and went back to allowing those who completed twenty years once again to receive 50 percent. At about the same time, the DOD also permitted retirees and their dependents who turned sixty-five to retain their medical benefits even after they became eligible for Medicare. Finally, after 1995, the DOD and Congress stopped raising premiums for the military health care program, Tricare,[18] and allowed individuals to pay $19 a month, or $38 for a family, a rate that remained in effect until October 2012, when it was raised by $3 a month for individuals and $5 a month for families.

After the attacks of 9/11, the Bush administration made preventive war the cornerstone of its national security strategy to win what it labeled the "war on terror." It invaded Afghanistan in October 2001 and Iraq in March 2003. Although the administration declared the "mission accomplished" in both theaters in spring 2003, it became clear that the United States would have to keep hundreds of thousands of troops on the ground in both countries for a significant period of time.

How would the military provide vast ground forces within the confines of the AVF? If the Joint Chiefs had followed the original blueprint for the AVF, they would have demanded that the secretary of defense and the president activate the Selective Service, which, by 2000, had on file some twenty million men between the ages of eighteen and twenty-four. But they lacked the political will to challenge their civilian superiors. Moreover, when General Eric Shinseki, the Army chief of staff, told Congress that the administration seriously underestimated the number of troops that would be needed to stabilize Iraq after the invasion, he was marginalized by his civilian superiors.

Similarly, the Bush administration's national security team did not want to raise the issue of Selective Service with Congress and the American people for fear that they might ask more questions about the necessity and cost of regime change and nation building in Iraq. And Congress did not want to broach the subject without support from the military or the administration.

Thus, the American military began to rely on the reserve forces to a degree not seen since World War II, but in this case without the support of conscription. It deployed both reserve and active forces more frequently, and for longer periods, than it knew was optimal for combat performance. It accepted more recruits at the lowest mental and moral standards deemed acceptable since the advent of the volunteer force.

The services also found that the racial and ethnic composition of the force was changing. Recruitment among African Americans, who had high propensities to serve and had been overrepresented in the volunteer force since its inception, declined. Recruitment among Hispanic Americans, who form the most rapidly growing sector of the population (but were not recognized as numerically important in 1973), increased. Women in the military, who until January 2013 were barred by policies and regulations from assignment to small ground combat units, found that the nonlinear battle spaces of Iraq and Afghanistan placed them in combat: the highways on which they operated military vehicles became the most dangerous places to be; and they have accompanied infantry units conducting patrols in hostile territory because, unlike male soldiers, they can both search and interrogate Muslim women without offending the local population.

As a result of waging these two large ground wars, which required the deployment of about two hundred thousand troops to Iraq and Afghanistan on a continuous basis from 2003 to 2009, the civilian and military leaders overstretched and abused the active and reserve components of the AVF, particularly the ground forces. Not only did this overextension undermine the readiness of the Army and Marines, but it was a moral outrage perpetrated against the troops and their families.

To understand how much strain the failure to activate the Selective Service has put on the troops, consider the horrendous situation of the Army, which bore the brunt of the wars in Iraq and Afghanistan. The Army has reorganized so that the brigade combat team, rather than the division, has become its major maneuver unit in ground combat. A brigade combat team consists of a combat arms brigade along with its artillery and support units and contains about two thousand soldiers, with some variation based on the type of combat unit at its core. In spring 2007, at the height of the so-called surge in Iraq, the Army had twenty of its forty-four combat brigades on the ground in either Iraq or Afghanistan.

Of these twenty brigades, nine were already on second tours, seven were serving a third tour, and two were on a fourth deployment of at least twelve months. Moreover, of the twenty-four brigades not deployed in spring 2007, ten had already been deployed for two tours, and three had been deployed three times in the previous five years.[19]

Of the twenty brigades in Iraq or Afghanistan in spring 2007, none had been back home for a full two years between deployments—the time period regarded as optimal for recovery from combat—and four had one year or less at home between combat tours. Of the twenty-four brigades not in theater, eleven had less than two years between deployments, and five had less than one year. Moreover, ten of the brigades had served longer than one year in theater. All told, by spring 2007, forty-three of the Army's forty-four brigades had served at least one tour (see table 5.2; only the brigade in Korea was not deployed to one of the combat zones).[20]

The reserve component, which includes the National Guard and the service or federal reserves, was also severely overstretched. Fifty-three percent of the Army's combat forces are in the National Guard;[21] by early 2007, about 600,000 reservists had been mobilized, and about 420,000, or 80 percent of the Guard and reserve, had been deployed to Iraq or Afghanistan, with an average of eighteen months per mobilization. Of these service members, about 85,000, or 20 percent, had been deployed more than once. Every one of the Army National Guard's sixteen enhanced brigades had been deployed overseas at least once, and two were deployed twice. Moreover, by the end of 2007, four more enhanced brigades were sent to Iraq, even though none of them had been demobilized for less than three years.[22] The members of the Guard had signed up to serve as part of a strategic reserve, training one weekend a month

Table 5.2 Deployment History of Currently Deployed U.S. Army Combat Brigades, as of Spring 2007

Combat Brigades Serving First Tour

1st Cavalry Division, 4th Brigade

2nd Infantry Division, 4th Brigade

Combat Brigades Serving Second Tour

1st Cavalry Division, 4th Brigade

2nd Infantry Division, 4th Brigade

1st Cavalry Division, 1st Brigade

1st Cavalry Division, 2nd Brigade

1st Cavalry Division, 3rd Brigade

1st Infantry Division, 2nd Brigade

1st Infantry Division, 4th Brigade

2nd Infantry Division, 2nd Brigade

2nd Infantry Division, 3rd Brigade

25th Infantry Division, 3rd Brigade

25th Infantry Division, 4th Brigade

Combat Brigades Serving Third Tour

3rd Infantry Division, 1st Brigade

3rd Infantry Division, 2nd Brigade

3rd Infantry Division, 3rd Brigade

82nd Airborne Division, 1st Brigade

82nd Airborne Division, 3rd Brigade

82nd Airborne Division, 4th Brigade

173rd Airborne Brigade Combat Team

Combat Brigades Serving Fourth Tour

10th Mountain Division, 2nd Brigade

82nd Airborne Division, 2nd Brigade

Source: Lawrence Korb, Peter Juul, Laura Conley, Myles Caggins, and Sean Duggan, *Building a Military for the 21st Century: New Realities, New Priorities* (Washington, DC: Center for American Progress, 2008).

and two weeks each summer to maintain their skills. They expected to serve primarily if needed for domestic contingencies such as natural disasters. Like their colleagues in the federal reserves, they could also serve as a strategic reserve for the active component until the Selective Service could be activated, or they could serve short tours in peacekeeping operations in places like the Balkans, or in short conflicts, such as the first Gulf War. But now they had effectively become an operational expeditionary force.

This abuse of the Total Force's Army component had severe repercussions on the service, the effects of which can be grouped into four categories. First, in order to meet its recruiting goals, the Army had to raise its recruiting budget as well as the bonuses paid to new recruits. It also had to increase the proportion of personnel it recruited at the lowest acceptable mental and moral standards for incoming soldiers. In the early years of the volunteer force, recruits were drawn largely from the middle range of the socioeconomic structure. That is, the bottom quartile was underrepresented because its members disproportionately did not qualify for service based on educational, aptitude, or legal grounds, and the upper strata disproportionately elected not to serve.[23] This pattern held throughout the remainder of the twentieth century,[24] a period in which the services recruited above the minimum standards set by the DOD.

From fiscal years 2005 through 2008, the Army did not achieve its goal of bringing in 90 percent Tier I recruits (those with high school diplomas and who scored at least average on the Armed Forces Qualification Test). In fact, in fiscal 2007, it did not even reach 80 percent.[25] The percentage of high school graduates recruited by the Army dropped from 92 percent in fiscal 2004 to 87 percent in fiscal 2005, and this downward trend continued.[26] The Army also reported a decline in recruits scoring high on its aptitude tests, from 72 percent in fiscal 2004 to 67 percent in fiscal 2005; at the same time, it accepted more recruits in the lowest acceptable mental category.

The Army compounded the problem by increasing the number of moral waivers that it issued. In fiscal 2004, about 12 percent of the recruits received waivers, including for criminal convictions and even felonies. In fiscal 2006, the Army approved waivers for 8,219 recruits; in fiscal 2007, the number rose to 10,258. Waivers for felony convictions for serious crimes, such as theft and assault, increased from 249 to 511.[27]

By fiscal 2008, the number of waivers exceeded 25 percent. All told, the Army gave eighty thousand moral waivers in the fiscal 2005–2008 period. Even though it lowered its standards and increased waivers, the Army had to increase its maximum enlistment bonus from $6,000 in fiscal 2003 to $40,000 by fiscal 2008.[28] Recruit quality improved toward the end of the decade, as unemployment, particularly among young people, increased dramatically with the economic recession. As the economy improves, and as unemployment decreases, recruit quality may once again decline.

Second, to meet its retention goals, the Army increased promotion rates for officers and enlisted personnel as well as retention bonuses. By 2008, virtually all first lieutenants and captains not only were promoted to captain and major, respectively, but also were promoted early and with significant bonuses. Typically, only 75 percent of captains are promoted to major and 90 percent of first lieutenants to captain, but by 2008, close to 100 percent of captains and first lieutenants were promoted to major and captain, respectively. Thus, the Army lost a decision point that it had used to weed out low performers among junior officers. For most of the volunteer-force era, company officers (lieutenants and captains) competed for promotion. Some who would have preferred to remain in service were passed over for promotion and had to leave under an up-or-out management policy. With a 100 percent promotion rate, the criterion for retention became simply a desire to remain in service. Rates of promotion to lieutenant colonel and colonel increased as well. For majors promoted to lieutenant colonels, the rate jumped from 60 percent to 90 percent. For lieutenant colonels promoted to colonel, the rate rose from 40 percent to 60 percent.[29]

Third, in 2007, to compensate for the failure to activate the draft, the Army and Marines increased their permanent end-strength by 92,500, or 15 percent. The Army also added another 22,000 on a temporary basis in 2009.

Fourth, repeated tours to combat zones without sufficient dwell time, or time between deployments, also took a toll on the individual men and women serving and their families. Close to five hundred thousand soldiers developed mental problems, and divorce and suicide rates skyrocketed.[30] For the first time since the advent of the AVF, the Army suicide rate surpassed that of the comparable civilian population. Prior to 2001, the military suicide rate rarely reached ten per one hundred thousand personnel. By 2009, a year in which more than three hundred soldiers took their own lives, the rate had doubled to more than twenty per one hundred thousand personnel.

Fifth, beyond repercussions for the force, failure to activate the Selective Service substantially increased military manpower costs. Partly motivated by guilt over what they were doing to the troops, the administration and Congress gave military personnel raises larger than required by the Employment Cost Index, and neither branch wanted to raise Tricare premiums. As a result, the DOD's budget for military personnel rose from $77 billion in fiscal 2001 to $180 billion in fiscal 2013, and health care costs jumped from $19 billion to $50 billion. These costs are projected to rise by at least 8 percent each year and if left untouched will consume the entire defense budget in twenty years.

Finally, the costs of the shift to an all-volunteer force were reflected not only in terms of personal costs to soldiers and financial costs to the nation, but also in terms of civil-military relations. Former Secretary of Defense William Cohen in 1997 suggested the possibility of a "chasm" between the military and civilian worlds in America,[31] and many commentators worried about an emerging civil-military "gap," with the military profession becoming monolithically conservative and estranged from civilian leadership and the nation. A major research program revealed that military officers were conservative, but not monolithically so, and that was no surprise. The gap was not as wide as anticipated.[32] In addition, the concern focused on the 15 percent of personnel who serve as officers. The 85 percent in the enlisted ranks reflected the attitudes of their civilian peers.[33] Interestingly, the major report of this research program was published on September 12, 2001, when the nation was focused on other military matters. The civil-military gap issue was raised again in 2011, not in terms of political ideology or civilian control of the military, but in terms of the readjustment of veterans to civilian society—particularly those who served after 9/11—and the failure of the majority who do not serve to understand the nature of military service.[34] This more recent survey again found that among post-9/11 veterans, there was a tendency toward conservatism, but not monolithically so. Republicans constituted 36 percent of these veterans, Independents were 35 percent, and Democrats 21 percent. (The comparable numbers for civilians are 23 percent, 35 percent, and 34 percent, respectively.) In terms of ideology, 40 percent of the post-9/11 veterans define themselves as conservative, 43 percent as moderate, and 12 percent as liberal.[35] (Respective numbers for civilians are 37 percent, 34 percent, and 22 percent.)

Both the secretary of defense and the chairman of the Joint Chiefs of Staff recognize that neither the Pentagon nor the country can afford the exploding personnel costs of the volunteer force.

And in January 2012, Secretary of Defense Panetta and the Joint Chiefs of Staff proposed reducing the size of the ground forces by one hundred thousand, as well as a number of modest changes to all three components of military compensation: base pay for current service members, military retirement pensions, and health care for military retirees.

The Pentagon proposes to reduce the annual pay raise for all military personnel by one-half percent less than the cost of living, beginning in 2015. The reason for this is that Congress, over the objections of former defense secretary Donald Rumsfeld and his successor, Robert Gates, increased military basic pay by one half point above the cost of living for the past five years.

Moreover, in deciding on the size of this military pay raise, Congress focused exclusively on base pay. This accounts for only about half of total military cash compensation because it doesn't include benefits like health care. As a result, total military compensation for the average enlisted person is more than $5,000 above the Pentagon's standard. Officers are more than $6,000 above accepted levels. In addition, the Pentagon requested the creation of a body similar to the Base Realignment and Closure Commission to reform the military's expensive and inflexible retirement system. Under this system, the government pays generous lifetime pensions—starting at 50 percent of base pay per year at retirement for those who serve at least twenty years.

Men and women unable or unwilling to serve twenty years get nothing. This creates a perverse incentive structure that punishes those who are not career officers or enlisted personnel—even if they serve in combat. Troops who might be productive for more than twenty years, meanwhile, have every incentive to leave the service.

Eighty-three percent of veterans don't serve twenty years and, therefore, leave with no retirement benefits. Perhaps most worrisome, enlisted ground troops—who have borne the brunt of the Iraq and Afghanistan fighting—are least likely to serve long enough to earn retirement benefits.

Though this system fails to cover the vast majority of veterans, it is still tremendously expensive. In fiscal 2013, the government is due to spend more than $100 billion on military retirement. If corrections are not made, these costs will grow to $217 billion by 2034.

The Pentagon has finally proposed increases in the enrollment fees paid by working-age military retirees—those younger than sixty-five—to remain on the military's Tricare health care system. When Tricare was introduced in 1995, enrollment fees for working-age retirees were set at $460 a year for a family—about 27 percent of health care costs. These fees were intended to be adjusted over time, in line with the private sector.

Sixteen years later, however, enrollment fees have been raised by just $5 per month—despite skyrocketing health care costs. So the Pentagon now covers about 89 percent of the health care costs for working-age retirees.

The Pentagon proposes to increase the cost share from 11 percent to 14 percent—still far less than the 27 percent of 1995. This is to be phased in over five years and means-tested. Active-duty service members will continue to receive health care at no cost. Nor will these changes affect wounded or disabled veterans, who receive free health care through the Department of Veterans Affairs.

For retirees older than sixty-five who are enrolled in Tricare for Life, a free Medicare supplement implemented in 2001, the Defense Department's proposals would introduce a small enrollment fee and some co-pays. This is far less than comparable private-sector Medigap insurance.

While these changes will be fought by the military lobby and veterans groups, most of these claims are baseless. These changes will not break faith with those who have served, nor are they a bait and switch. Rather, they are an attempt to bring military compensation back into line with accepted standards.

In the twentieth century, citizens of the United States believed that when America's army went to war, America went to war. Thus, when we engaged in significant conflicts, like the two world wars, or even more limited conflicts like Korea and Vietnam, we drafted men to augment the standing force. But our civilian and military leaders misled us about Vietnam, and many of the political elites—including the current and former vice presidents and the forty-second and forty-third presidents—avoided combat service. Largely as a result of Vietnam, conscription was ended in 1973, and America, its leaders, and its army have been dealing with the consequences ever since.

To ensure that America could go to war but would not take the decision to do so lightly, the creators of the AVF kept the Selective Service in place. In their view, draftees would augment the volunteers in the active and reserve component, who would handle small contingencies or the opening days of significant conflicts. Not only would activating the Selective Service compel citizen involvement in war making, but it would prevent the country from putting undue strain on volunteers.

Despite the fact that the George W. Bush administration deployed more than two hundred thousand people on a continuous basis in Iraq and Afghanistan, and although Congress approved these conflicts, our political and military leaders did not have the courage to activate the draft. Many of the volunteers in the active and reserve ground forces were abused, physically and psychologically, while Americans went shopping. The military and the nation will pay the costs of this moral failure for a long time. Let us hope that the next time we engage in large campaigns, political and military leaders will not again forget their obligations to the country and those who serve it.

Notes

1 For an excellent analysis on this topic, see Beth Bailey, *America's Army: Making the All-Volunteer Force* (Cambridge, MA: Belknap Press of Harvard University Press, 2009).

2 See Molly Clever and David R. Segal, "After Conscription: The United States and the All-Volunteer Force," *Sicherheit und Frieden, no. 1* (2012), 5–26.

3 David R. Segal, *Recruiting for Uncle Sam: Citizenship and Military Manpower Policy* (Lawrence: University Press of Kansas, 1989), 36–38.

4 Clever and Segal, "After Conscription."

5 Mady W. Segal, Meridith Hill Thanner, and David R. Segal, "Hispanics and African Americans in the U.S. Military: Trends in Representation," *Race, Gender & Class* 14, nos. 3–4 (2007): 48–64.

6 Clever and Segal, "After Conscription."

7 Bureau of Labor Statistics, 2007.

8 Mady W. Segal, "Women's Military Roles Cross-Nationally: Past, Present, and Future," *Gender & Society* 9, no. 6 (1995): 757–75.

9 Michelle Sandhoff, Mady W. Segal, and David R. Segal, "Gender Issues in the Transformation of an All-Volunteer Force: A Transnational Perspective," in *The Decline of Citizen Armies in Democratic States*, ed. Stuart Cohen (New York: Routledge, 2010), 111–31.

10 David R. Segal and Mady Wechsler Segal, "America's Military Population." *Population Bulletin* 59, no. 4 (2004), 10–11.

11 Pew Research Center, *War and Sacrifice in the Post-9/11 Era* (October 5, 2011), 25–26.

12 Segal and Segal, "America's Military Population," 25–26.

13 Charlotte E. Hunter and Lyman M. Smith, "Religious Diversity in the U.S. Military." Defense Equal Opportunity Management Institute Technical Report 05–10. March 2010.

14 Clever and Segal, "After Conscription."

15 Bailey, *America's Army*, 227.

16 Deborah D. Avant, "Selling Security: Post-Cold War Security Services in Historical Perspective," paper presented at the annual meeting of the American Political Science Association, San Francisco, 2001.

17 Deborah D. Avant, "From Mercenary to Citizen Armies: Explaining Change in the Practice of War," *International Organization* 54 (2000): 41–72.

18 Tricare is the current health care program of the DOD military health care system. It was formerly known as Champus (Civilian Health and Medical Program of the Uniformed Services), which was established in 1966 as part of the legislation that established Medicare.

19 Lawrence Korb, Peter Rundlet, Max Bergmann, Sean Duggan, and Peter Juul, *Beyond the Call of Duty: A Comprehensive Review of the Overuse of the*

Army in the Administration's War of Choice in Iraq (Washington, DC: Center for American Progress, 2007).

20 Lawrence Korb, Peter Juul, Laura Conley, Myles Caggins, and Sean Duggan, *Building a Military for the 21st Century: New Realities, New Priorities* (Washington, DC: Center for American Progress, 2008).

21 The National Guard consists of units that evolved from state militias and that therefore have responsibilities to state governments. Guardsmen in peace-time generally train for one weekend each month and two weeks during the summer and can be mobilized by the governors of their states in the event of natural disasters or civil unrest. They also are members of the armed forces mobilization base and can be activated and called to federal service by the president. Members of the federal reserve forces, by contrast, have no state responsibilities.

22 Lawrence Korb and Sean Duggan, *Caught Off Guard: The Link between Our National Security and Our National Guard* (Washington, DC: Center for American Progress, 2007).

23 Thomas J. Burns, David R. Segal, Michael P. Silver, William W. Falk, and Bam Dev Sharda, "The All-Volunteer Force in the 1970s," *Social Science Quarterly* 79 (1998): 390–411.

24 Jerald G. Bachman, David R. Segal, Peter Freedman-Doan, and Patrick O'Malley, "Who Chooses Military Service? Correlates of Propensity and Enlistment in the United States Armed Forces," *Military Psychology* 12 (1998): 1–30. Cf. Robert L. Goldich, "American Military Culture from Colony to Empire," in this volume. Drawing on data reported by the Heritage Foundation, which uses census tract data where available to estimate the socioeconomic status of volunteers, Goldich suggests that the highest strata of society are overrepresented in the American military. However, while census tracts exist for the most part in urban or high-population-density areas, the military recruits primarily in rural or low-density areas. Only six states and the District of Columbia are fully tracted. Existing tracts range from about 2,500 to 8,000 people, and while they are initially designed to be relatively homogeneous demographically, there is still considerable internal variance. Moreover, there has been great resistance to changing tract bound-aries, which would eliminate the ability to make comparisons across decen-nial censuses. Thus, the homogeneity of tracts might well decrease with increasing population diversity. Methodologists refer to using geographical measures to estimate individual characteristics as the "ecological fallacy." The Heritage Foundation reports that recruits who cannot be located in a census tract are randomly assigned to one based on zip code data. Other survey-based research agrees that recruits from the bottom of the socioeco-nomic scale are underrepresented because of the military's education-based selectivity, but it disagrees with the interpretation at the top of the scale.

Census-tract estimates of individual status require an assumption that recruits' income is at the mean for their tract or is randomly distributed around that mean. We find these assumptions problematic. See Shanea J. Watkins and James Sherk, *Who Serves in the U.S. Military? Demographic Characteristics of Enlisted Troops and Officers* (Washington, DC: Heritage Foundation Center for Data Analysis, August 21, 2008).

25 See Karin K. De Angelis and David R. Segal, "Building and Maintaining a Post-9/11 All-Volunteer Military Force," in *The Impact of 9/11 on Politics and War: The Day That Changed Everything*, ed. Matthew J. Morgan (New York: Palgrave Macmillan, 2009), 43–60.

26 Korb, Juul, Conley, Caggins, and Duggan, *Building a Military for the 21st Century.*

27 Ibid.

28 Ibid.

29 Ibid.

30 Korb, Rundlet, Bergmann, Duggan, and Juul, *Beyond the Call of Duty.*

31 William S. Cohen, remarks at Yale University, September 26, 1997.

32 Peter D. Feaver and Richard H. Kohn, eds., *Soldiers and Civilians: The Civil-Military Gap and American National Security* (Cambridge, MA: MIT Press, 2001).

33 David R. Segal, Peter Freedman-Doan, Jerald G. Bachman, and Patrick M. O'Malley, "Attitudes of Entry-Level Enlisted Personnel: Pro-Military and Politically Mainstreamed," in *Soldiers and Civilians: The Civil-Military Gap and American National Security*, ed. Peter D. Feaver and Richard H. Kohn (Cambridge, MA: MIT Press, 2001), 163–212.

34 Pew Research Center, *War and Sacrifice in the Post-9/11 Era.*

35 Ibid.

6 :: Military Contractors and the American Way of War

Deborah Avant and Renée de Nevers

Abstract: Contractors are deeply intertwined with the American military and U.S. foreign policy. Over half the personnel the United States has deployed in Iraq and Afghanistan since 2003 have been contractors. Their relationship with the U.S. government, the public, and domestic and international law differs from that of military personnel, and these differences pose both benefits and risks. America's use of private military and security companies (PMSCs) can provide or enhance forces for global governance. Yet PMSCs can also be used to pursue agendas that do not have the support of American, international, or local publics. Thus far, the use of PMSCs has proved a mixed bag in terms of effectiveness, accountability, and American values. Moving forward in a way that maximizes the benefits of contractors and minimizes their risks will require careful management of the uncomfortable trade-offs these forces present.

More than one-half of the personnel the United States has deployed in Iraq and Afghanistan since 2003 have been contractors. Contractors—part of the global private military and security industry—are deeply intertwined with the American military and U.S. foreign policy.[1] Whatever one chooses to call them—mercenaries, contractors, or private military and security companies (PMSCs)—their relationship to the U.S. government, the American public, and domestic and international law differs from that of military personnel. These differences pose both benefits and risks to the effectiveness, accountability, and values represented in American actions abroad.

In the best case, American use of PMSCs can provide or enhance forces for global governance. PMSCs can recruit from around the world to quickly mobilize expertise as needed. If their employees are instilled with professional values and skills and engaged in a way that is responsive to the demands of the U.S. public, the international community, and local concerns, these forces could contribute to managing a global demand for security that U.S. forces alone cannot meet. In the worst case, PMSCs can provide a means for pursuing agendas that do not have the support of American, international, or local publics. They may siphon off U.S. dollars for practices that are wasteful, are antithetical to U.S. interests, or undermine global stability. Thus far, the use of PMSCs has produced mixed results: it has increased military effectiveness somewhat, but often at the expense of accountability and with dubious attention to the values the United States and the international community hold dear. Moving forward in a way that maximizes the benefits of contractors and minimizes their risks will require careful management of the uncomfortable trade-offs these forces pose.

The degree to which the United States relies on private security vendors has become clear during the hostilities in Iraq and Afghanistan, as contractors have provided logistical support for U.S. and coalition troops. Less well known is that as U.S. forces were stretched thin by the lawlessness resulting from the fall of Saddam Hussein in 2003, the first "surge" involved private personnel mobilized to protect expatriates working in the country and train the Iraqi police force and army; and a private Iraqi force was hired to guard government facilities and oil fields.[2] Retired military or police from all over the world, employed by a wide array of PMSCs, worked for the U.S. government (and others) throughout the country.

Although precise figures are difficult to determine, by 2008 the number of personnel in Iraq under contract with the U.S.

government roughly equaled or was greater than the number of U.S. troops on the ground.[3] In September 2009, two months prior to the Obama administration's announcement of the troop surge in Afghanistan, contractors made up an estimated 62 percent of the U.S. presence in that country.[4] The use of contractors in these conflicts represents a dramatic expansion in the U.S. military's reliance on PMSCs. During the 1991 Gulf conflict, the ratio of troops to contractors was roughly ten to one; in 2007, the ratio of troops to contractors in Iraq was roughly one to one.[5] In Afghanistan in 2010, there were roughly 1.43 contractors for every American soldier.[6] The Commission on Wartime Contracting (CWC), established by Congress in 2008, estimates conservatively that at least $177 billion has been obligated in contracts and grants to support U.S. operations in Afghanistan and Iraq since 2001.[7]

PMSCs offer a wide range of services, including tasks associated with military operations, policing, and the gray area between the two that is an increasingly large part of twenty-first-century conflict. Common services include support for weapons systems and equipment, military advice and training, logistical support, site security (armed and unarmed), crime prevention, police training, and intelligence.[8] While some firms specialize in a specific area, others provide an array of services, and a few offer the entire range. The CWC divides the services provided by contractors into three categories: logistics, security, and reconstruction.[9]

Logistics services include the supply of food, laundry, fuel, and base facility construction. Kellogg Brown & Root (KBR) held the U.S. Army's logistics civil augmentation contract (LOGCAP) in the early years of the Iraq and Afghanistan conflicts. In June 2007, the new contract (LOGCAP IV) was awarded to three companies: DynCorp International LLC, Fluor Intercontinental Inc., and KBR. In Iraq alone, the LOGCAP contract paid out $22 billion between 2003 and 2007.[10]

Security services include guarding people, buildings, and convoys. Many security contractors are armed; in carrying out their duties, they routinely shoot and are shot at.[11] The Congressional Budget Office estimated that in 2008, thirty thousand to thirty-five thousand of the contractors working in Iraq were armed; in late

2012, the Department of Defense employed over twenty-one thousand private security contractors in Iraq and Afghanistan.[12] Blackwater (now Academi) employees, recruited to support both the military and the U.S. State Department, have received the most notoriety for their security work in Iraq and, more recently, in Afghanistan. Working under the State Department's Worldwide Personal Protective Services contract in Iraq, Blackwater personnel carried weapons, had their own helicopters, and defended against insurgents in ways hard to distinguish from military actions.[13] They were later joined by companies such as Triple Canopy, Crescent Security Group, and Custer Battles.[14]

Reconstruction services incorporate everything from building physical infrastructure (for roads, communication, water, and power) to strengthening institutions (for example, by training government employees, including military, police, and justice personnel at the national, provincial, and local levels; supporting civil society groups; and promoting rule of law and democratization). A wide range of PMSCs, along with other contractors, have delivered these services. DynCorp, a well-established company with roots in technical support and an increasing presence in policing and police training, has trained Iraqi police, constructed police and prison facilities, and built capacity for a justice system.[15] Three companies that provided training for the new Iraqi army early in the conflict are Vinnell Corporation, a company with a long history of providing military training in Saudi Arabia; MPRI, a firm that gained prominence by training Croatian and then Bosnian troops in the 1990s; and USIS, which was established as the result of an Office of Management Personnel privatization effort in 1994.[16] Parsons Corporation, another well-known firm with a long record in the building of infrastructure, has worked on many large infrastructure projects. Myriad others have delivered various capacity-building services.[17]

Though their use in Iraq and Afghanistan dominates the discussion of contractors in the U.S. context, PMSCs are important players in all aspects of the U.S. military and U.S. foreign policy.[18] Contractors working for the Department of Defense (DOD) and the State Department contribute significantly to U.S. foreign policy projects aimed at enhancing development and security in a number of states; they also support U.S. troops and diplomats. Their tasks cover all three categories noted above. Consider, for instance, the contractor support for U.S. foreign assistance policies in Africa and Latin America.

In Africa, the United States has relied on the private sector to support missions such as military training and peacekeeping operations. These programs fall within AFRICOM, the U.S. military command for Africa established in 2007, and the State Department's Africa Peacekeeping program (AFRICAP), which is similar in structure to the Army's LOGCAP contract. In 2008, AFRICAP's stated objectives were to enhance regional peace and stability in Africa through training programs in peacekeeping and conflict management and prevention for African armed forces, as well as through logistics and construction activities in support of peace-keeping and training missions.[19] AFRICOM's stated purposes are "to build strong military-to-military partnerships," to help African countries better address the threats they face by improving African military capacity, and to bolster peace and security there.[20] Since its inception, AFRICOM has awarded contracts for training, air transport, information technology, and public diplomacy to companies such as DynCorp, which has trained armed forces in Liberia and the Democratic Republic of Congo, and PAE, a company specializing in infrastructure, mission support, and disaster relief.[21]

U.S. foreign policy in Latin America, dominated since at least 2000 by antinarcotics and counterterrorism efforts, also relies heavily on contractors.[22] Plan Colombia, the central element of a counter-drug initiative focused on the Andean region, has sought to reduce drug production in Colombia and strengthen Colombian security forces to better secure the state against threats posed by terrorists, drug traffickers, and paramilitary groups. The program has failed to slow drug production there, but military and police training conducted by both U.S. troops and civilian contractors has led to security improvements.[23] Roughly half of the military aid to Colombia is spent on private contractors funded by the DOD and the State Department. Like Plan Colombia, the 2007 Mérida Initiative, a U.S.-Mexico assistance agreement, seeks to disrupt drug-trafficking activities by providing equipment and training to Mexican security forces.[24]

PMSCs are incorporated in many countries and employ a mix of U.S. citizens, local citizens, and "third-country nationals" (recruits from neither the United States nor the host state). That combination changes over time and from contingency to contingency. For example, an April 30, 2008, census by the U.S. Army Central Command found that the 190,200 contractors in Iraq included about 20 percent (38,700) U.S. citizens, 37 percent (70,500) Iraqis, and 43 percent (81,006) third-country nationals.[25] In March 2010, the total number of contractors had dropped to 95,461, of which 26 percent were U.S. citizens, 56 percent third-country nationals, and 18 percent Iraqis.[26] The number of locals working as private security contractors (as opposed to logistics or reconstruction contractors) in Iraq has been relatively low: about 6 percent of private security contractors in 2011 were Iraqi; 82 percent were third-country nationals. In Afghanistan, the DOD has relied more heavily on locals. The total number of contractors in March 2011 was 90,338, of which 21 percent were private security contractors. The numbers of locals who work in private security is higher than those who provide other services. About 95 percent of the 18,971 private security contractors in 2011 were Afghans; 4 percent were third-country nationals, and 1 percent Americans.[27]

When the United States hires PMSCs to train militaries abroad, the contractor may take a small team of U.S. personnel (as MPRI did in Croatia), or it may recruit an international team (as DynCorp did in Liberia). Companies providing logistics support abroad often rely on locals or third-country nationals to cut costs. Hiring locals or third-country nationals can also avoid a variety of political restrictions and diminish visibility when the United States is undertaking more-controversial missions. For instance, Congress restricted the number of American contractors the United States could use under Plan Colombia to three hundred (raised to four hundred in 2001); PMSCs bypassed this restriction by hiring personnel from Peru, Guatemala, and other Latin American countries.[28]

In addition to nationality, personnel hired by PMSCs vary in their employment backgrounds. PMSCs that offer military training

primarily hire former military officers. Those that offer armed security services hire a broader range of military veterans. Those that
offer police training often hire former police officers. As the number
of companies and the range of services they offer have expanded to
meet market demand, companies have hired employees with more
diverse experience.

Contracting for military and security services has raised questions about the effectiveness of using force, political accountability
for the use of force, and the social values to which force adheres.
Some concerns vary according to which service is provided, while
others apply more generally across different tasks.

Military *effectiveness* rests on a range of components, including
skill of personnel, quality of matériel, and military responsiveness
to contextual or external constraints. A critical component noted in
recent research is integration: that is, the degree to which military
plans follow from overarching state goals and to which activities are
internally consistent and mutually reinforcing.[29]

Contracting can influence both the military's effectiveness
and its broader mission. For example, when U.S. goals change,
as they did after the Cold War's end, contracting enhances the
military's ability to integrate forces with (new) political goals.
Speed and flexibility are the hallmark benefits of contracting, and
contractors can quickly provide tools or skills for new missions
that regular military forces may lack, or cannot identify rapidly
within their ranks. Using a contract with MPRI, for instance, the
Africa Crisis Response Initiative military training courses for
French-speaking African countries were staffed with employees
who spoke French. The U.S. military was also able to mobilize
civilian police forces, first for Haiti in 1994, and then for contingencies in the Balkans, via contracts with DynCorp. With a
reduction in the size of the joint force, as outlined in the new
Defense Strategic Guidance, the likelihood that the United States
will rely on the flexibility of contractors in the future will only
increase.[30]

Different concerns regarding effectiveness emerge with contracting for logistics, security, and reconstruction services. Logistics services are fundamental to the military's ability to operate. Without

personnel to provide logistics services, the U.S. military simply cannot go to war. Contracting for logistics also requires strong oversight. Early in the Iraq conflict, serious concerns were raised about adequate staffing for logistics contracts. General Charles S. Mahan Jr., then the Army's top logistics officer, complained of troops receiving inadequate support because of problems deploying contractors.[31] After the Coalition Provisional Authority appointed Brigadier General Stephen Seay the new head of contracting authority in February 2004, Seay hired more acquisition staff, enabling overburdened contracting officers to do their jobs more effectively.[32] More recently, military personnel have expressed general satisfaction with the quality of logistics services.[33] Many worries over logistics contracting in Iraq and Afghanistan have focused on lack of oversight (particularly inadequate numbers of contract officers), along with waste and fraud.[34] But logistics contracts require fewer skills specific to military personnel, and logistics contractors do not need to work as closely with military personnel on the ground as do security and reconstruction contractors.

The activities of contractors who provide security services are most similar to those performed by soldiers. Many are armed and, in carrying out their duties, pose deadly risks to those working around them. Periodic tensions between contractors and regular forces—aggravated by disparities in pay and responsibilities—have raised the issue of whether these two types of forces can work together effectively. A 2010 survey of DOD personnel and their perceptions of private security contractors suggests that combining these forces in conflict zones is problematic. Lower-ranking and younger personnel in particular claim that pay disparities between military personnel and contractors are detrimental to the morale of their units in Iraq.[35] However, many security service tasks do not require close interaction with military personnel. Roughly one-third of military personnel surveyed in Iraq, for example, had no firsthand experience with private security contractors.[36] These tasks are also frequently less crucial to the performance of military units than are logistics services.

Nonetheless, the behavior of contracted security personnel matters to the overall U.S. mission. The hazards of questionable behavior were demonstrated most vividly in the September 2007 Blackwater shoot-out in Baghdad's Nisoor Square. Both Iraqis and Americans, however, had consistently reported this type of behavior long before that dramatic incident. Private forces have tended to focus on the strict terms of their contracts (protecting particular people or facilities) rather than on the overarching goals of the United States (effectively countering the insurgency). Some of the tactics developed to protect clients, such as driving fast through intersections and rapid resort to force, alienated the local population in ways that undermined the broader counterinsurgency strategy. Similar problems persist in Afghanistan. Among military personnel who had experience with security contractors, approximately 20 percent reported firsthand knowledge of PMSC failure to coordinate with military forces "sometimes"; another 15 percent of this population witnessed such coordination problems "often."[37]

In today's conflicts, reconstruction tasks—particularly training— are often more crucial for achieving the goals of the war effort than either logistics or security services. Often, reconstruction tasks must be coordinated so that police training and justice reform, for instance, complement one another, and so that civilian leaders understand the military they are expected to oversee. Contractors who provide reconstruction services must not only deliver quality work but also coordinate that delivery with other contractors, the U.S. military, and other government agencies. Thus, these services are among the most crucial for U.S. goals *and* the most challenging to coordinate. Moreover, concerns have been raised about the military's ability to ensure that these tasks are carried out effectively when they have been outsourced. Notably, DynCorp's training of the Afghan national police and army is widely regarded as a failure, but the DOD was unable to move the training contract to a different company because of DynCorp's legal protest regarding contract competition.[38] Yet these jobs are less important than logistics support to the functioning of military units, and they pose less deadly risk than security operations do. Problems with integration of activities—or unity of effort—were among the most significant challenges to reconstruction, as noted by the CWC's 2009 interim report.[39]

Thus, the overall picture of how contractors shape effectiveness is complicated. Clearly, contractors can quickly deploy skilled personnel, and the majority of contractors are good at what they do. But the United States does not have the capacity to oversee these contracts successfully, and this failure has led to waste, fraud, and, particularly with regard to security contracts, abuse. Furthermore, the level of integration needed for the most effective delivery of services has lagged in Iraq and Afghanistan.

How does contracting for military and security services affect the United States' capacity to take political *accountability* for forces? Mobilization via contract operates differently from military enlistment, with consequences for the relationship between the force and civilians—the political elite and the public included. The U.S. experience in Iraq suggests that forces raised via contract operate much more opaquely than military forces. Largely because of this reduced transparency, Congress has struggled to exercise constitutional authorization and oversight. Furthermore, the public has less information about the deployment of contractors. Though evidence suggests that the public is just as concerned about the deaths of contractors as it is about military deaths, statistics on the former are much less likely to be known.[40]

Using contractors speeds policy response but limits input into the policy process. As the insurgency grew in Iraq, for example, the United States mobilized 150,000 to 170,000 private forces to support the mission there, all with little or no congressional or public knowledge—let alone consent. President Bush was not required to appeal to Congress or the public for these additional forces, which doubled the U.S. presence in Iraq. Indeed, he may not have even realized the extent to which these contractors were deployed. As negative reaction to the request for a mere twenty thousand troops for the 2007 surge suggests, the president may well not have been able to deploy additional personnel if he had been required to assess exact needs and obtain congressional permission. Because the use of PMSCs garners little attention, their employment reduces public arousal, debate, commitment, and response to the use of force.

How contracted forces relate to civilian leaders is an important question. Some claim contracted forces can be more responsive (given the potential for losing their contracts) than the military bureaucracy. Flexibility in contracts can accelerate mobilization in ways that military organizations often cannot deliver. Certainly, contractors are designed to deliver whatever the client wants. They are thus much less prone to standard operating procedures or organizational bias that can inhibit responsiveness in military organizations.

Not at all apparent, however, is the U.S. government's capacity to oversee contracts in a manner sufficient to generate responsiveness. Even as DOD contract transactions *increased* by 328 percent between 2000 and 2009, the staff responsible for reviewing contractor purchasing at the Defense Contract Management Agency *declined* from seventy in 2002 to fourteen in 2009.[41] Contracting in individual service branches faced similar problems. The dearth of contract officers makes it difficult to effectively oversee contracts at home, but concerns about adequate oversight are even more pressing when PMSCs are operating abroad. The relevant contracting officer is often not even in theater. Inadequate contract staffing and oversight have been important complaints in both Iraq and Afghanistan and have been tied to numerous problems—from poor performance to waste, fraud, and abuse. Though the risks of poor oversight vary according to task, difficulties in overseeing contractors have been common to all three areas of contract services. The challenge of overseeing expeditionary operations may undermine companies' responsiveness to contractual obligations.

Overall, then, the use of contractors has skirted accountability, making half of U.S. mobilization largely invisible to Congress and the public; as a result, it has masked the number of conflict-related casualties.[42] Though one could argue that contractors are more responsive to political leaders, this likelihood can only be the case once political leaders know what contractors are doing— and evidence shows that this has not been the case in Iraq and Afghanistan.

A final point of evaluation is to look at whether contractors allow the exercise of force in a way that is consistent with the larger *values*, culture, and expectations of the society they represent. Over the course of the Cold War and in its aftermath, military professionalism within advanced industrial states increasingly enshrined principles drawn from theories of democracy (civilian control of the military and abidance by the rule of law), liberalism (respect for human rights), and the laws of war.[43] Though marginal differences exist, the values that govern U.S. military personnel are largely shared with their Western partners. The ease of mobilization that contracting offers is viewed by some as consistent with the United States' evolving concerns with global security and global governance. But in practice, the use of PMSCs has not fit well within the normative and legal frameworks that underpin global security.

Two factors regarding contracting place strains on the values represented by military forces. First, precisely which professional norms inform the PMSC industry remains unclear. Americans employed by PMSCs have a range of military and law enforcement backgrounds—some distinguished and others less so. However, PMSCs increasingly recruit from a global market. As recruiting and subcontracting have become more transnational, personnel are from countries as diverse as the United Kingdom, Nepal, Fiji, South Africa, El Salvador, Colombia, and India. These geographic differences bring an even more diverse array of professional norms. Concerns about lax industry vetting of employees have raised the question of whether PMSCs are increasingly hiring employees with less distinguished service records.[44] Finally, many PMSCs also hire local personnel. In addition to lower costs, these forces bring many benefits: local knowledge and ties that can aid companies' effectiveness. However, they also bring local values that may not be consistent with democracy, liberalism, or the laws of war. For instance, evidence suggests that local companies hired by the United States to provide convoy security in Afghanistan funneled money to Taliban forces or were otherwise engaged in corrupt practices that worked against U.S. goals and values in Afghanistan.[45]

Even if all contractors were well-socialized military or police professionals, they nonetheless operate in a different environment—vis-à-vis both the law and command and control—than troops do. Commanders are less likely to notice or to punish offenses committed by contractors than offenses committed by troops. Over time, a lack of punishment can be expected to lead to more lax behavior;

indeed, many have claimed that this outcome is the case in Iraq and Afghanistan. Though reliable, systematic evidence is not yet available, a wealth of anecdotal evidence lends credibility to this conclusion.[46] Military officers have expressed their concern that the "culture of impunity" surrounding PMSCs has become a real problem.[47]

The increasing reliance on contractors suggests that U.S. national military forces have not been sufficient to meet the foreign policy goals that U.S. leaders consider vital to national security. Yet, as the United States plans for a smaller force, and support for a draft is nowhere to be found, the use of contractors provides an escape valve of sorts.[48] The fact that leaders can turn to contractors means that neither the U.S. leadership nor the U.S. public is forced to reconcile foreign policy goals and the size of forces—by revising goals, using other means, or building an adequate force.

While potentially beneficial to effectiveness, the availability of contractors has also permitted leaders to avoid squaring foreign policy tools with national values and institutions. Enhancing effectiveness in this way has undermined the accountability of U.S. forces. Even as the United States works to make the use of contractors more efficient and effective, part of the attraction is that private forces are accountable to leaders, not publics or their representatives, thereby allowing elected representatives to pursue a global mission without first convincing the electorate to make the sacrifices required.

Efforts to make contractors more broadly accountable, though, can undermine the flexibility that makes them effective. For instance, spelling out more clearly in each contract the limits of action can address congressional concerns and enhance accountability, but it diminishes the flexibility that PMSC personnel can deliver on the ground. Furthermore, contractors are even more important to the State Department than they are to the DOD. Attempts to rein in contractor numbers, then, would further fuel questions about the appropriate balance between civilian and military activities in U.S. foreign policy initiatives. Although interagency efforts have sought to ensure that U.S. assistance in Africa, for example, extends beyond military training, the budgetary and personnel imbalance between the DOD and the State Department makes such a realignment of programs unlikely to occur in the near future.[49]

Finally, efforts to implement professional and legal standards for contractors promise to improve behavior but may also limit reliance on local residents in a way that could increase costs and inhibit the input of local knowledge. To the extent that U.S. standards are perceived as national rather than global, they may omit a large portion of the global industry. The United States has taken pains to engage with transnational processes to develop an International Code of Conduct and work toward global standards of behavior for private security providers.[50] The effort to coordinate regulatory and legal mechanisms for the PMSC industry has great potential. Its development, though, will require continued cooperation between the United States, other governments, NGOs, journalists, industry groups, and additional stakeholders.[51]

Reliance on contractors has generated tensions between the effectiveness of forces, their accountability, and the degree to which they represent U.S. values. These tensions, though not insurmountable, are not easily resolved. They require persistent management by U.S. leaders in cooperation not only with the American public but also with other governments and the variety of additional stakeholders that have an interest in how contractors behave. Thus, while contracting is likely to remain, it is also likely to continue to generate unease in U.S. foreign policy.

Notes

1 The contemporary "Total Force" concept explicitly includes contractor personnel. For general overviews of the private military and security industry, see Peter Singer, *Corporate Warriors: The Rise of the Privatized Military Industry* (Ithaca, NY: Cornell University Press, 2003); Deborah Avant, *The Market for Force: The Consequences of Privatizing Security* (New York: Cambridge University Press, 2005). For a discussion of the role of contractors in U.S. foreign policy more generally, see Allison Stanger, *One Nation under Contract: The Outsourcing of American Power and the Future of Foreign Policy* (New Haven, CT: Yale University Press, 2009).

2 David Isenberg, "A Government in Search of Cover: Private Military Companies in Iraq," in *From Mercenaries to Market: The Rise and Regulation*

of Private Military Companies, ed. Simon Chesterman and Chia Lehnardt (New York: Oxford University Press, 2007), 83.

3 Determining exact numbers is difficult because the Department of Defense did not begin to collect reliable information on the contractors it employed until 2007. Furthermore, contractors were hired by many other government agencies in addition to the DOD; Moshe Schwartz, *Department of Defense Contractors in Iraq and Afghanistan: Background and Analysis* (Washington, DC: Congressional Research Service, December 14, 2009), 4.

4 In Afghanistan's case, this percentage represents a drop in the ratio of contractors to uniformed personnel, from a high of 69 percent contractors in December 2008; Schwartz, *Department of Defense Contractors*, 5–13.

5 This ratio was at least 2.5 times higher than the ratio during any other major U.S. conflict; Congressional Budget Office, *Contractors' Support of U.S. Operations in Iraq* (Washington, DC: CBO, August 2008).

6 T. X. Hammes, "Private Contractors in Conflict Zones: The Good, the Bad, and the Strategic Impact," *Strategic Forum* no. 260 (Washington, DC: Institute for National Strategic Studies, October 2010). By mid-2012, the ratio of contractors to troops in Afghanistan had declined to 1.13 to one. DASD, "Contractor Support of U.S. Operations in the USCENTCOM Area of Responsibility to Include Iraq and Afghanistan," October 2012, http://psm.du.edu/media/documents/reports_and_stats/us_data/dod_quarterly_census/dod_quarterly_census_oct_2012.pdf.

7 Commission on Wartime Contracting, *At What Risk? Correcting Over-reliance on Contracting in Contingency Operations* (Washington, DC: CWC, February 2011), 1.

8 Avant, *Market for Force*.

9 Commission on Wartime Contracting, *At What Cost? Contingency Contracting in Iraq and Afghanistan* (Washington, DC: CWC, June 2009).

10 Congressional Budget Office, *Contractors' Support of U.S. Operations in Iraq*.

11 Ibid.

12 DASD, "Contractor Support of U.S. Operations," 2.

13 Dana Priest, "Private Guards Repel Attack on U.S. Headquarters," *Washington Post*, April 6, 2004.

14 See descriptions of these companies in Steve Fainaru, *Big Boy Rules: America's Mercenaries Fighting in Iraq* (Philadelphia: Da Capo Press, 2008); T. Christian Miller, *Blood Money: Wasted Billions, Lost Lives, and Corporate Greed in Iraq* (New York: Little, Brown, 2006); and Tom Ricks, *Fiasco: The American Military Adventure in Iraq* (New York: Penguin Press, 2006).

15 See DynCorp International, "A Brief History of DynCorp International," http://www.dyn-intl.com/history.aspx.

16 See the discussion of Vinnell Corporation in Avant, *Market for Force*, 18, 114, and 148. MPRI stands for Military Professional Resources Incorporated; the company is now a part of L-3 Communications. For a discussion of its role

in the Balkans, see ibid., chap. 3. For the history of USIS (US Investigations Services), see http://www.usis.com/Fact-Sheet.aspx.

17 See Parsons, "About Parsons," http://www.parsons.com/pages/default.aspx.

18 Stanger, *One Nation under Contract*.

19 Office of Logistics Management, *AFRICAP Program Re-Compete* (Washington, DC: U.S. Department of State, February 6, 2008), https://www.fbo.gov/index?s=opportunity&mode=form&tab=core&id=4fbad7bde428a5595aca7bfe3cdb co2d&_cview=1 (accessed May 6, 2010).

20 Government Accountability Office, *Actions Needed to Address Stakeholder Concerns, Improve Interagency Collaboration, and Determine Full Costs Associated with the U.S. Africa Command*, GAO Report, GAO-09-181 (Washington, DC: GAO, February 2009).

21 See David Isenberg, "Africa: The Mother of All PMC," *Huffington Post*, March 22, 2010, http://www.huffingtonpost.com/david-isenberg/africa-the -mother-of-all_b_509111.html; Tim Watson, "DynCorp International Wins AFRICAP Training Task Order," http://www.govconwire.com/2011/06/dy ncorp-international-wins-africap-training-task-order/; PAE, "Capabilities and Operations," http://www.paegroup.com/capabilities-operations.

22 Connie Veillette, Clare Ribando, and Mark Sullivan, *U.S. Foreign Assistance to Latin America and the Caribbean*, Congressional Research Service Report, RL32487 (Washington, DC: CRS, January 3, 2006), 2.

23 Government Accountability Office, *Plan Colombia: Drug Reduction Goals Were Not Fully Met, but Security Has Improved*, GAO Report, GAO-09-71 (Washington, DC: GAO, October 2008), 15.

24 Clare Ribando, *Mérida Initiative for Mexico and Central America: Funding and Policy Issues* (Washington, DC: Congressional Research Service, April 19, 2010), 1–3.

25 Congressional Budget Office, *Contractors' Support of U.S. Operations in Iraq.* http://www.cbo.gov/ftpdocs/96xx/doc9688/08-12-IraqContractors.pdf.

26 Schwartz, *Department of Defense Contractors*, 9.

27 Moshe Schwartz, *The Department of Defense's Use of Private Security Contractors in Afghanistan and Iraq: Background, Analysis, and Options for Congress*, CRS Report R40835, May 13, 2011, 7–14.

28 Lora Lumpe, "U.S. Foreign Military Training: Global Reach, Global Power, and Oversight Issues," *Foreign Policy in Focus* Special Report, May 2002, 11–12.

29 Risa Brooks and Elizabeth Stanley-Mitchell, eds., *Creating Military Power: The Sources of Military Effectiveness* (Stanford, CA: Stanford University Press, 2007).

30 Department of Defense, *Sustaining U.S. Global Leadership: Priorities for 21st Century Defense* (January 2012), http://www.defense.gov/news/Defense_ Strategic_Guidance.pdf.

31 This complaint was aired in a draft of what became Gregory Fontenot, E. J. Degen, and David Tohn, *On Point: The United States Army in Operation Iraqi Freedom* (Fort Leavenworth, TX: Combat Institute Press, 2004). In the final version of the document, however, the discussion of the difficulty with logistics did not mention contractors. General Mahan's complaints were also reported by Anthony Bianco and Stephanie Anderson Forest, "Outsourcing War," *Business Week*, September 15, 2003; and David Wood, "Some of Army's Civilian Contractors Are No-Shows in Iraq," Newhouse News Service, July 31, 2003.

32 Office of the Special Inspector General for Iraq Reconstruction, *Hard Lessons: The Iraq Reconstruction Experience* (Washington, DC: U.S. Government Printing Office, 2009), 172–73. Another example of the negative consequences of poor oversight is seen in the contractor abuses at Abu Ghraib prison; see Steve Schooner, "Contractor Atrocities at Abu Ghraib: Compromised Accountability in a Streamlined, Outsourced Government," *Stanford Law and Policy Review* 16 (2005): 549–72.

33 On troop satisfaction, see Commission on Wartime Contracting, *At What Cost?* 45.

34 Ibid., 39–59.

35 Sarah Cotton, Ulrich Petersohn, Molly Dunigan, Q. Burkhart, Meghan Zander-Cotugno, Edward O'Connell, and Michael Webber, *Hired Guns: Views about Armed Contractors in Operation Iraqi Freedom* (Santa Monica, CA: Rand Corp., 2010), figure S1.

36 Ibid.

37 Ibid.

38 Christine Spolar, "Military Training of Afghan National Police Mired in Contract Dispute," Huffington Post Investigative Fund, February 22, 2010, http://huffpostfund.org/stories/2010/02/military-training-afghan-national-police-mired-contract-dispute (accessed February 23, 2010).

39 Commission on Wartime Contracting, *At What Cost?* 3.

40 Deborah Avant and Lee Sigelman, "Private Security and Democracy: Lessons from the US in Iraq," *Security Studies* 19, no. 2 (2010).

41 Commission on Wartime Contracting in Iraq and Afghanistan, *Defense Agencies Must Improve Their Oversight of Contractor Business Systems to Reduce Waste, Fraud, and Abuse*, CWC Special Report 1, September 21, 2009, http://www.wartimecontracting.gov/index.php/reports. See also Jacques S. Gansler et al., *Urgent Reform Required: Army Expeditionary Contracting* (Washington, DC: Commission on Army Acquisition and Program Management in Expeditionary Operations, October 31, 2007), 4.

42 T. Christian Miller, "Contractors in Iraq Are Hidden Casualties of War," ProPublica, October 6, 2009, http://www.propublica.org/feature/kbr-contractor-struggles-after-iraq-injuries-1006 (accessed December 31, 2009).

43 See Charles Moskos, John Allen Williams, and David Segal, *The Postmodern Military* (New York: Oxford University Press, 2000).

44 Senate Committee on Armed Services, *Inquiry into the Role and Oversight of Private Security Contractors in Afghanistan*, 111th Cong., 2nd sess., September 28, 2010, http://info.publicintelligence.net/SASC-PSC-Report.pdf (accessed October 15, 2010).

45 Dexter Filkins, "Convoy Guards in Afghanistan Face an Inquiry: U.S. Suspects Bribes to Taliban Forces," *New York Times*, June 7, 2010.

46 See, for instance, Fainaru, *Big Boy Rules*.

47 Schwartz, *Department of Defense's Use of Private Security Contractors*, 19. There are international efforts to establish standards for PMSCs, codes of conduct for personnel, and standards for the legal responsibilities of companies and individuals that may begin to address some of these concerns. See International Committee of the Red Cross and the Swiss Federal Department of Foreign Affairs, *The Montreux Document on Private Military and Security Companies* (Montreux, Switzerland: ICRC, September 17, 2008); Swiss Directorate of Political Affairs, *International Code of Conduct for Private Security Service Providers* (Bern: Federal Department of Foreign Affairs, November 9, 2010).

48 According to a recent Pew Report, 80 percent of post-9/11 veterans and 74 percent of the public opposed returning to a draft. See Pew Research Center, *War and Sacrifice in the Post-9/11 Era: The Military-Civilian Gap* (October 5, 2011), http://www.pewsocialtrends.org/2011/10/05/war-and-sacrifice-in-the-post-911-era/.

49 Government Accountability Office, *Actions Needed*.

50 See Office of the Deputy Assistant Secretary of Defense, "Private Security Companies (PSCs)," http://www.acq.osd.mil/log/PS/psc.html.

51 See International Commission of the Red Cross and the Swiss Federal Department of Foreign Affairs, *Montreux Document*; Swiss Directorate of Political Affairs, *International Code of Conduct*.

7 :: Filming War

Jay Winter

Abstract: There is a shape to the history of war films, and a set of directorial choices, too, which have varied over time. Those choices can be summarized very roughly in this way: One school of film-making, which I term "war cinema realism," predominant from 1940 to 1970, is a style that, through sound, scenery, and special effects, enables a viewer to leave behind the knowledge that violence and destruction are staged and to accept while watching it that the film is portraying war as it actually is. In contrast, there was and is an alternative school, which I term "war cinema indirection," that never lets the viewer leave behind the knowledge that the violence and destruction on-screen are staged, and never lets the viewer accept the illusion, while watching it, that the film is portraying war "as it actually is." By and large, war film indirection dominated the silent era, and has become more important since the 1970s. In between, the majority of films made about war in the period 1940–1970 were "realistic" in the terms I use here, and frequently spectacular. Over time, I argue, the spectacle of war has become less dominant and less important in cinematography than the pathos of victimhood.

Language frames memory. What most of us know of war is always mediated knowledge, shaped and refracted by the stories we are told. Film is one such storyteller, an exceptionally powerful one, reaching a public much larger than that comprising readers of memoirs, fiction, and poetry, and viewers of the visual arts. This chapter focuses on the mediation of nondocumentary, commercial film in the formation and dissemination of popular representations of war.

Doing so enables us to see that imagining war has a history, in film as in the other visual arts, parallel to that of waging war. The arts of the imagination reflect changes in the material conditions and forms of warfare, and thereby contribute to the evolution of armed conflict, by framing the ways contemporaries understand what war is. In the twenty-first century the complexities of counterinsurgency warfare are both material and perceptual. Frameworks of thinking about war are not constructed out of documents alone; images matter. Policy makers always bring to the table what the historian James Joll termed the "unspoken assumptions" of their generation, and many of them arise from images of war in photography, in the visual arts, and especially in film.

Film itself has developed dramatically over time, but some elements remain constant. In cinematic history, we must attend to the marketplace at all times. The portrayal of military conflict in film is a mainstay of the industry. Box office considerations are never absent in the framing and gestation of commercial film, and the perennial popularity of films about combat—terrestrial or extra-terrestrial—requires us to take measure of their power to represent war and men at war.

It was an accident that the film industry came of age as a centerpiece of mass entertainment at precisely the moment industrialized warfare arrived in 1914. That first global war helped globalize the film industry, which saw exponential growth in particular in American film marketing at the same time the U.S. position in the war remained neutral.[1] It is impossible, however, to treat film in strictly national terms, because the upheavals of the 1930s produced a massive hemorrhage of talent from Germany to Britain and elsewhere, and from continental Europe to London and Hollywood, among other destinations. European filmmakers such as Fritz Lang, Ernst Lubitsch, and Billy Wilder brought their art with them, and braided it together with American approaches to the medium. I examine representations of war from a transnational perspective, while recognizing the significance of national institutions and codes, many of which are explicitly political in character.

In this effort, it makes sense to speak of roughly three periods in the cinematic history of war. The first is the silent epoch, from about 1900 to 1930. I extend this first period beyond 1926, when sound was initially introduced, because many directors schooled in silent film imported silence into the talkies. They framed sound by its absence, and did so in dramatically important ways. Consider the famous scene in Fritz Lang's classic film *M* (1931), in which a child murderer, played by Peter Lorre, faces a kangaroo court made up of hundreds of Berlin criminals. The faces of those criminals are scanned in a forty-five-second soundless tracking shot that seems to last for hours. Silence did not disappear with the talkies; it entered into and inflected the medium in a host of ways, even years after the introduction of sound.

We frequently lose sight of the artistic and affective power of silence. Suggestion is more hypnotic than instruction. Recall the remark of the great British journalist Alistair Cooke, whose "Letter to America" was broadcast on BBC radio every Sunday morning for forty years. He was asked one day why he preferred to work in radio. His answer was, the pictures are better. And silent film arguably delivered better sound, by drawing on viewers' pulse and heartbeat and internal voices. It is best to treat silent film not as a simple precursor of the talkies, but as a powerful art form in its own right, one that launched the cinematic history of war.[2] Recently, we have been reminded of the power of silent film by the artistic and critical success of *The Artist*, directed by Michel Hazanavicius, which won the Oscar for best motion picture of 2011.

The second phase of filmic history of war takes place from the lead-up to World War II through its aftermath, from 1933 to 1970. I include pre-1939 films because the fear of the return of total war is evident in 1930s cinema. War was both unthinkable and just around the corner. Images of war in the 1930s were seen by audiences that included millions of veterans, many of whom would take up arms again: first in Manchuria, then in Ethiopia, next in Spain, and finally throughout Europe and the Pacific. European filmmakers who later fled the Continent, such as Jean Renoir, did some of their greatest work in the later 1930s. This period also saw the production of some of the few pacifist classics in the history of the medium.

I have somewhat arbitrarily chosen 1970 as the end of this second phase of the cinematic history of war, but I base that dating on two interlaced developments. First, the Holocaust assumed a central place in the history of World War II and, increasingly, became a subject of powerful cinematic treatment in and of itself. Second, the Vietnam moment arrived, both repeating many of the heroic stereotypes of the World War II era and, to a degree, subverting them. Films of Vietnam drew on World War II tropes but went beyond them, too. Defeat mattered, yet so did dissent and disaffection, muting the unflinchingly patriotic posture of early Vietnam films, such as *The Green Berets* (1968), and producing in the next, the third period of war films, much darker and more ambiguous treatments of the conflict: for example, *The Deer Hunter* (1978), *Apocalypse Now* (1979), and *Full Metal Jacket* (1987). For these reasons, it makes sense to separate war films made between 1933 and 1970 from silent films before and from the films of so-called asymmetrical war that came after.

The third phase of representations of war in film covers the period from the 1970s to our own times, when changes in the face of war itself have inflected the face of war in film. Historian Charles Maier has described what he terms the end of the age of territoriality at around 1960,[3] an insight that forces us to see war over the last forty years or so not in national terms alone, but in subnational and transnational terms as well. War is no longer primarily a classic military encounter between nation-states and armies, but rather a messy and chaotic array of violent clashes between national troops— say, American forces in Somalia, Iraq, or Afghanistan—and a wide variety of insurrectionary groups, not nations. Since the 1970s, war has often meant "dirty wars" waged by military elites against their own people, including in Central America, South America, Africa, and the Middle East. Not surprisingly, film has followed the tides of war into these destinations, too.

Asymmetrical war also means civilian casualties on a scale, and as a proportion of all losses, greater than ever before. In the Second World War, civilian casualties constituted more than half of all war-related deaths. By 2001, some analysts and the International Committee of the Red Cross put the ratio of civilian to military deaths in modern conflicts as ten to one.[4] Some commentators are unconvinced by this claim, and see substantial variation in the distribution of casualties in asymmetric wars. Even then, their estimates of civilian casualties to all casualties in many post-1960 conflicts are substantially above the Second World War levels of 50 percent.[5]

This distinction matters in the history of film because the shadow of the Holocaust is also cast on the victims of wars remote from those of Nazi-occupied Europe. War as horror is not new, but the horror is no longer limited essentially to the battlefields: it is present in cities, in the countryside—indeed, everywhere. One reason the Holocaust has become metonymical, standing for victims of war and violence elsewhere, is that no one of Jewish origin was safe anywhere within the Nazis' reach.[6] Wars of extermination are wars without limits; for that reason, among others, the war against the Jews was a transformational event.

Let me add an additional analytical distinction. In each of these three phases of war-film history, I believe, filmmakers have operated in one of two registers, or in combinations of two registers— that of *spectacle* or of *indirection*. Film has always flourished in the atmosphere of the spectacular drama of war.[7] But the power to convey the spectacle was limited in the first phase by the absence of sound, and in the third phase by the absence of the kind moral transparency distinguishing "good" and "evil" in the war against the Axis powers. World War II was the cinematic "good war" par excellence in that its power to simplify and dramatize latched on to a cause that was clearly intelligible in precisely those terms: the war of good against evil. In the evolution of that moral calculus, the Holocaust became more and more important as time went on. Here, the cinematic tools of indirection were necessary because the problem of representing the Holocaust defies conventional protocols of representing warfare.

The third, post-1970 generation of war films did not leave World War II behind, but instead oscillated between morally simplifying war and recognizing unsanitized glimpses of its horrors and moral predicaments. These films are one important source of the moral ambiguity with which the public has come to view war in the last few decades. In the history of cinema, as in the history of the military, the 1970s constituted a breaking point, when perceptions and practices changed markedly.

The effects of this shift in perspective about war have been significant. As war has changed, it has been increasingly difficult to construct moral certainties about its meaning. Yet most films that show the ugliness of war in recent years stop short of pacifism. They suggest not that war is always immoral, but rather that it is always out of control and leaves men and women broken in its wake, whatever the outcome. If these films have anything positive to say, it is to visualize the camaraderie, courage, and sacrifice of warriors, affirming the power of war to bring out not only the worst but also the best in ordinary people. Over the course of a century, war films have developed from studies of conflict to studies of combatants, their loves, their hatreds, their inner lives.

Within this chronological framework, I note what may be termed a pendulum theory in the choices directors of war films make. Early filmmakers' first forays were perforce not realistic; they were indirect, allusive, suggestive, performative. They had to be so, because the texture and the roar of war—the sound of battle and of artillery and of airpower—were not reproducible. The films' technological weakness was their strength. They gestured toward images of battles rather than pretending to show war "as it really was." No one could, and I assert more generally, no one can, do that.

In the second generation of war films, the quest for cinematic "realism" dominated, to the great profit of the industry. Over and over, audiences saw combat, sacrifice, and killing and were led by filmmakers to believe they "were there," on Guadalcanal, Iwo Jima, at Bataan. Technical effects and massive injections of cash produced this mighty canvas of war, but however hard they tried, filmmakers could as little show the face of war realistically as they could show the dark side of the moon. In the World War II period, the pendulum swung too far toward what was taken to be verisimilitude.

That urge to show the "real face of war" is still apparent, but it exists alongside another powerful impulse, one that moves away from realism and toward suggestions of the unrepresentability of war in film. In part, the emergence of this new element reflects the literariness of cinematic culture. War literature, from Robert Graves's *Goodbye to All That,* to Ernest Hemingway's *A Farewell to Arms,* to Erich Maria Remarque's *All Quiet on the Western Front,* to Joseph Heller's *Catch-22*, has made the madness of war part of our cultural landscape. The literary witnessing of the victims of the Holocaust has brought that madness into an even more haunting register, which is increasingly at the heart of World War II narratives. But the change in representations of war is also a consequence of the change in war itself: its civilianization, its transformation into the asymmetrical struggles that made the (misleadingly named) Cold War and its proxy wars so bloody, wars between men in uniform and ordinary people, brutalized, mutilated, killed by the millions since the 1970s. The Cold War was "cold" or bloodless only if we myopically interpret it as confined to the Soviet-American standoff. Ask people in Indonesia, in Colombia, in Sri Lanka, in Vietnam, in Cambodia, in Rwanda what was "cold" about the "Cold War" and you are likely to get a different answer.[8]

In this period of new forms of warfare, war films introduce us to different kinds of landscapes of violence, doing so in new and indirect ways. There is very little in the pre-1970 period to match the hallucinatory effects of the Israeli film *Waltz with Bashir* (2008), a cartoon exploration of shell shock. Innovative approaches have the power to move beyond realism to explore the face of war—at a tangent, at an angle, indirectly, and with great power. And that face is a soldier's face, not the face of war.

The central arguments advanced in this chapter are these: first, that there is a shape to the history of war films, and second, that there is a set of choices too, which we can see in all three periods. Those choices can be summarized very roughly in this way: There was one school of filmmaking, predominant in the years 1940–1970, which I term that of "war cinema realism." War cinema realism is a style of filmmaking that, through sound, scenery, and special effects, enables a viewer to leave behind the knowledge that violence and destruction are staged and accept while watching it that the film is portraying war "as it actually is." In contrast, there was and is an alternative school, which I term "war cinema indirection," evident before 1930 and more so after 1970. It is a style of filmmaking that never lets the viewer leave behind the knowledge that the violence and destruction on-screen are staged, and never lets the viewer accept the illusion, while watching it, that the film is portraying war "as it actually is." A few films of the Second World War adopted this indirect style, both before and after 1970, but by and large the bulk of films made about that war were "realistic" in the terms I use here, and frequently spectacular. Over time, the spectacle of war became less important in cinematography than the pathos of victimhood.

First, silent film. War stories were at the core of D. W. Griffith's *The Birth of a Nation* (1915), which wandered through the Civil War and Reconstruction with a romantic brush, memorably presenting heroism in battle, the assassination of President Lincoln, and the "chivalry" of the Ku Klux Klan. But silent filmmakers soon turned to the 1914–1918 conflict, which formed the perfect setting for adventure stories, melodramas, romances, and the like. But aside from good box office entertainment, cinema contributed to popular narratives of the war by locating it within identifiable and mundane themes, thereby humanizing it. By suggesting the monumental scale of the conflict, in a way prose rarely could do, cinema mythologized the war as a vast earthquake against the backdrop of which the petty conflicts and hopes of ordinary mortals were played out. Here again, the superior power of images over words has had a greater impact on popular attitudes to war than most commentators have recognized. This is as true today as it was a century ago when war cinema was in its infancy.

The balance between what I call the *cinema of indirection* and the *cinema of spectacle* differed in each period of the history of war film. In the silent period, the realistic genre was perforce indirect because sound was absent, and silence was either preserved or replaced by impromptu or arranged piano or organ music. Audiences brought their own sound effects with them and thereby were drawn into the story in even more compelling ways. Consider the contrast after 1926, when the score, inscribed on a sound track, told us (and still tells us) how to react to what we see. With sound came emotional *dirigisme*, a kind of authorial instruction that we should feel suspense at one moment, relief later, and resolution at last.

In 1916, the British government produced a film titled *The Battle of the Somme*, which was distributed and shown while soldiers were still engaged in that six-month operation. Perhaps two million people saw it in six weeks, the equivalent in today's Britain of six million people going to the same film at roughly the same time. At the center of the film was an entirely false reconstruction of what it meant to "go over the top." A line of soldiers in a trench crawl up to its lip, then stand and proceed through smoke and fire to engage the enemy. One man is "hit" and slides down the trench. Entirely silent, without any musical accompaniment, the scene had a devastating effect on the audience, many of whom had relatives serving in the war at that very moment. Women fainted; others cried out and had to be escorted from the cinema. Silence provided the visceral punch.[9]

Sound films framed audience reactions in ways that tended to reduce their own affective choices to the ones the cineaste or his composer provided. Silent films were more open-ended emotionally, and hence potentially more powerful. Yet whatever the sound or silence accompanying the scene, those screen images carried a kind of authenticity, a surface realism, with them. They appeared to be about real people: a real man hit on the lip of a trench, who could have been the husband, brother, or son of someone in the audience. The power of film to lie about war was revealed at its inception, though the power of sound expanded this field of invention in significant ways. Indeed, the introduction of sound effects enabled viewers to believe that they could actually imagine war. What is thinkable is what is doable, and one ramification of the introduction of the talkies was that war films helped domesticate a set of violent events that, at their core, resist representation. To be sure, all films misrepresent war; but talkies do so with gusto and with even more powerful effect.

Part of the reason for the unrepresentability of war in all film is its chaotic character. Battle has no vanishing point, no center of gravity, and the rubble of destruction accompanying industrialized warfare in 2013—just as in 1916—makes it difficult to see what is happening and why. Films have a proscenium arch, just like the theaters and music halls out of which they were born; they frame action and draw our eyes to some central point of action. Yet the oddness of war and the weird, uncanny sights it presents to soldiers are frequently beyond even today's special effects.

If the physical landscape of battle is almost always trivialized or reduced to mundane proportions, the emotional landscape of battle also eludes cinematic portrayal. We cannot capture the smell of cordite or decaying bodies, or the stench of the detritus war leaves in its wake. Fear can be suggested but never tasted in film, and without that dimension, cinematic representations of war always remain stylized or worse. Thus, both the material and the affective framing of war in film tend to reduce it to formulas or clichés. Exceptions prove the rule.

Silence had another major advantage in the early interwar years. Silent film, which can be defined as a set of cinematic non-speech acts,[10] framed the mourning process in ways rarely, if ever, matched by talkies. Music and banal dialogue frequently turn filmic treatments of this theme into kitsch and worse. By saying less, and leaving viewers to create the words and voices in their own minds, silent film had the power to portray the predicament of men and women alive in the aftermath of wars that took life, not by the scores but by the millions.

Spiritualism had wide appeal in both Europe and America both before and after World War I, and it gave a mournful character to many war films. When viewers reached the end of Lewis Milestone's *All Quiet on the Western Front* (1930), they encountered the faces of the dead looking back at them before they marched off to eternity. This was, in a sense, a very American film, spoken with American accents and intentionally without inflection. Five years earlier, King Vidor's *The Big Parade* had also offered a downbeat version of war, including the hero's loss of a leg in combat and his rejection by his prewar sweetheart. His French *petite amie* managed to come to the rescue afterward. *The Big Parade* was the biggest box office hit of the silent era—more than *The Birth of a Nation*.[11]

In the 1930s, a number of talking films presented the dread of war to a public more and more concerned with the menace of a new war. Frank Borzage's 1932 film *A Farewell to Arms* was downbeat, as was Sidney Franklin's *The Dark Angel* (1935). More elegiac, and marked by a deep sense of the futility of war, was Jean Renoir's masterpiece *La Grande Illusion* (1937). Sympathetic to German soldiers, filled with the fierce and defiant patriotism of French prisoners of

war, Renoir's film humanized not war but the men trapped in it. I
am not alone in considering it in a class of its own as a war film. It
said so much about war without showing a single battle scene. That
is indirection as cinematic genius.

．．．．

It is indeed arbitrary to choose to bracket films about World War
II in the period from 1940 to 1970, and to claim that most of them
adopted a realist's pose in presenting war to cinematic audiences.
World War II films were certainly produced long after 1970,[12] and I
return to this matter in a moment. In addition, there were nonre-
alistic, indirect, and unusual war films in this era. One such film,
René Clément's *Jeux interdits* (*Forbidden Games*) from 1952, directs
our attention away from the battlefield of 1940 and to the ways two
children, ages four and seven, deal with war and death in the French
countryside. They puzzle over how to bury a little girl's pet dog
killed by strafing in her family's escape from Paris in May 1940. The
answer they come to is simple: they build a cemetery for animals,
large and small, with room for people too, but get into terrible trou-
ble by stealing all the crosses from the local church and cemetery
to provide the crosses they need for their own. Brigitte Fossé, age
four, never played a better role.[13] Another is the Japanese masterpiece *Biruma no tategoto* (*The Burmese Harp*), first released in 1956
in black and white and rereleased in color in 1985. Kon Ichikawa's
tale concerns a Japanese soldier who, at the end of the war, is sent by
his Allied captors to persuade his comrades not to fight on after the
Armistice. He fails in his mission and is nearly killed. In his effort to
rejoin his comrades, he traverses old sites of combat and is horrified
by the hundreds of unburied Japanese corpses he sees. He decides to
put on the robes of a Buddhist monk and stays to tend the graves of
his fellow soldiers. His lonely vigil transforms the landscape of war
into an eternal landscape of mourning.

Stanley Kubrick's *Paths of Glory* (1957) is a devastating portrait
of evil or incompetent commanders saving their careers by executing soldiers for cowardice in World War I. Charged with failing to
succeed in a senseless and impossible operation, the three men shot

are chosen at random; none was a coward. What constitutes courage or cowardice had already made American cinematic history in Borzage's *A Farewell to Arms*, starring Helen Hayes and Gary Cooper. Cooper, who plays an American volunteer ambulance driver in Italy in 1917, deserts from the chaos of the Italian defeat at Caporetto to find his lover, a British nurse. They are reunited, but Hayes's character dies in childbirth. Indirection, indeed, plays out in the story of loss of a mother's life in wartime.

While death is ever-present in most films set in World War II, it is not the central element in this body of work. As historian John Bodnar has recently shown, the movie industry presented many different facets of World War II, but the primary focus was internal, in the sense that what mattered was what Americans had done in the war "and what type of people they were." This guiding theme left room for both national celebration and meditation on the rocky road many veterans faced in returning to civilian life.[14] Here, we see an important transition in film from a focus on war to a focus on men at war. Once again, this is a matter of emphasis, not precision, but it may be useful to bear in mind nonetheless.

However nuanced their positive view of World War II as "a good war," most filmmakers aimed at a kind of verisimilitude that made audiences believe they could actually know "what it had really been like." The most spectacular instance of this approach is *The Longest Day* (1962), directed by Ken Annakin and Andrew Martin. Filming in black and white to highlight the film's "authenticity," producer Darryl Zanuck managed to acquire substantial support and military hardware from Britain and France as well as from American authorities. Cameo performances by an array of stars helped make this film the biggest box office success before Steven Spielberg's *Schindler's List* (1993), a classic of the third generation of war films. Similarly admiring of the swagger of military masculinity and the American way of waging war was George C. Scott's portrayal of Patton in Franklin Schaffner's eponymous film of 1970. Bringing viewers onto the battlefield meant bringing them into the minds of the men who imposed their will on it and on the enemy; no one did that with more panache than Patton.[15]

The presentation of the home front was another matter entirely, and in William Wyler's *The Best Years of Our Lives* (1946), the troubled return of veterans emerges without much sugarcoating. The film generated twice the box office earnings of *Sands of Iwo Jima* (1949), demonstrating that filmgoers were prepared to deal with the difficult aftermath of military service, though within certain conventional limits.[16] Indeed, the theme of return and recovery unites films spanning the silent era—*The Big Parade*, for instance—to later cinematic work such as Hal Ashby's 1978 film *Coming Home*.

What I term the *direct* or *realistic* approach to presenting war in film had plenty of room for nuance and contradiction. By no means were all World War II films formulaic presentations of sadistic Japanese or snarling Nazis, subdued in turn by simple, small-town, honest GIs. Realism in war cinema was not exclusively the domain of American films. It marked British approaches to the ambiguities of war, too. In *The Bridge on the River Kwai* (1957) and *In Which We Serve* (1942), both directed by David Lean, we find counterparts to the American filmic presentation of "realistic" war scenes and "realistic" approaches to the home front. In one controversial film, which Winston Churchill tried to scrap, a vision of British decency as an obstacle to victory was presented in terms of getting rid of the old guard who were too old school and not nasty enough to win the war. Churchill took the message personally, but Michael Powell and Emeric Pressburger's *The Life and Death of Colonel Blimp* (1943) survived anyway.[17]

Other pre-1970s European film presentations of the war are similarly heroic and realistic in their account of combat. Jean-Pierre Melville's 1969 film *L'armée des ombres* (*Army of Shadows*) presented a gritty, harsh, unvarnished picture of the impossible choices Resistance fighters had to face. Their war was indeed a dark one, and honoring it was the least the film industry could do while nations like France were recovering from defeat, humiliation, and collaboration.[18]

Indirection was evidently not an invention of the post-1970 period, but it has carried different messages about war ever since. After 1970 or so, filmic representations of World War II changed in important ways. The lid came off the story of collaboration and the

Holocaust, both on-screen and in wider discussions of the war. The effect of Marcel Ophüls's 1969 film *Le chagrin et la pitié* (*The Sorrow and the Pity*) was palpable. The narrative of collaboration and resistance turned from one of black and white to many shades of gray.[19]

The rewriting of the World War II narrative to include the Holocaust in a central role coincided with American defeat in Vietnam. The combination opened up a new phase in the history of war films. The focus shifted from the war the soldiers waged to the victims of violence in the midst of a new kind of asymmetric warfare. This new form of war ushered in a renewed and deepened concentration on the psychological and moral effects of war on combatants themselves.

In this way, the meaning of what is now termed asymmetric war was inflected by its growing linkage to the Holocaust, the only war the Nazis won. Asymmetric wars of a different kind emerged after the end of the Vietnam conflict, pitting Western forces, mostly American, against insurgents in many parts of the world.[20]

Vietnam and After

Film followed the flag, first into Vietnam and then into these transnational or subnational conflicts. I have already noted the transition from *The Green Berets* to the much more complex landscape of *The Deer Hunter*. At the end of the latter film, the group of young, working-class men and women at the heart of the story wind up singing "God Bless America." One is paraplegic, another is scarred mentally, and one of their circle, who lost his mind in Vietnam, has just been brought home and buried. The tone of the anthem is muted: are they still patriotic? Probably, but the message can be read another way. In a world of ugly choices, God had better bless America, for Americans cannot find answers in the old patriotic tags. War as madness takes over in *Apocalypse Now* and in *Full Metal Jacket*, both tales of disillusionment and savagery.

Oliver Stone's *Platoon* (1986) added a different dimension to the cinema's representation of the Vietnam War. Stone drew on his own service in Vietnam. His ambivalence about the war emerged in his treatment of two sergeants: one humane, the other a brute who commits war crimes with impunity. Open the Pandora's box of war, Stone says, and who knows how any of us will be transformed by it? Atrocities are built into war, he shows; no one is unscarred by it. Here, Stone echoes many literary accounts of the passage in wartime from innocence to savagery; the film is both reminiscent of World War I poetry and anticipates Tim O'Brien's *The Things They Carried*, published four years later in 1990.

The link with the Holocaust is especially evident in the work of Steven Spielberg. His masterpiece *Schindler's List* was followed five years later by *Saving Private Ryan* (1998). The films both show the essential elements of the new cinema of war. The first is a powerful and realistic account of the morally ambiguous figure of Oskar Schindler, who lived on the tightrope of the Nazi bureaucracy surrounding the Holocaust and managed to save hundreds of Jews thereby. World War II is only the backdrop of the story, but there are few portrayals more powerful of precisely what Hitler's war against the Jews meant than the *Aktion* (or murderous round-up) in Krakow. In *Saving Private Ryan*, war is the central subject. Spielberg starts with blood and guts, in a boldly realistic manner, in his portrayal of the Normandy landings, and then segues to a more conventional account of the rescue of a surviving soldier whose three brothers had died in combat. The film ends with the survivor asking his wife, in the cemetery where one of the men who rescued him is buried, if he is a good man—if the loss of life in his rescue had produced something good to ennoble it.

Iraq and Afghanistan

Once the wars in Iraq and Afghanistan began, moral ambiguity became dislocated from nostalgia, and films increasingly portrayed war as cruelty, bloodshed, and (at times) butchery without redemption. In Sam Mendes's *Jarhead* (2005), set in the first Gulf War, the brutality of Marine Corps training echoes Kubrick's *Full Metal Jacket*; but this time, the men itching to get into the action "only" manage to mutilate corpses and do not even shoot at the enemy. The Air Force gets in first, and the frustrated Marines fire off a fusillade only at the end of the film. Impotent killers indeed.

The lies about weapons of mass destruction are the subject of Paul Greengrass's *Green Zone* (2010), which features Matt Damon as a decent GI betrayed by those in the CIA and higher up in the administration who invented the story. *Rendition* (2007) tells the tale of the George W. Bush administration's complicity in torture by allies through the fictionalized tale of one man mistaken for a militant who disappeared into the Bush administration's twilight zone. In a much more poignant, though downbeat, account of the costs of the Iraq War, *The Messenger* (2009), directed by Oren Moverman, focused on the work of the U.S. Army's Casualty Notification Service—the men who brought home the news of a soldier's death on active duty.

The theme of decent soldiers locked in an indecent war recurs in Kathryn Bigelow's *The Hurt Locker* (2008). The film features a bomb-disposal unit composed of men whose primary aim is to get home alive. Their sergeant, William James, played by Jeremy Renner, is a more puzzling man, someone who seizes danger by the throat. He appears to enjoy the Russian roulette of disarming booby-trapped bombs, and even when he makes it back home, he cannot re-embrace civilian life. At the end of the film, we see him returning for another tour of service in Iraq. Whether or not he was suicidal before the war, he certainly was during and after it. War as a home for suicidal men is hardly an advertisement for the military, and yet *The Hurt Locker* won the Oscar for both best director and best picture of the year.

The unending character of the "war on terror" was also the subject of Steven Spielberg's 2005 film *Munich*. Spielberg tells the story of the assassination squad that liquidated the men who masterminded the Munich massacre at the Olympics of 1972. After the killings have been avenged, the Israeli agent who is the central figure in the story tells his boss that he is through with assassination because it changes nothing of importance. He walks away from his mission against the backdrop of the World Trade Center. The script says nothing about the juxtaposition of words and scene; it doesn't have to. Silence does it better.

War Films in the Era of the All-Volunteer Army

The advent of all-volunteer armed forces was not solely an American phenomenon. In Britain the last man conscripted on "national service" left the army in 1963. In the United States, the draft came to an end in 1973. In both countries armies downsized. These developments

reinforced the trend of focusing not on war but on individual soldiers in film. It is hardly surprising that when armies were reduced
radically in size, films moved away from the spectacle of war to the
predicament of the warrior and of those civilians trapped in war.
And yet this turn in narrative framework introduced a tension. The
shift from heroic warfare to the troubled warrior individualized his
moral dilemmas and personal risks that at times ran counter to the
ethos of "the corps" or other collective identifications with a service arm or a division. This tension mirrored a wider trend. War
was individualized in film, at the very time that a kind of radical
individualism achieved cultural ascendancy in both Britain and the
United States. By the early 1980s, the collective experience of the
Second World War was over; in its place came a new focus on individual liberties over collective rights and shared experiences.

This interpretation helps explain the market for filmic align-
ments of the warrior alongside other paladins, men of honor facing dishonor not only from the enemy but frequently from within
their own ranks. Cowboys and spies have performed similar functions in cinema, and millions of viewers have paid to see them in
action. These loners are men apart, men who still retain vestiges
of moral thinking in an immoral world, and thereby have to live
outside "conventional" society. These filmic motifs were present before the 1970s, but grew rapidly thereafter. It makes sense,
therefore, to see the development of the work of Clint Eastwood as
a continuum, moving from westerns to police films to war films
with a sure hand for the representation of scarred individuals facing a hostile and indifferent world. Steven Spielberg's oeuvre is
more interested in innocence than in embittered experience, but
he too is a cinematic student of betrayal, usually of the young by
their elders.

The post-1970 phase of cinematic history resembled the early
years of film in a number of ways. The authoritative historian of
silent film, Kevin Brownlow, saw it as focusing on "The War, the
West, and the Wilderness." The first two are easily identified settings for recent film. As in Spielberg's corpus, the "wilderness" we
imagine in the early twenty-first century is in the skies, in outer
space, or in other futuristic landscapes.

Espionage

The lone man in the wilderness has been a pillar of the film industry from its early years in the form of the spy. Espionage films take us back to the beginning of the cinematic representation of war. The First World War spawned them, and so did the unstable international climate of the 1930s. Hitchcock's *The Man Who Knew Too Much* appeared in 1934. The next year, his *39 Steps* (1935) recycled a First World War story written by John Buchan. *Secret Agent* (1936) and *Notorious* (1946) explored the same genre. From the 1960s, some filmmakers portrayed the Cold War as more of a moral wilderness than a crusade against the "Great Satan." Martin Ritt's 1965 adaptation of John Le Carré's novel *The Spy Who Came in from the Cold* was the first of a number of spy films that offered a plague on both the houses of the great powers. Cartoon-strip cinema was available too: the highly profitable James Bond series of spy films also dated from the early 1960s, and they have gone on earning money for fifty years.

And yet in recent years, more cynical and critical portrayals of spies at work have appeared. British director John Madden's 2010 film, *The Debt*, showed the lies surrounding a botched operation by Israeli agents attempting to kidnap and transport to Israel for trial a man resembling Dr. Josef Mengele. A year later, *Tinker Tailor Soldier Spy* (2011), directed by Tomas Alderson, took up the same theme, and offered a sardonic antidote to the cult of spies as heroes. No doubt, both currents—the heroic and the antiheroic—will carry on in parallel in future years.

If espionage was a core element of the Cold War, the use of private contractors to provide services for the American armed forces is an important departure in post-1989 military history. And yet there have been few films that focus on the effects of outsourcing war services to corporations. One is Stephen Gaghan's 2005 film *Syriana*, in which George Clooney and Matt Damon come to grief in a tale of corruption, greed, and betrayal. Rodrigo Cortés's *Buried* (2010) follows the travails of a civilian driver kidnapped and confined in Iraq; no rescue and no redemption follow.

War and Civil Wars in Film

Civil war is another subgenre of war films that spans all three periods of cinematic history. What the Irish call "the troubles" has left
a number of filmic accounts of their predicaments, all of which
point to the moral ambiguity of the struggle for independence
from Britain, first in the south and then in the north of Ireland.
There is a long and distinguished tradition of filmmakers exploring Ireland's multiple civil wars. In the interwar years, Hitchcock
entered this divided country with *The Shame of Mary Boyle* in 1930.
The film was originally called *Juno and the Paycock*, the title Sean
O'Casey gave to the play on which the film was based. John Ford
followed with *The Informer* (1935), and a year later with his adaptation of another O'Casey play, *The Plough and the Stars*. In more
recent years, Neil Jordan's 1996 portrait of *Michael Collins* (2001)
described the treacherous world of betrayal in the second Irish civil
war, between those who followed Collins into accepting the parti-
tion of Ireland, and those—including his killers—who did not. Ken
Loach's *The Wind That Shakes the Barley* (2006) explores the same
subject, with the same bleak view of the havoc civil war wrought.[21]
A more unusual take on the subject of the IRA and Britain is Neil
Jordan's *The Crying Game* (1992). This film is a subtle portrayal of
ambivalence and equivocation, both political and sexual, in men
serving both in the IRA and the British army. The subject of civil
war is prone to highlight the gray areas of conflict between neighbors and within families themselves. Recent films focusing on the
Algerian war, on the civil war in Yugoslavia, or in Lebanon, among
others, follow this darker, less stirring, agenda in showing the cruelties and uncertainties of societies torn apart by intercommunal violence. On balance, ambivalence is at the heart of much, though not
all, cinematic forays into the terrain of civil war in recent decades.

The American Civil War continues to attract cinematic treatment of varying kinds. Edward Zwick's *Glory* (1989) highlighted the
story of black soldiers fighting for freedom in the Union army, and
pointed back to the more comfortable moral terrain and noble sentiments (on the southern side) of *Gone with the Wind* (1939) and many
Second World War movies. More in line with the third phase of

moral uncertainty about war and the mindless cruelty and senseless death it leaves in its wake is Anthony Minghella's *Cold Mountain* (2003). This film tells of the struggle of a wounded deserter from the Confederate army to reach home. He does so, but is killed in the arms of his wife.

There are other evocations of a similarly downbeat kind in films concerning the civil war in Nicaragua (Roger Spottiswoode's *Under Fire*, 1983), in Somalia (Ridley Scott's *Black Hawk Down*, 2001), and in the former Yugoslavia (Danis Tanovic's *No Man's Land*, 2001). What they all have in common is a recognition of the cruelty and moral ambiguity of all sides in civil wars.

Dignity without Voyeurism

In this all-too-brief survey of film and war, I have had to omit many facets of the cinematic history of military conflict—Eisenstein, Wajda, Tarkovsky, Kurosawa are all important contributors to the war film genre, but space limitations preclude discussing them here.

I have omitted, too, the vexed question of filmmakers as ideologues, as representatives of certain powerful interests that want to "sell" war to the public. Consider as one example Gary Cooper's pacifist-turned-sniper in Howard Hawks's 1941 film *Sergeant York*. My aim is more modest. It is to point to certain trends in the way filmmakers have tried to portray war. I have emphasized the choices filmmakers have to make, choices that are embedded in the medium itself. Their business has been to choose the cast, to find ways to interchange silence and dialogue, to select a particular musical setting, to try to "re-create" a battlefield or base camp, to turn a rough cut into a final product. Some do better than others. But all, in my view, fall short of faithfully representing war.

Samuel Fuller, the director of *The Big Red One* (1980), was once asked what constituted a good war film. His answer was "one which cultivates dignity and does not pursue voyeurism." He saw service in Africa, Sicily, Normandy, Belgium, and Czechoslovakia, and was present at the liberation of the Falkenau concentration camp. He was one of the few directors with extensive combat experience.[22]

Dignity without voyeurism is indeed a good measure of the balance war films aim to achieve. And yet few succeed. The reason is that showing war without terror is a recipe for voyeurism, and spectacular war films rarely make terror come alive. Here is the central point about silence: it carries terror within it much more readily than the scariest movie score does. Stop the sound and terror is one of the elements of the story that rushes to the surface. The subject of terror is present in all war narratives, but it is differently configured in the age of asymmetrical wars. The terror of children, women, and the aged is etched into the history of the Holocaust, and into the story of brutality from Biafra in 1968 to Sudan, Somalia, or Afghanistan today. Post-national warfare is therefore less about soldiers and more about victims. Terry George's *Hotel Rwanda* (2004) is a film about genocide, and the hotelier who saves hundreds of lives; he is a Schindler without the moral shadows. The friendship between two men is at the heart of the 1984 film *The Killing Fields*, and despite the monstrous evil he faces, Dith Pran's survival is what leaves us with hope, even now.

Surveying such films, we can see the force of Fuller's plea for dignity. Films can portray men and women at war, whose dignity, integrity, and existence are threatened, but who, if they are lucky, emerge from war as recognizable human beings nonetheless. We are left, therefore, with a modest conclusion: war defies simple representation, but men at war can be presented, with clichés or human qualities attached, depending on the actor, the director, and the audience the producers want to reach.

In a vast array of nondocumentary films, soldiers of many nationalities have been represented as frail, complex men as well as cartoon-strip figures. What differs is the framing of the wars in which these soldiers fight. Here, we can take note of an evolution, which I have presented in this chapter. Film in the silent age stood back from realism: it could hint, suggest, gesture; but without sound, it could not portray war. In the World War II generation, a kind of spectacular realism took over, with mixed effects. Phony wars were presented as real wars, and given the moral clarity of the 1939 to 1945 conflict, in most cases, that was enough. But from the 1970s on, soldiering has been framed differently. It was darker, more tragic, more morally ambiguous, more focused on victims than on heroes. Heroic images of war were still on offer, but the colors of war grew somber, muted. Thus, the portrait of the soldier came to be more important than that of the war in which he served.

In countries with a volunteer army, that was not a negative outcome; masculine virtues still matter, especially among the young. One television ad in the United States for enlistment offers not to make men strong, but to make them "Army strong." Yet once the broader public began to see war as morally precarious, as it did beginning in the 1970s, public support for the men who wage war became uncertain, too. Supporting the men but not the war is a hard act to pull off. It usually winds up in disillusionment and disengagement.

As for the legacy of one hundred years of war films, we ignore it at our peril. The search for a balance between the spectacular and the indirect in visual portrayals of war goes on, tilted toward the spectacular by the immense popularity of computer war games. Indirection in that context is nonexistent, but the film industry is different. It does not speak with one voice. To take but one very recent box office success, Steven Spielberg's *War Horse* continues his immensely popular set of cinematic meditations on war and its cruelties. Speaking of war through the story of an animal and the young boy who searches for him, Spielberg tries to capture the futility of war in one of his many tales of the way innocent children are betrayed by their elders. The spectacular elements of the film are impressive enough: the horse confronted by three tanks is filmmaking at its best. The sheer sentimentality of the story, though, outweighs its moral message, much more powerfully conveyed indirectly in the stage version of the story. A model of a horse, designed brilliantly by a South African company to approximate the uneven cadence of the animal, conveys the horror of war silently and in a way that puts the so-called "real" presentation to shame. My first response to seeing this film was to hope that someone would turn off the sound.

Filming war, like configuring war, and writing war, always works through mediation. The technical framework of cinema both limits what can be done and at times distorts war beyond recognition.

That is true of painting, sculpture, and writing as well. But time and again exceptions appear that make us reaffirm a belief that the best defense we have against the ravages of war is the human imagination itself. At its best, cinema is today and has been from its birth a century ago an indispensable resource for those who are fascinated or puzzled or horrified about war. The flaws of those films that attempt to show what war "is really like" are evident, but in the hands of masters, film is today and is bound to remain an essential point of reference for those who try to understand what happens to soldiers in combat and for those who try time and again to imagine war, our brutal companion, past, present, and future.

Notes

1 Jay M. Winter, *The Experience of World War I* (London: Macmillan, 1988), 238.

2 Kevin Brownlow, *The War, the West, and the Wilderness* (New York: Alfred A. Knopf, 1979).

3 Charles Maier, "Consigning the Twentieth Century to History: Alternative Narratives for the Modern Era," Forum Essay, *American Historical Review* 105, no. 3 (June 2000): 807–31.

4 For the source and use of this statistic, see Sabrina Tavernise and Andrew W. Lehren, "A Grim Portrait of Civilian Deaths in Iraq," *New York Times*, October 22, 2010; Ruth Leger Sivard, *World Military and Social Expenditures 1991* (Washington, DC: World Priorities, 1991), 20.

5 Adam Roberts, "Lives and Statistics: Are 90 Percent of War Victims Civilians?" *Survival* 52, no. 3 (June–July 2010): 115–36.

6 Giorgio Agamben, *Homo Sacer: Sovereign Power and Bare Life*, trans. Daniel Heller-Roazen (Stanford, CA: Stanford University Press, 1998).

7 James Chapman, *War and Film* (London: Reaktion Books, 2008).

8 Hoenik Kwon, *The Other Cold War* (New York: Columbia University Press, 2010).

9 Roger Smither, "'A Wonderful Idea of the Fighting': The Question of Fakes in *The Battle of the Somme*," *Historical Journal of Film, Radio and Television* 13, no. 2 (1993): 149–68.

10 Jay M. Winter, "Thinking about Silence," in *Shadows of War: The Social Construction of Silence*, ed. Efrat en Zeev, Ruth Ginio, and Jay Winter (Cambridge: Cambridge University Press, 2010), 1–30.

11 Michael T. Isenberg, *War on Film: The American Cinema and World War I, 1914–1941* (London: Fairleigh Dickinson University Press, 1981), 118–22.

12 Carl Boggs and Tom Pollard, *The Hollywood War Machine: U.S. Militarism and Popular Culture* (London: Paradigm, 2007).

13 A.V. Club, "Film," *Forbidden Games*, at http://www.avclub.com/articles/forbidden-games,63508/.

14 John Bodnar, *The "Good War" in American Memory* (Baltimore: Johns Hopkins University Press, 2010), 165.

15 Ibid., 144–45.

16 Ibid., 151.

17 Robert Murphy, *British Cinema and the Second World War* (London: Continuum, 2000).

18 Sylvie Lindeperg, *Les écrans de l'ombre: La Seconde Guerre mondiale dans le cinéma français (1944–1969)* (Paris: CNRS, 1997).

19 Henry Rousso, *Le syndrome de Vichy: 1944–198—*(Paris: Seuil, 1987).

20 Mary Kaldor, *New and Old Wars: Organized Violence in a Global Era* (Cambridge: Polity Press, 1999).

21 CAIN (Conflict Archive on the Internet), http://cain.ulst.ac.uk/images/cinema/nimovies.htm.

22 Norbert Multau, "Quand la guerre est un spectacle," in *Le cinéma et la guerre*, ed. Philippe d'Hugues and Hervé Coutau-Bégarie (Paris: Economica, 2006), 148.

8 :: The Future of Conscription

SOME COMPARATIVE REFLECTIONS

James Sheehan

Abstract: This chapter provides a historical and comparative perspective on contemporary American military institutions. It focuses on the origins, evolution, and eventual disappearance of conscription in Western Europe. By the 1970s, Europeans had developed civilian states in which the military's traditional role steadily diminished; the formal abolition of conscription after 1989 was the final step in a long, largely silent revolution. A brief survey of military institutions outside Europe suggests why mass conscript armies will remain politically, culturally, and militarily significant in many parts of the world. Seen in a global context, the American experience appears to combine aspects of Western European civilian states with the willingness and ability to project military power.

> [Conscription] is always a significant index of the society where it is found; to view it solely as a method of conducting war is to see very little of it.
>
> Victor Kiernan[1]

When Alexis de Tocqueville listed the advantages of democracy in America that came "from the peculiar and accidental situation in which Providence has placed the Americans," he had no doubts about which was most important. Americans, he wrote, "have no neighbors, and consequently they have no great wars … nor great armies, nor great generals."[2] Shielded from potential aggressors by its two great ocean glacis, the United States was, for much of its history, able to avoid building those mass armies on which European states lavished so much energy and resources. When, during the Civil War and World War I, great armies were built, they were dismantled as soon as the war was over. We should not underestimate the reluctance with which Americans abandoned this tradition: the Selective Service Act of 1940 was renewed a year later with a one-vote majority in the House of Representatives and included a prohibition on sending draftees out of the Western Hemisphere. The abolition of the draft and the creation of an all-volunteer Army in 1973 were in response to the immediate crisis of Vietnam, but these actions also represented a return to deeply rooted traditions in American political culture.

In the 1830s, as Tocqueville was writing his great book on American democracy, European states were in the process of creating new kinds of armies, founded on some form of conscription. The term itself first appeared in a French law of 1798 that called for compulsory military service for all young men between twenty and twenty-five. The system evolved in the nineteenth century, first in Prussia and then throughout Europe. The theory and practice of conscription were inseparable from the larger ideals and major institutions of the modern state. First, conscription is essentially democratic because every male (in theory, although rarely in practice) is liable to be called on to fight. Military service is linked to citizenship, that complex blend of rights and obligations that binds people to their state. The citizen army, therefore, is not simply a military institution, but also a way of expressing and acquiring those patriotic commitments essential for the nation's survival. Second, conscription requires the administrative capabilities and material resources that states did not possess until the modern era. For the system to work, governments had to be able to identify, select, assemble, train, equip, and deploy a significant percentage of their male population, retaining some of them on active duty for several years, with the rest on reserve status for several more.[3]

In the nineteenth century, European states developed conscript armies to prepare for massive territorial conflicts in which the fate, perhaps even the existence, of the nation might be at stake. Among the great powers, only Britain did not adopt conscription, relying instead on naval power and a small professional army. Outside of Europe, Japan was the first non-Western state to adopt conscription, based on a careful study of the Prussian model. In 1873, as part of a larger program of political and social modernization, Japan introduced compulsory military service, including three years on active duty and four in the reserves. From then on, the army became the key instrument in Japan's initially successful but ultimately doomed attempt to be a great power. In the twentieth century, governments throughout the world imported the idea of conscript armies, which, like so many other European institutions, seemed to be an essential part of what it meant to be a modern state.[4]

Although the creation of mass armies was an essential function of European states, their uses were limited. Throughout the nineteenth and early twentieth centuries, governments were unwilling to dispatch their citizen-soldiers to fight "small wars" of colonial conquest or pacification. "Conscripts," the German statesman Otto von Bismarck once remarked, "cannot be sent to the tropics." Like Britain, whose army was constantly deployed in defense of its empire, every colonial power left these overseas battles to professionals or, whenever possible, to native forces recruited from local populations but usually commanded by European officers.[5]

Yet conscripts fought the two world wars of the twentieth century, and despite the horrendous losses suffered by their citizen armies between 1914 and 1918 and again between 1939 and 1945, every European state either retained or restored conscription after World War II. Britain, which had only belatedly and reluctantly introduced a draft in both world wars, preserved national service until 1960. Perhaps even more remarkably, Nazi Germany's three postwar successor states—West and East Germany and the Austrian Republic—eventually reintroduced conscription. On both sides of the Iron Curtain, therefore, the members of NATO and the Warsaw Pact prepared mass armies in anticipation of a new land war between East and West. At the same time, Western European states all sent conscripts in a succession of final, futile efforts to defend their overseas possessions. Of the 135,000 troops dispatched to the Dutch East Indies in 1945, two-thirds were draftees; conscripts also represented a significant percentage of the French army stationed in Algeria in 1961. Political opposition engendered by the loss of citizen-soldiers in defense of colonial rule was one reason that governments were forced to abandon those campaigns—as well as, eventually, their empires. Not accidentally, Portugal, the least democratic of the colonial powers, was also the last to surrender its overseas possessions.

By the end of the 1960s, the security environment in Europe had begun to change. Except for Portugal's struggles in Africa, the colonial powers had already liquidated their imperial enterprises, some of them centuries old, and had done so with remarkable speed and relatively little political resistance. Equally important, the Cold War order imposed by the two superpowers essentially removed the danger of conventional war between European states; in the West, this new state of affairs made possible the growing cooperation of national economies and rising aspirations for political integration. Of course, the potential for armed conflict persisted, especially on the German-German border, which bristled with the largest amount of lethal hardware in history. Nevertheless, to more and more Europeans, the possibility of a continental land war seemed increasingly remote. The sort of limited war that had been fought in Korea and was still going on in Vietnam hardly seemed possible in the only place in the world where the superpowers directly confronted one another. The risk of escalation to nuclear catastrophe was simply too high.[6]

These changing assessments of the military situation are clearly reflected in public opinion polls: when asked what they wanted their governments to do, Europeans consistently stressed domestic issues—a stable currency, education, health care, retirement benefits, law and order—and rarely mentioned national defense or effective military institutions. These polls do not suggest that Europeans no longer cared about being conquered; they simply didn't think that it was going to happen.[7]

The end of imperial wars and the waning salience of security concerns produced a silent revolution in European politics, a revolution that can be measured in budgets, where defense spending stagnated, in popular attitudes toward the military, and in the symbols and ceremonies of public life. The army, once regarded as essential for both national defense and national identity, moved to the margins of most people's consciousness. "Security" ceased to denote issues of national defense and came to be identified with individual welfare.

This revolution in Europeans' views of security gradually—and once again, silently—transformed their conscript armies. Every Continental country retained conscription until the 1990s. But everywhere its character changed. Armies reduced the time required in active service, as well as conscripts' reserve obligation. Exemptions from the draft became much easier to get, as did the right to perform alternative service, both of them ways to drain off potential political opposition to the military. The percentage of those actually conscripted and the size of the armed forces declined throughout Europe. Within the armies themselves, regulations were eased, punishments made less severe, and training less rigorous. In a few states, enlisted men were allowed to form unions, work a forty-hour week, and even receive overtime pay. The semiofficial motto of the Dutch armed forces was said to be "As civilian as possible, as military as necessary." In fact, where European armies had once been seen as a way of instilling discipline and patriotic commitment in civilian society, by the 1970s they were becoming increasingly "civilianized," the products of a gradual but unmistakable readjustment of the citizen's sense of obligations to the nation.[8]

During the 1990s, after more than two decades of gradual decline, conscript armies were finally abolished in most of Europe. The most obvious reason was the end of the Cold War and the subsequent withdrawal of Soviet forces, which removed even the remote possibility of a territorial threat from the East. Fiscal pressures, too, encouraged governments to take a hard and critical look at their defense budgets. Most important, it had become painfully clear that Europe's armed forces, while quite large, were militarily worthless, especially for the kind of technically sophisticated, fast-moving, and intensive combat made possible by the so-called revolution in military affairs. European states no longer needed mass armies to defend the homeland, but rather a relatively small number of professionals who could, if necessary, be sent on expeditions abroad, perhaps as part of a multinational peacekeeping mission. As Bismarck had warned in the nineteenth century, such missions were not for conscripts.[9]

In the Netherlands, where the number of conscripts had plummeted since the 1950s, the draft was abolished in 1993; two years later Belgium ended it. France, despite the powerful historical memories of the revolutionary nation in arms and a deep distrust of professional soldiers, announced the end of the draft and introduction of an all-volunteer army in 1996. Spain, Italy, and most of the former Communist states of Eastern Europe soon followed. By the beginning of the twenty-first century, the overwhelming majority of NATO's armed forces were professionals. The speed and ease with which European states abandoned compulsory military service reflected the long erosion of conscription's political, cultural, and military significance.[10]

Germany held on to conscription longer than the other major European states. In part this was because of postwar Germany's historically rooted anxiety about professional soldiers and pride in the democratic army created after the war. Significantly, as the proponents of conscription also pointed out, the increasing number of those choosing alternative service provided the relatively inexpensive caregivers and hospital orderlies who are essential for the Federal Republic's welfare system. Without a military draft, Germany's civilian institutions might suffer. In practice, however, conscription in the Federal Republic disappeared well before it was formally suspended: between 2000 and 2009, the total number of men performing military service dropped by more than half, from 144,647 to 68,304. In any case, it was difficult to describe as compulsory a system in which a civilian alternative was now granted automatically, making the German army what one expert called "an all volunteer force in disguise." Needless to say, the German troops serving as part of the NATO contingent in Afghanistan are all professionals.[11]

In 2010, responding to severe pressure to cut his budget and recognizing the need for a smaller but more effective force, the energetic minister of defense, Karl-Theodor zu Guttenberg, decided to suspend the draft (abolition would require a constitutional amendment) and introduced substantial reforms in the composition of Germany's armed forces. The last German conscripts, some twelve thousand young men, were inducted in January 2011. It is striking that in the German discussions of these reforms, as had been the case in debates about ending conscription in other European states, the level of engagement, among both politicians and their constituents, is low. Well before they were abolished formally, Europeans' conscript armies had ceased to be politically or culturally salient, either as a source of positive commitment or a target of active opposition.

Now that the Germans have suspended conscription, only a handful of Western European states still have a draft. These include Norway and Denmark, where military service continues to be a part of a citizen's duty to the nation. In neither country, however, does conscription have a military purpose. There are, for example, no conscripts in the small but quite effective unit that Denmark has contributed to the NATO mission in Afghanistan. In addition to Norway and Denmark, three of the five Cold War neutrals—Austria, Switzerland, and Finland—still have conscript armies. (Ireland always had a small professional force; Sweden abolished conscription in summer 2010.) Austria requires six months of active duty in what has traditionally been an underfunded and poorly equipped army. In Switzerland, on the other hand, the army has always had a significant role, as a deterrent to aggression and as a source of national identity. There are indications, however, that in the current security environment, both of these functions are losing their central place in Swiss politics. It may be that among European states, only Finland retains a conscript army on the traditional model. In a country where 80 percent of the male population has served in the military, the prestige and importance of the armed forces remain high. Moreover, the Finnish military's strategic objective remains territorial defense, a purpose persistently nourished by memories of the heroic Winter War against the Soviet Union in 1940 and recently reinforced by the example of Russia's invasion of Georgia in 2008.[12]

With few exceptions, European military institutions continue to be profoundly affected by the global economic crisis that began in 2008. In fact, expenditures for defense, which were stagnant for decades, have been in sharp decline since the turn of the century: the European members of NATO spent 2.05 percent of GDP for defense in 1999, 1.65 percent in 2008. This trend is not likely to be reversed in the austerity budgets now being formulated throughout Europe. The British government, for example, announced drastic cuts in troop strength and equipment in a comprehensive defense review published in October 2010.[13] One result of these budgetary pressures may be greater cooperation among European states. Britain and France, Europe's two most important military powers, have already taken steps in this direction. Promises of greater cooperation among NATO members were reaffirmed at the alliance's summit held in Chicago in May 2012. But such promises have been made before, while accomplishments remain modest. In fact, the road to effective transnational military institutions is bound to be long and difficult, and the most likely consequence of Europe's budgetary problems will be a continuation of its dependence on the United States. The question now facing NATO is how long Washington will pay for this dependence in the face of America's own economic problems and its growing uneasiness over Chinese ambitions in Asia. There is no reason to think that the existence of the alliance is in doubt, but it does seem that in the future, as the *Economist* wrote in March 2012, "NATO will end up just doing less with less."[14]

An unspoken assumption behind Europeans' budgetary debates is that military spending has become discretionary, an expense to be weighed against a variety of other demands on the state's resources— not, as was long the case, a necessary price to ensure national survival. European governments recognize that they still face profound dangers: terrorism, organized crime, and, in some countries, increasingly violent social protests. And there are occasions when states may want to project power by sending an expeditionary force abroad. But the preservation of order and the deployment of troops on some distant mission are very different from the defense of the nation from existential threats, the purpose for which the mass conscript army had originally been created.

Soon after the end of the Cold War and the dissolution of the Soviet Union, the American political scientist Robert Keohane remarked that "one of the most vexing questions in Europe today is where the frontier between the West European zone of peace and Eurasian zone of conflict will be."[15] On the western side of this line, conscription has largely disappeared, and military service has become limited to a relatively small group of professionals who are compensated, like firefighters and police officers, for the risks they are asked to take on behalf of their fellow citizens. On the other side of the line, however, where the survival of the nation might still be at stake, military service remains both a political obligation and a strategic necessity.

But while the line between the peaceful and conflictual parts of Eurasia may be ill-defined—frontiers are, by definition, contested and imprecise—there is good reason to suppose that it runs directly through the former Soviet imperium. On the peaceful side are the Soviet Union's former Eastern European satellites and the three newly autonomous Baltic republics. Despite some hesitation and reluctance on both sides, these states eventually joined NATO; with the exception of Estonia, Latvia, and Lithuania, they, like their new allies in the West, have abolished conscription in favor of small professional forces. In 2008, there were only 4,000 conscripts among the 317,000 military personnel in the new NATO members from the East. Moreover, again as in the West, military expenditure in the East has continued to decline: except for Bulgaria (2 percent), Poland, and Romania (each 1.9 percent), the Eastern European states are well below the stated NATO goal of allocating 2 percent of GDP to defense. What the eminent military sociologist Martin Shaw once called "the last bastions of classical militarism in the northern industrial world," the former Communist regimes of Eastern Europe have become, within little more than a decade, civilian states on the Western European model.[16]

On the other side of the frontier are the remaining Soviet European and Central Asian successor states. All these states retain conscript armies. Some, such as Belarus, are among the most militarized states in the world. Where there are still external threats and ongoing territorial disputes, as in Georgia, Armenia, and Azerbaijan, military institutions have an importance far greater than in the civilian West.

With just over half of the old Soviet Union's population and three-fourths of its territory, the Russian Federation is far and away its most important successor state. Russia's military capacity was among the casualties of the Soviet Union's extraordinary implosion. Even before the USSR disappeared in 1991, the Soviet military suffered a series of stunning blows, including defeat in Afghanistan and the loss of its bases in Eastern Europe. After 1991, morale and cohesion deteriorated precipitously, attended by endemic corruption, criminality, and brutality. At present, Russia is supposed to have over one million men on active duty, with another twenty million reservists, but in practice only a small percentage of these forces are deployable. Since the 1990s, there have been several efforts at reforming the military, the latest and most ambitious of which was introduced in September 2008, following the rather mixed results of Russia's brief invasion of Georgia that summer. Although conscription remains in effect (early in 2008 the length of service was reduced to one year), the reformers want to create a smaller, better trained and equipped force that is permanently ready for deployment. But formidable barriers to effective reform remain, including the pervasive weakness of the Russian administrative apparatus, the economic problems created by the global decline in energy prices, and, perhaps most serious of all, the long-term effects of Russia's devastating demographic decline. According to the chief of the Russian general staff, in 2012 the number of draft-eligible males will be half of what it was in 2001.[17]

Among the members of NATO, only Turkey clearly occupies a position on the conflict side of Keohane's frontier. Turkish troops have long defended a contested border on Cyprus and fought a long, bloody civil war against the Kurds. How the creation of a semiautonomous Kurdish territory in Iraq will affect Turkey is by no means clear. In any case, Turkey's military budget, unlike those of its European counterparts, has not dramatically declined; conscription remains in force, exemptions are rare, alternative service is virtually impossible. Militarily and politically, the army played a central role in the emergence of the republic from the ruins of the Ottoman Empire. Since becoming prime minister in 2002,

Recep Tayyip Erdogan has tried, with increasing success, to reduce the army's power. Some forty high-ranking officers were recently arrested on suspicion of plotting against the government. In July 2011, the commanders of Turkey's armed forces resigned in protest against government policies, thus enabling the prime minister to appoint a new high command. This represented, as one Turkish journalist put it, "the symbolic moment where the first Turkish republic ends and second republic begins."[18] Nevertheless, despite the decline of the army's role, it is clear that, unlike the rest of the EU, Turkey is not a fully developed civilian state; the possibility of international and domestic violence remains very much a part of Turkish political life.[19]

In most of Eurasia, the political role of the army is closer to the Turkish model than to the civilian states of Western Europe. In a few places, like Myanmar, the influence of the military remains direct and widely extended despite recent efforts at democratic reform; sometimes, as in Thailand, its power is veiled by a diaphanous curtain of civilian authority. Most often, the army acts, as it traditionally did in the Turkish case, as a kind of "deep state," using the threat of a coup to set limits on what governments can and cannot do. Nowhere is this situation more dramatically clear than in the political upheavals in Egypt that followed the fall of Hosni Mubarak in February 2011. For decades, the Egyptian army has had enormous political and economic power. ("It is," notes one well-informed observer, "an open question how much power the military has, and they might not even know themselves.")[20] Any successful transition to a stable, post-Mubarak regime, therefore, will depend on some kind of collaboration between the army and the civilian opposition. At the moment (May 2012), it is still an open question whether a newly elected Egyptian government will be able to find the means to cooperate with the military without losing its legitimacy or provoking a coup.

In North Korea, when Kim Jong Il sought to extend his family's control into the third generation, he made Kim Jong Un, his son and heir apparent, a four-star general before he was appointed to the Central Committee of the Korean Workers' Party, a sequence that underlined how the army has consolidated its hold on political power. In Kim Jong Un's first public appearance following his father's death, the new leader reaffirmed Kim Jong Il's emphasis on the military: it was, he declared, his government's "first, second, and third" priority. With terms of active duty from five to twelve years and reserve obligations up to the age of sixty, North Korea has what is perhaps the world's most extensive and socially intrusive system of conscription.

The border between the two Korean states may be the most heavily fortified, but it is by no means the only contested frontier in East Asia. Some of the territories involved in these disputes are very small, and in others the conflict is largely inert; but there are some—Kashmir, for instance, or parts of the Sino-Indian border— that remain volatile enough to erupt into large-scale international violence. With two major powers, India and China, and a number of unstable and potentially aggressive smaller states, the rivalries and tensions within Asia somewhat resemble the European international system before 1914. Not surprisingly, it is here that the mass conscript army continues to provide the foundation of national defense.

In the past few years, a number of experts have argued that conscription, like the modern state from which it developed, was on its way to historical oblivion. The international studies scholar Eliot Cohen, for example, recently declared that "the age of the mass army is over."[21] Perhaps. There is no question that in many parts of the world, conscript armies have been dissolved or diminished; quality, represented by the ability to use complex new weapon systems, has replaced quantity as a measurement of military power. Even in China, where the massive People's Liberation Army has traditionally been at the core of security policy, there has been a shift toward more mobile, technologically sophisticated weapons systems. In much of Europe, the rise of civilian states has changed the balance between rights and duties that had once made military service inseparable from citizenship. But in many parts of Eurasia, especially on the wrong side of the frontier separating zones of peace and conflict, conscript armies designed to protect the territorial interests of states are still centrally important, and a war between states remains a constant danger. Here, civilian states on the European model have not developed: military service remains an important part of young men's lives, conscript armies have political and cultural significance, and the officer corps often plays an important role. In countries such as Egypt, North Korea, Thailand, Burma, and Pakistan, conscription still has a future, which will help shape the future of these nations.

Where does the United States fit into this picture? With its massive military budget and globally deployed armed forces, it is surely not a civilian state on the European model. However divided they may be on the use of force in specific situations, most Americans agree that as a world power, the United States must be willing and able to project military power to defend its interests throughout a dangerous world. And yet, unlike those states where military service remains a national obligation, the United States counts on professionals to meet its extensive global commitments. The burden of America's mission in the world, therefore, is carried by a relatively small portion of the population, whose sacrifices are honored but not shared by the larger society. In a sense, the United States is a civilian state with significant military obligations. Many of the other essays collected in this volume examine the tensions that arise from this uneasy mix of values and aspirations.

Notes

1 Victor Kiernan, "Conscription and Society in Europe before the War of 1914–1918," in *War and Society: Historical Essays in Honour and Memory of J. R. Western, 1928–1971*, ed. M. R. D. Foot (New York: Barnes & Noble Books, 1973), 141.

2 Alexis de Tocqueville, *Democracy in America* (New York: Everyman's Library, 1994), 288–89.

3 The classic analysis of conscription's political significance is Morris Janowitz, "Military Institutions and Citizenship in Western Societies," in *The Military and the Problem of Legitimacy*, ed. Gwyn Harries-Jenkins and Jacques Van Doorn (Beverly Hills, CA: Sage Publications, 1976), 77–92.

4 See David Ralston, *Importing the European Army: The Introduction of European Military Techniques and Institutions into the Extra-European World, 1600–1914* (Chicago: University of Chicago Press, 1990).

5 See Bruce Vandervort, *Wars of Imperial Conquest in Africa, 1830–1914* (Bloomington: Indiana University Press, 1998).

6 On the changing security environment in postwar Europe, see James Sheehan, *Where Have All the Soldiers Gone? The Transformation of Modern Europe* (Boston: Houghton Mifflin, 2008), chap. 7.

7 For some examples, see the data in Ronald Inglehart, *The Silent Revolution Changing Values and Political Styles among Western Publics* (Princeton, NJ: Princeton University Press, 1977).

8 See Sheehan, *Where Have All the Soldiers Gone?* chap. 8. The best collection of information on military institutions is *The Military Balance*, published annually since 1959 by the International Institute for Strategic Studies in London. On the Netherlands, see F. Olivier and G. Teitler, "Democracy and the Armed Forces: The Dutch Experiment," in *Armed Forces and the Welfare Societies: Challenges in the 1980s*, ed. Gwyn Harries-Jenkins (New York: St. Martin's Press, 1983), 54–95.

9 For changing patterns of conflict, see Lotta Harbom and Peter Wallensteen, "Armed Conflicts, 1946–2009," *Journal of Peace Research* 47, no. 4 (2010): 501–9; Andreas Wenger et al., *Strategic Trends 2010* (Center for Security Studies, ETH Zürich, 2010); and the essays in Isabelle Duyvesteyn and Jan Angstrom, eds., *Rethinking the Nature of War* (London: Frank Cass, 2005).

10 See James Burk, "The Decline of Mass Armed Forces and Compulsory Military Service," *Defense Analysis* 8, no. 1 (1992): 45–59; and Curtis Gilroy and Cindy Williams, eds., *Service to Country: Personnel Policy and the Transformation of Western Militaries* (Cambridge, MA: MIT Press, 2007). There is a careful study of the French case in J. Justin McKenna, "Towards the Army of the Future: Domestic Politics and the End of Conscription in France," *West European Politics* 20, no. 4 (1997): 125–45.

11 Enlistment data from *Der Spiegel*, July 29, 2010. Quotation from Gerhard Kümmel in Gilroy and Williams, *Service to Country*, chap. 8.

12 Henning Sørensen, "Conscription in Scandinavia during the Last Quarter Century: Developments and Arguments," *Armed Forces & Society* 26, no. 2 (2000): 313–34. Pauli Järvenpää, "Finland's Defence Policy: Sui Generis?" *Baltic Defense Review* 11, no. 1 (2004): 129–34.

13 See Judy Dempsey, "The Peril That NATO Can't Ignore," *New York Times*, November 10, 2010, and "Briefing: The Cost of Weapons," *Economist*, August 28, 2010, 20–21.

14 *Economist*, March 31, 2012, 70.

15 Robert Keohane, Joseph Nye, and Stanley Hoffman, eds., *After the Cold War: International Institutions and Strategies in Europe, 1989–1991* (Cambridge, MA: Harvard University Press, 1993), 6.

16 Martin Shaw, *Post-Military Society: Militarism, Demilitarization, and War at the End of the Twentieth Century* (Philadelphia: Temple University Press, 1996), 163. On the armed forces of the former Communist states, see the data in *The Military Balance 2010* and the useful summary by Jeffrey Simon,

"NATO's Uncertain Future: Is Demography Destiny?" *Strategic Forum*, no. 236 (October 2008): 1–7.

17 On the difficulties of reform, see Carolina Pallin, *Russian Military Reform: A Failed Exercise in Defence Decision Making* (London: Routledge, 2009). For the most recent efforts, see the chapter on the Russian Federation in *The Military Balance 2010*. Russia is by no means the only state in which demographic trends will reduce the pool of available recruits: see the essays in Jack Goldstone et al., eds., *Political Demography: How Population Changes Are Reshaping International Security and National Politics* (New York: Oxford University Press, 2011).

18 *New York Times*, July 30, 2011.

19 On the Turkish armed forces, see *The Military Balance 2010* and "A Special Report on Turkey," *Economist*, October 23, 2010.

20 Thanassis Cambanis, "Succession Gives Army a Stiff Test in Egypt," *New York Times*, September 12, 2010.

21 Quoted in Colin Gray, *Another Bloody Century: Future Warfare* (London: Weidenfeld & Nicolson, 2005), 172.

9 :: Whose Army?

Andrew J. Bacevich

Abstract: When Americans think of civil-military relations, they tend to think of the interaction, sometimes fractious, between very senior military officers and very senior civilian officials. Yet the civil-military relationship that really matters is the one between the U.S. armed forces and American society. For the first two centuries of the republic's existence, the citizen-soldier was the defining figure in that relationship. As a direct result of the Vietnam War, Americans jettisoned the concept of the citizen-soldier in favor of the warrior-professional. Few at the time considered the implications of creating what the founders had termed a "standing army." Today, the implications have become clear, and they are troubling. Between the military and society a large gap has emerged. Worse, the American people have largely forfeited any say in how the state employs its soldiers, with fateful consequences for both the nation and those who serve.

As a public policy issue, U.S. civil-military relations suffer from perennial neglect. Given the importance that the United States assigns to maintaining and wielding military power, such neglect is not only surprising but deeply unfortunate.

The interaction of civilians and soldiers takes place in two distinct domains. On the one hand is the relationship between very senior military officers and very senior civilian officials. Call this "elite" or "inside the Beltway" civil-military relations. On the other hand is the relationship between the armed forces of the United States and American society as a whole. Call this civil-military relations for the rest of us, taking place, for the most part, beyond the Washington Beltway.

At the elite level, the well-known principle of civilian control, implemented jointly by Congress and the chief executive, is said to exercise a governing influence. Article I, Section 8, of the Constitution assigns the legislative branch the power to declare war and to raise, support, and regulate the nation's armed forces. Article II, Section 2, designates the president as commander in chief of federal forces and state troops "when called into the actual Service of the United States." The president also commissions and promotes officers, albeit with the advice and consent of the Senate.

Adherence to the principle of civilian control by no means guarantees effective national security policy. It does, however, serve to guard against the danger of a military dictatorship. For this reason, students of civil-military relations view civilian control as foundational—that which needs to be preserved and protected at all costs.

In the realm of civil-military relations for the rest of us, another well-known principle once exercised a governing influence: namely, the conviction that national defense qualifies as a collective responsibility. According to this principle, citizenship and military service are inextricably linked. Writing in 1783, General George Washington put it this way: "It may be laid down as a primary position, and the basis of our system, that every Citizen who enjoys the protection of a free Government, owes not only a proportion of his property, but even of his personal services to the defence of it."[1] In 1792, President Washington signed legislation that incorporated this principle into law. The Uniform Militia Act declared that "each and every free able-bodied white male citizen of the respective States, resident therein, who is or shall be of age of eighteen years, and under the age of forty-five years...shall severally and respectively be enrolled in the militia."[2]

Truth to tell, in the implementation of these principles, Americans have always played fast and loose. Whether in the elite domain or out in the hustings, the realities of civil-military relations have seldom conformed to the reigning theories. For example, Americans have never, in practice, paid much attention to ensuring that the commander in chief has an unambiguously civilian identity. They have routinely voted for and sometimes elected as president former generals, several of whom evinced few qualifications for high office other than having achieved passing fame as war heroes. Winning a World Series, a Nobel Prize, or an Olympic medal won't earn you a place in the quadrennial White House sweepstakes, but have a hand in winning a war and you can be sure to see your name floated as a potential chief executive.

Moreover, although General Washington himself conscientiously deferred to civilian authority during his tenure in command of the Continental army, the history of the United States features any number of examples of senior officers who have marched to a decidedly different drumbeat. Some dabbled in partisan politics or bridled against civilians having the temerity to stick their noses into military matters. Others asserted the prerogative of deciding exactly what U.S. policy ought to be. A partial list of offenders includes such outsize personalities as Andrew Jackson, Winfield Scott, George McClellan, Fighting Joe Hooker, Nelson Miles, Leonard Wood, Billy Mitchell, and, most persistently and notoriously, Douglas MacArthur.

Likewise, when it comes to the bond between the military and society, principle has tended to be honored in the breach. Note that the citizen's obligation to serve, as legislated in 1792, mandated enrollment in the militia, not in the regular Army. This stipulation is significant for several reasons, most of them lost to memory. To begin, from the founding of the Republic until World War II, when it came to turning back prospective attacks on the United States or its institutions, Americans looked upon the militia (today's National Guard)—not the regular Army—as the nation's primary fighting force. Throughout the nineteenth century and well into the twentieth, the United States Army was neither organized nor equipped for serious large-scale combat. It served chiefly as a constabulary force, assisting in the project of territorial expansion and internal development. The militia was the varsity in the eyes of most Americans; the small regular Army qualified as the B team.

Yet the varsity seldom suited up and almost never practiced. With actually existing threats to the United States ranging from negligible to nonexistent, Americans had little incentive to treat seriously the requirement to keep the militia in fighting trim. Although imposing enough on paper, its actual capabilities were slight, a fact that suited most citizens just fine. They didn't much cotton to armies as such anyway, didn't want to spend money supporting them, and fancied themselves a peace-loving people to boot.

When peace-loving Americans found themselves periodically going to war anyway—launching ethnic cleansing campaigns against Native Americans or giving in to the impulse to invade Canada, Mexico, or Cuba, for example—they extemporized the forces needed for the task at hand. Rather than relying on none-too-ready militia-men or barely more capable army regulars, federal authorities called on volunteers to rally to the colors. Notwithstanding their general antipathy for things military, Americans responded to each such summons with surprising alacrity. Never was this more vividly the case than in 1861, when Americans from the South and the North formed two very large volunteer armies and spent the next four years killing one another in staggering numbers. In short, when the nation required a fighting force, it conjured one up. When the need passed, the citizen army vanished and Americans returned to other, more pressing priorities.

For all its evident inefficiencies, this arrangement worked toler-ably well. The country prospered. Except perhaps on the far edges of the frontier, Americans slept soundly, unworried about a possible invasion by alien hordes. Practically speaking, for most Americans most of the time, the notion of a civic obligation to defend the country was more symbolic than real. Yet however symbolic, the obligation to serve retained a psychic significance, much as the idea of obligatory Sunday Mass remained a hallmark of Roman Catholicism long after most self-identified Catholics had ceased to honor any such obligation. Although largely ignored and unen-forced, the Militia Act stayed on the books for more than a century,

the basis of a military system that, in a formal sense, hardly qualified as a system at all.

The small regular Army produced a few dissenters who railed
against this system that was hardly a system. One such dissident,
important even if today largely forgotten, was Emory Upton. A fascinating, charismatic, and ultimately tragic figure, Upton graduated
from West Point in 1861 and, as a young officer, performed prodigious feats of heroism during the Civil War. Yet the bloodletting
Upton had witnessed appalled him. Amateurism and sheer incompetence, in his view, had needlessly wasted tens, perhaps hundreds
of thousands of lives. The antidote was clear: scrap the tradition
of the citizen-soldier; rely instead on a professionalized and much
larger regular army to defend the country when it came time to
fight; entrust the conduct of war to officers who devoted their lives
to studying war.

Upton dedicated the remainder of his life to a crusade aimed at
junking the existing military system and replacing it with a new one—
this at a time when the American people were about as interested in
military reform as they are today in reciting Elizabethan poetry.

Among the few people Upton did manage to persuade were members of the officer corps itself. Succeeding generations of regulars
came to regard him as a prophet; Upton's aspirations became theirs.[3]
In the country as a whole, however, Upton's legacy was negligible. In
America, "We the People"—not hired guns or mercenaries—continued to bear primary responsibility for safeguarding the nation.

During the first half of the twentieth century, U.S. participation
in two successive world wars changed all this. War transformed
America's role in the world. War also transformed American
civil-military relations. In both domains, inside the Beltway and
far removed from Washington's orbit, the implications proved to be
enormous—and almost entirely problematic.

To be sure, change did not come all at once. At the conclusion of
World War II, for example, consistent with past practice, the citizen army raised up to fight Germany and Japan almost instantly
dissolved. American citizen-soldiers responded to the end of hostilities in 1945 pretty much as they had in 1848, 1865, 1898, and 1918:
they clamored to shed their uniforms and go home. Yet events soon

revealed this as a valedictory homage to a tradition rapidly headed toward extinction.

During World War II, as never before, military elites had gained access to the inner circles of American power. Those at the very top of the military hierarchy enjoyed enormous prestige and wielded enormous clout. Once having acquired such influence, they did not willingly surrender it. After 1945, Washington's newly asserted role of global leadership affirmed the elevated status that senior admirals and generals had acquired in the war. These officers used their status to press for the creation of a large and powerful *standing* military establishment—something that was entirely alien to the American experience. Rather than a sometime thing, war was becoming an anytime thing, at least in their estimation. Instead of raising up forces in response to a particular emergency, the brass (and their civilian allies) saw a need for forces held in readiness for rapid employment. During the first half-decade of the postwar era, military *demands* (the term is not inappropriate) produced continuous and remarkably open discord between the leadership of the armed services and the president. Issues that became the subject of civil-military conflict included the size of the Pentagon budget, the design and procurement of major weapons, control of the nation's nuclear arsenal, service roles and missions, and even racial integration.

Faced with decisions or guidance not to their liking, military leaders complained, stalled, shirked, or simply disobeyed. The Navy and Marine Corps waged all-out bureaucratic warfare to frustrate President Harry Truman's efforts to unify the armed services. The Air Force likewise strove to prevent the newly established Atomic Energy Commission from taking possession of the nation's stockpile of atomic bombs. For their part, Army leaders took umbrage when the commander in chief ordered the Pentagon to abolish racial separation, and at first made only token efforts toward integrating the Army's ranks.

Only with the onset of the Korean War in the summer of 1950, and Truman's approval of major increases in military spending, did civil-military conflict subside. The views promoted by senior military leaders had prevailed. The year 1950 proved to be a watershed.

U.S. foreign policy became unambiguously militarized. The United States garrisoned forces around the world, global presence becoming a signature of the American military posture. It configured each of the armed services as instruments of global power projection. In short order, global presence married to global power projection capabilities found expression in a penchant for global intervention, both overt and covert, with protecting the homeland, once the overriding priority, now figuring as an afterthought. During the Cold War, these became the hallmark of American statecraft. Even today, this "sacred trinity" remains fully intact, never having been subjected to serious reconsideration.

Yet if civil-military disharmony eased after 1950, it by no means disappeared. Indeed, civil-military tugging and hauling enshrined itself as a permanent feature of Washington politics—part of the way the game gets played. The vast apparatus of the national security state affirmed and institutionalized the exalted role that senior military officers now enjoyed. In the 1950s and 1960s, when presidents ventured into the White House Rose Garden to make some portentous national security announcement, they took care to have the Joint Chiefs of Staff (JCS) festooned with ribbons lined up behind them. The message was clear: "Look, I have consulted the chiefs; they concur; therefore my decision deserves to be treated with respect."

That the officer corps' ultimate loyalty to the Constitution remained intact was beyond question. Yet the very implausibility of an outright coup made all manner of shenanigans permissible. It's like the married man who flirts outrageously with women: he knows in his heart that he could never actually cheat on his wife, so as long as he adheres to some neatly legalistic definition of what cheating entails, his innocence remains intact, and within that self-defined boundary he is free to do as he pleases. So too with regard to relations between the top brass and their putative political masters.

At the upper echelons of the military profession, effectiveness came to require political savvy. The "simple soldier"—if such a creature ever existed—won't get very far in the E-Ring of the Pentagon. After all, politics is a blood sport. The making of national security policy is nothing if not political, with blood and treasure, power and access, ego and ambition all on the line. So senior officers learned to lobby, leak, ally with strange bedfellows, manipulate the media, and play off the Congress against the White House. In Washington, that's how things get done.

Theoretically, the top brass should place the national interest above parochial concerns, render disinterested advice when asked, and then loyally implement whatever decisions competent civilian authorities may make. Theoretically, civilian authorities should treat their military counterparts with the respect owed to professionals. They should allow the military wide latitude in matters pertaining to war. To use a term that acquired all manner of negative connotations during the Vietnam era, civilians should avoid "meddling" in soldiers' business. Theory, however, does not conform to reality. Conflict exists between the top brass and top civilian officials for precisely the same reason that conflict pits Republicans against Democrats, the White House against Capitol Hill, and the Senate against the House of Representatives: because power is at stake.

Reality is the fact that when Army Chief of Staff Eric Shinseki speculated to a Senate committee—just prior to the invasion of Iraq—that occupying that country could well turn out to be a costly mess requiring "several hundred thousand troops," Secretary of Defense Donald Rumsfeld and his deputy, Paul Wolfowitz, instantly retaliated by publicly rebuking Shinseki and declaring him persona non grata within the Pentagon—an object lesson to any other officers inclined to speak their minds. Reality is the chorus of retired and retiring senior officers who subsequently saddled Rumsfeld and Wolfowitz with blame for everything that went wrong in Iraq, thereby giving the generals in command an unearned free pass.

Reality is General Stanley McChrystal's highly sensitive assessment of how to proceed in Afghanistan finding its way into the hands of Washington Post reporter Bob Woodward, thereby hijacking the Obama administration's internal policy review process. It's McChrystal's enlisting as "consultants" various known commodities from Washington think tanks certain to promote his views in op-eds and television talk show appearances; it's McChrystal himself making public presentations—a speech in London and an interview on 60 Minutes—in which he declared that alternatives to his plan simply did not exist, thereby handcuffing the president. It's the Pentagon responding to Obama's request for serious options on Afghanistan by offering three variations of a single option—the one McChrystal himself was so insistent upon implementing.

The ideal of civilian control stands in relation to actual civil-military relations as the ideal of the common good stands in relation to actual politics: it represents an aspiration rather than a fact. It will never define reality. Responsibility for this unhappy circumstance does not lie with one side or the other but with both. To insist that senior officers and senior civilians should find ways to work in harmony recalls Rodney King's plaintive appeal during the 1992 Los Angeles riots, when the now-famous victim of police brutality asked, "Can't we all just get along?" Any such expectation of human behavior, applied to politics, flies in the face of history. As with the poor, so too will the competition for power be ever with us.

Now, when generals overreach, they deserve to have their hands slapped indeed; Obama did eventually hand General McChrystal his walking papers, and rightly so.[4] When ignorant or arrogant civilians ignore their military advisers and thereby commit costly blunders, they, too, should be held accountable. To the delight of the officer corps, George W. Bush ultimately replaced the bumbling Donald Rumsfeld as Pentagon chief—again, rightly so. Yet inside the Beltway, civil-military conflict is not a problem to be solved; it is a situation to be managed.

Elite civil-military relations require constant policing. Whenever evidence of inappropriate conduct leading to defective policy becomes evident, editorial writers and TV commentators decry the latest civil-military "crisis." This is necessary and honorable work. Once critics raise a sufficient ruckus, the system's mechanism for internal self-correction kicks in. It's the same thing when people get up in arms about potholes or lousy service at the bureau of motor vehicles. To quiet complaints (and preserve their status and prerogatives), the people in charge eventually respond.

Indeed, the decades since World War II have seen recurring efforts to find legislative remedies to civil-military dysfunction. At regular intervals, Congress has passed "landmark" legislation aimed at bolstering civilian control while simultaneously providing policy makers with improved access to cogent, timely military advice and improved mechanisms to ensure the effective conduct of war. Three themes have dominated these efforts: concentrating ever-greater authority in the hands of the secretary of defense; empowering the chairman of the JCS at the expense of the service chiefs; and emphasizing "jointness" as the antidote to crippling service parochialism.[5]

With the 1986 passage of the Goldwater-Nichols Act, this penchant for institutional tinkering reached a climax. This legislation stripped the service chiefs of their advisory function, designating the JCS chairman as the principal military adviser to the secretary of defense and the president. It also enhanced the standing of senior field commanders, having them report directly to the secretary of defense. Finally, it elevated *jointness* to the level of theological precept. Henceforth, the armed services were to be "intellectually, operationally, organizationally, doctrinally, and technically" joint, the operative assumption being that "jointness" provided "the key to operational success in the future."[6] For a time during the 1990s, Washington convinced itself that it had fixed the problem. Events since 9/11 have told a different story, with calls for a "Goldwater-Nichols II" the predictable result.[7]

The point here is not that legislative efforts have been a waste of time. It's simply that results routinely fall short of what reformers promise. The earnestly sought panacea remains elusive. Still, even if corrective action achieves only partial or cosmetic success, reforms initiated in Washington suffice to quiet the clamor and restore a semblance of order. That's probably the best we can hope for when it comes to civil-military relations inside the Beltway. Yet there is a larger point to be made here: this preoccupation with dysfunction in the realm of elite civil-military relations distracts attention from the far more significant problem of dysfunction in the realm of civil-military relations for the rest of us.

Put simply, more or less contentious civil-military relations within the Beltway are inevitable. Within limits, such contention is also tolerable. Meanwhile, an unharmonious relationship between the military and society is *not* inevitable. Here, Americans *should* view dysfunction—which has become endemic and pervasive—as intolerable. By way of elaborating on this point, let's go back to World War II.

George C. Marshall, Army chief of staff throughout the war, was a great soldier. He was also a very adept politician. Long before the war's end had come into view and without consulting his civilian masters, Marshall began to put in place his own plan for postwar U.S. civil-military relations. Yet his interest was not in how his successors were going to interact with presidents and cabinet secretaries. Instead, Marshall was concerned about the connection between America's Army and the American people. In other words, it was not elite civil-military relations that interested him, but civil-military relations for the rest of us. Toward that end, the Army chief of staff enlisted the help of an old friend, John McCauley Palmer, a retired brigadier general long since put out to pasture. Marshall restored Palmer to active duty and charged him with laying the basis for a postwar military establishment.

Palmer stands in relation to American *military* thought and practice as Eugene V. Debs does in relation to American *political* thought and practice. Like Debs, he was a romantic and a radical of gentle mien. Like Debs, he diligently and persistently argued against tendencies that in his eyes were subverting authentic American ideals. Like Debs, Palmer's substantive impact turned out to be negligible. Yet both men left behind an intellectual legacy worth pondering.

Also like Debs, Palmer was a son of the Middle Border, born in 1870 in downstate Illinois. The Palmers played a prominent role in state politics. Instead of entering the family trade, however, John McAuley left his home state as a young man, heading east to attend West Point. Graduating with the Class of 1892, he entered the military profession. There he found considerable satisfaction and achieved modest success even as he cultivated views that placed him at odds with those prevailing in the officer corps. The Army to which Palmer devoted several decades of service was well into its Uptonian moment. Indeed, Elihu Root, a reform-minded secretary of war from 1899 to 1904, had drawn explicitly on Upton's writings in reorganizing and modernizing the War Department. The prophet had received a posthumous vindication of sorts.

John McAuley Palmer saw things differently. Among regular officers, he was a rare anti-Uptonian. With a passion equal to Upton's, he defended the citizen-soldier tradition. Not only was that tradition sound, Palmer insisted; it also expressed fundamental and irreplaceable American ideals. Advocating for and striving to update the citizen-soldier tradition became his life's work. In 1916, his first book on the subject appeared. Called *An Army of the People*, it was an exercise in fantasy, Palmer spinning a tale in which the United States embraced the Swiss concept of the people in arms, thereby constituting an impregnable defense.

Neither the Army's leadership nor President Woodrow Wilson was especially interested in impregnable defenses, however. Within a year of Palmer's book appearing, the United States was indeed raising up a new army of citizen-soldiers. Yet this army's purpose was not to defend America per se, but to fight Germans in far-off France, a campaign in which Palmer himself participated.

Following World War I, the issue of military reform briefly commanded attention in Congress. Palmer's views had made him sufficiently well known that, in 1919, he was seconded to the Senate Committee on Military Affairs, where he assisted in drafting the bill that became the National Defense Act of 1920. Much to the dismay of the Uptonians, this legislation reaffirmed the primacy of the citizen-soldier. With that issue settled, Congress proceeded to ignore the practical requirements of national defense. Throughout the ensuing interwar period, the United States ended up with the worst of all worlds: the National Guard, repository for the citizen-soldier tradition, was underfunded, untrained, and unready; the regular Army, now with its own reserve, was too small and too poorly equipped to qualify as a serious fighting force.

When Palmer retired from the Army in 1926, he turned full-time to campaigning for a modern and capable citizen-soldier army, producing a series of books that fall into the category of "advocacy history." Essentially, he ransacked the past, telling different versions of the same story and reaching the same conclusion every time. Here is the gist of his argument, taken from his 1927 book *Statesmanship or War*:

From the dawn of history wise men have seen that the perpetuation of free institutions depends on the power of self-defense. To be permanent, democratic political institutions must include a democratic system of military security.... A free state cannot continue to be democratic in peace and autocratic in war. Standing armies threaten government by the people, not because they consciously seek to pervert liberty, but because they relieve the people themselves of the duty of self-defense. A people accustomed to let a special class defend them must sooner or later become unfit for liberty. An enduring government by the people must include an army of the people among its vital institutions. For this reason, the maintenance of a single professional soldier more than necessary threatens the very groundwork of free institutions.[8]

Recent German history provided an example of what the United States needed to avoid: as Germany's "military power extended, its political aims expanded."[9] To maintain military power in excess of that needed for self-defense was to pave the way for militarism and empire. However inadvertently, means could end up dictating—and perverting—ends. The citizen-soldier, in Palmer's view, served not only as a safeguard of democracy but also as a bulwark against imperial adventurism. Americans, Palmer wrote in 1930, had to choose one of two military visions: that of "[George] Washington or [Emory] Upton."[10]

Or as he emphasized in yet another book, published on the eve of U.S. entry into World War II, "We should never maintain professionals to do things that can be done effectively by citizen soldiers."[11] Military policy that looked to the regular Army as the primary instrument of national defense, he insisted, "could have no congenial place among the political institutions of a self-governing free people." Such an approach to policy flunked this essential test: that "a nation's military institutions should be in harmony with its political traditions."[12]

Given the paper trail that Palmer had left over a period of three decades, George Marshall knew exactly what he was getting when he recruited his old comrade, now seventy years of age, to define the parameters of postwar military policy. So Palmer holed up in a small office in the Library of Congress and went to work. The results of his labors appeared in a document issued over Marshall's signature on August 25, 1944. The title of this document was "Military Establishment," or, more prosaically, War Dept Circular No. 347. With fighting far from over in either Europe or the Pacific, Circular 347 declared the following:

> There are two types of organization through which the manpower of a nation may be developed. One of these is the standing army type.... This is the system of Germany and Japan. It produces highly efficient armies. But it is open to political objections.... It, therefore, has no place among the institutions of a modern democratic state based on the conception of government by the people.
>
> The second type of military institution ... is based upon the conception of a professional peace establishment (no larger than necessary to meet normal peacetime requirements) to be reinforced in time of emergency by organized units drawn from a citizen army reserve, effectively organized for this purpose in time of peace.... This is the type of army which President Washington proposed to the First Congress as one of the essential foundations of the new American Republic.... It will therefore be made the basis for all plans for a post-war peace establishment.[13]

Notably, Palmer's reference to a "peace establishment" echoed George Washington's use of that same phrase in his "Sentiments on a Peace Establishment," written back in 1783.

In his final report as chief of staff, Marshall expanded on Palmer's admonition. "War has been defined by a people who have thought a lot about it—the Germans," he wrote. The German view held that "an invincible offensive military force ... could win any political argument." He continued:

> This is the doctrine Hitler carried to the verge of complete success. It is the doctrine of Japan. It is a criminal doctrine, and like other forms of crime, it has cropped up again and again since man began to live with his neighbors in communities and nations. There has long been an effort to outlaw war for exactly the same reason that man has

outlawed murder. But the law prohibiting murder does not of itself prevent murder. It must be enforced. The enforcing power, however, must be maintained on a strictly democratic basis. There must not be a large standing army subject to the behest of a group of schemers. The citizen-soldier is the guarantee against such a misuse of power.[14]

Creating a citizen army reserve would require universal military training (UMT). The idea was not to turn every able-bodied citizen into a fully equipped warrior, but to provide individuals with rudimentary training, thereby facilitating the mobilization of the citizen reserve when it was needed. Palmer described the concept thus:

> Every able-bodied young American should have a course of recruit training during his nineteenth, twentieth, or twenty-first summer. After his recruit training he would be enrolled in one of the local units of the National Guard or the Organized Reserves formed in the vicinity of his home. Twice during this four-year period each soldier in the Organized Reserves would be required to attend maneuvers for two weeks with his company.[15]

General Marshall fervently believed that UMT should form the cornerstone of U.S. military policy after World War II. Here lay the key to harmonizing a postwar military establishment with American political traditions. "The entire idea," one historian has aptly written, "resembled the old nineteenth-century militia program, except it would be run by the national government rather than the states."[16]

By the time the war ended, Marshall had persuaded President Truman, himself a former citizen-soldier from Missouri, to sign on. Dwight D. Eisenhower, who succeeded Marshall as Army chief of staff, concurred, albeit with reservations. Although Congress took up the idea, it went nowhere. UMT was stillborn. The United States instead chose the course that spelled the demise of the citizen-soldier tradition. Instead of a peace establishment, Americans opted for a war establishment. Incrementally, over time, the concept of a standing army lost its negative connotations. Creating an impregnable defense no longer sufficed. The phrase *national security*, which was displacing *national defense* in the lexicon of everyday politi-cal discourse, implied more expansive and ambitious requirements. Among many Americans, the prospect of creating "an invincible offensive military force" that "could win any political argument" found increasing favor.

Why did efforts by Palmer and Marshall to revise and sustain the citizen-soldier concept fail? Two factors stand out as especially important. First, whatever its merits in forging a harmonious rela-tionship between the armed forces and society, UMT could not satisfy immediate and pressing military requirements. The end of World War II generated requirements to station large U.S. occupa-tion forces in Europe and the Pacific. UMT offered nothing to fulfill this mission. With the onset of the Cold War, the forward deploy-ment of U.S. forces became a core element of national security pol-icy and served to emphasize this shortcoming.

Second, although proponents described UMT as inherently dem-ocratic and a safeguard against militarism, wary Americans didn't necessarily see it that way. After all, UMT implied compulsion. In the eyes of critics, it looked like a backdoor way of impressing the entire male population into military service, in essence making per-manent the system of conscription that Americans had accepted as a wartime emergency measure. In short, UMT was hard to explain and hard to sell. So Congress rejected it. Responding to the per-ceived imperatives of the Cold War, it opted instead for "Selective Service," a system of peacetime conscription that was not universal and eventually proved to be anything but democratic.

Selective Service provided federal authorities with mechanisms to manage the entire military-age male population. The prospect of being drafted spurred some young Americans to volunteer for mili-tary service, while General Lewis Hershey, director of the Selective Service System, protected others with deferments and augmented the supply of willing recruits by adjusting monthly draft quotas upward or downward. In this guise, a vestige of the citizen-soldier tradition survived through the 1950s and into the 1960s—this was the era of Sergeant Elvis Presley, after all—yet it was a system that neither George Washington nor Emory Upton would likely have found completely satisfactory.

Then came Vietnam. Under the strain of an unpopular and protracted war, the entire system collapsed. Vietnam handed Emory Upton a belated triumph and dealt John McAuley Palmer a seemingly decisive defeat. It drove a stake through the heart of the citizen-soldier tradition. President Richard M. Nixon killed that tradition. Disregarding concerns voiced by the Joint Chiefs, he persuaded Congress once and for all to terminate the draft.

Out of the wreckage of Vietnam emerged the so-called all-volunteer force. This was a standing army par excellence, existing quite apart from American society. For a time, however, divorcing the American military from the American people seemed a masterstroke. Rather than harmonizing military policy with political values, the all-volunteer force appeared to resolve a much thornier issue. It reconciled American culture, now celebrating unencumbered individual autonomy, with the dogged insistence of political elites in Washington that exercising global leadership made it essential for the United States to have available for immediate use immensely capable armed forces. Rather than a state-based militia activated in emergencies, the National Guard became an adjunct of the standing military. In the Pentagon's view, guardsmen were part-time regulars, expected to conform fully to professional standards. This, at least, was the premise informing the so-called Total Force doctrine.

The creation of a new class of warrior-professional made everyone happy. Those residing outside the Beltway could live their lives, unbothered by the prospect of receiving a summons from the likes of General Hershey. Inside the Beltway, meanwhile, elites could still find satisfaction in sending American soldiers off to Beirut, Panama, Somalia, or elsewhere. By the 1990s, something close to unanimity existed: the military created after Vietnam was perhaps the most successful federal innovation since the self-adhesive postage stamp.

Then came 9/11 and in its wake another unpopular and protracted war—two wars, in fact, one in Iraq and another in Afghanistan. Somewhere around 2004 or 2005, Americans began awakening to the real implications of having deep-sixed the citizen-soldier. Inside the Beltway, it became apparent that the United States faced the problem of having too much war and too few warriors. To ease the burden on a badly overstretched force, and with few allies stepping up to the plate to help, the Pentagon turned increasingly to corporate mercenaries, referred to euphemistically as "private security firms." No one much cared for the result except the contractors, who raked in huge profits at taxpayer expense. Even then, sending troops back for a third or fourth combat tour became commonplace, and the sustainability of the situation seemed precarious.

Outside the Beltway, the American people retained negligible say in the employment of an army over which they had forfeited any ownership. Long since cast as spectators, citizens found that they had little voice in deciding when Team America suited up or where it played. If there remained any doubts on that score, President Barack Obama's decision to escalate the Afghanistan War in December 2009 ended them. Having promised to "change the way Washington works," Obama instead conformed to the dictates of standard practice.

In that regard, the president's claim in early 2012 that "we're turning the page on a decade of war" deserves a prize for artful phrasing.[17] Obama could rightly claim credit for ending the Iraq War. Rather than closing the books on the larger conflict begun in response to 9/11, however, his administration succeeded mostly in opening a new chapter, not only in Afghanistan but also in Pakistan, Yemen, Somalia, and Libya.

"We the People" need to understand: it's no longer *our* army; it hasn't been for years. It's *theirs*, and they intend to keep it. The American military belongs to Bill Clinton and Madeleine Albright, to George W. Bush and Dick Cheney, to Hillary Clinton and Leon Panetta. They will continue to employ that military as they see fit. If Americans don't like the way the army is used, they should reclaim it. Doing so will require resuscitating the tradition of the citizen-soldier, thereby reasserting the connection between citizenship and military service. Bluntly, Americans need to heed the counsel of George Washington, George Marshall, and John McAuley Palmer.

The likelihood of this happening is nearly nil. With rare exceptions, members of the national security establishment remain wedded to the all-volunteer force and adamantly oppose any measure that might invite increased popular influence on policy. Worse, American civic culture continues to evince a very low tolerance for anything that smacks of collective obligation. Americans might feel uneasy about the fact that one-half of 1 percent of their fellow citizens bear the burden of service and sacrifice. But uneasiness has yet to translate into demands for change.[18] The few willing to entertain the notion that military service should constitute an obligation tend to be long in the tooth—aging veterans of World War II or Korea.

Yet as long as the tradition of the citizen-soldier remains moribund, reversing the militarization of U.S. foreign policy will remain a pipe dream. In the nation's capital, the halls will resound with calls for peace, but war is likely to remain a permanent condition. In Washington, people will periodically wring their hands over the unseemly state of relations between civilian and military elites, as brass hats and politicians maneuver against the other for advantage. That's *their* problem.

The problem for the rest of us is a far greater one: grasping the implications, moral as well as political, of sending the few to engage in endless war while the many stand by—passive, mute, and yet, whether they like it or not, deeply complicit.

Notes

1 George Washington, "Sentiments on a Peace Establishment" (1783), http://www.potowmack.org/washsent.html (accessed May 11, 2010).

2 U.S. Congress, the Militia Act of 1792, 2nd Cong., 1st sess., May 8, 1792, http://www.constitution.org/mil/mil_act_1792.htm (accessed May 11, 2010).

3 The Uptonian bible is *The Military Policy of the United States*, a history left unfinished at the time of Upton's death and published several decades later at the behest of Secretary of War Elihu Root; Emory Upton, *The Military Policy of the United States* (Washington, DC: Government Printing Office, 1904).

4 What cost General McChrystal his job was not aggressive policy promotion but a willingness to tolerate among his immediate subordinates casual expressions of contempt for senior civilians. For the *Rolling Stone* article that led to his firing, see http://www.rollingstone.com/politics/news/17390/119236 (accessed November 30, 2010).

5 Although not included in the official *Department of Defense Dictionary of Military and Associated Terms*, "jointness" identifies seamless interservice collaboration as the sine qua non of military effectiveness.

6 U.S. Congress, Goldwater-Nichols Department of Defense Reorganization Act of 1986, 99th Cong., 2nd sess., October 1, 1986; available at the National Defense University Library, http://www.ndu.edu/library/goldnich/goldnich.html (accessed December 22, 2010).

7 See "Beyond Goldwater-Nichols," a project undertaken by the Center for Strategic and International Studies, http://csis.org/program/beyond-goldwater-nichols (accessed November 30, 2010).

8 John McAuley Palmer, *Statesmanship or War* (Garden City, NY: Doubleday, 1927), 74.

9 Ibid., 29.

10 John McAuley Palmer, *Washington, Lincoln, Wilson: Three War Statesmen* (Garden City, NY: Doubleday, 1930), 361.

11 John McAuley Palmer, *America in Arms: The Experience of the United States with Military Organization* (New Haven, CT: Yale University Press, 1941), 203.

12 Quoted in I. B. Holley Jr., *General John M. Palmer, Citizen Soldiers, and the Army of a Democracy* (Westport, CT: Greenwood Press, 1982), 89. This volume combines Palmer's unfinished and previously unpublished memoir with a biography that takes up where the memoir leaves off.

13 Ibid., 659–60.

14 United States War Department General Staff, *Biennial Report of the Chief of Staff of the United States Army July 1, 1943, to June 30, 1945, to the Secretary of War* (Washington, DC: Infantry Journal Press, 1945), 117.

15 Palmer, *America in Arms*, 174.

16 George Q. Flynn, *The Draft, 1940–1973* (Lawrence: University Press of Kansas, 1993), 90.

17 "Defense Strategy Guidance Briefing from the Pentagon" (January 5, 2012), http://www.defense.gov/transcripts/transcript.aspx?transcriptid=4953 (accessed January 20, 2012).

18 Pew Research Center, *War and Sacrifice in the Post-9/11 Era: The Military-Civilian Gap* (October 5, 2011), http://www.pewsocialtrends.org/2011/10/05/war-and-sacrifice-in-the-post-911-era/ (accessed January 20, 2012). This Pew survey notes that nine out of ten Americans "express pride in the troops" while "three-quarters say they [have] thanked someone in the military." Pew does not comment on how many of those surveyed thereby felt inspired to enlist.

10 :: Reassessing the All-Volunteer Force

Karl W. Eikenberry

Abstract: As both a former U.S. ambassador to Afghanistan and commander of the U.S.-led coalition forces in the Afghanistan War, Karl Eikenberry offers a unique perspective on important issues in civil-military relations that have evolved out of the successful establishment of America's all-volunteer force (AVF) in 1973. Eikenberry argues that the unmatched power and effectiveness of today's U.S. military has not come without costs to traditional democratic ideals. With America's armed forces growing more isolated from civilian society, political authorities have increasingly committed them to security operations abroad. At the same time, oversight both by civilian leaders and the media has weakened, internally enforced professional accountability standards have slackened, and respect for civilian control of the military has begun to falter. The decline in oversight by those responsible is attributable to a lack of military expertise and a fear of being depicted as "unwilling to support the troops." Only by acknowledging these problems can Americans address them adequately and preserve the constitutional principles that have successfully guided their society for over two hundred years.

When America ended the military draft in 1973 and transitioned to the all-volunteer force (AVF), the success of this ambitious enterprise was not guaranteed. Yet by the early 1990s, decisive victories in the Cold War and Operation Desert Storm convincingly validated the AVF. Today, U.S. military forces are unmatched globally and historically in terms of lethality, speed, and agility.

Though expensive to organize, equip, and maintain, the AVF is deemed by most Americans to be a necessary part of the high price tag that comes with securing the nation's interests in a dangerous world. Our society's cost-benefit calculus is based upon its volunteer military's demonstrated deterrent effect and battlefield performance, the amount of defense expenditures, and the societal premium associated with liberation from the burden of conscription.

Yet, while the majority of Americans hold their soldiers in high esteem and consider the well-endowed AVF a worthy bargain, we have collectively ignored the severe political and strategic consequences of its implementation.[1] By two important but rarely acknowledged metrics, the advantage of the volunteer over the conscript military is less certain.

First is the question of "political ownership" of the military within our democracy. The defense establishment lays claim to vast amounts of taxpayers' dollars and plays a consequential role in deciding vital matters of war and peace. Just as most town dwellers take a keen interest in the cost and conduct of their police force, so should citizens at the national level have a broad sense of responsibility for the behavior of our armed forces.

Second is the degree of congressional and media oversight of the volunteer armed forces, and the extent to which the military's senior leadership holds itself accountable for shortcomings in its performance.

In this essay I argue that the AVF, which has compiled an extraordinary operational record over the past three decades, has liabilities—some quite serious—when viewed through the prism of the above two considerations. I do not urge a return to the draft. There is little public or political appetite for its implementation. Moreover, it is not clear that a sufficiently capable conscript force could even be fielded, given the extensive training required to meet the demands of highly technical and specialized twenty-first-century warfare. However, we cannot simply continue ignoring such weighty issues as the political ownership and oversight of the armed forces and their internal accountability. Doing so is an abdication of the first principles of good republican governance that removes from public discourse a search for corrective policy measures.

My presentation is in three parts. To provide context, I first briefly review America's historical experience in filling the ranks of its armed forces, with emphasis on the decision to establish the AVF. There follows an assessment of the volunteer force through the prism of political ownership and oversight as well as internal accountability. I conclude with some thoughts on the implications for our national security and global democratic example.

In the more than two centuries since the U.S. Constitution went into effect in March 1789, our government has only four times relied on conscription to field an armed force: the Civil War (draft in effect 1863–1865), World War I (draft 1917–1918), World War II (draft 1940–1945), and the Cold War (draft 1946–1947 and 1948–1973), a total of thirty-five years. Moreover, throughout the Cold War era, only during the Korean and Vietnam conflicts were sizable numbers of draftees needed to supplement the pool of volunteers, reservists, and guardsmen.[2]

Whenever proposed, conscription has usually been a point of political contention in the United States. When President Madison proposed to draft a mere forty thousand men during the War of 1812, Daniel Webster argued that the Constitution did not provide the government with the authority to conscript citizens, and the measure failed.[3] Civil War conscription triggered occasionally violent civil protests, but the drafts associated with the two world wars were generally supported. And though Congress periodically debated the Cold War draft, it was not until 1965, when President Johnson significantly increased the number of U.S. troop deployments to Vietnam, that popular opposition to the draft became a politically salient issue.

Indeed, it was the growing unrest on American college campuses in reaction to the Vietnam War levies that in part inspired the 1968 Republican presidential candidate Richard Nixon to promise to end military conscription if elected.[4] The next year, President Nixon appointed an Advisory Commission on the All-Volunteer Armed Forces to develop a plan for eliminating conscription. In early 1970, this group, known as the Gates Commission after its chair, former secretary of defense Thomas Gates Jr., unanimously recommended the adoption of an all-volunteer force. The commission's report, accepted and acted upon by the Nixon administration with some modifications, also acknowledged five major objections to the establishment of an AVF: (1) the potential isolation of such a force from society and the threat to civilian control; (2) with isolation, an erosion of civilian respect; (3) ranks likely to be disproportionately filled with blacks or those from low-income backgrounds; (4) a decline in the population's concern with foreign policy issues; and (5) the nation becoming more inclined to embark on "military adventurism."[5] Some of these concerns have proven to be quite prescient. In addition, while the report argued persuasively that the AVF would not lead to significant increases in the defense budget, it did not estimate future outlays for retirement and health care costs. That proved to be a serious omission, as the contribution by Lawrence J. Korb and David R. Segal in this volume documents.[6]

Several summary observations follow. First, conscription has only been adopted in the United States when the country faced a significant security threat calling for a manpower-intensive military response, including the first twenty-five years of the Cold War. Second, with the exception of periods of the Civil War and the later years of the Vietnam War, the public widely accepted the imposition of the draft, albeit against a backdrop of frequent political contention.[7] Third, as Princeton professor Julian Zelizer has noted, "By eliminating the draft, Nixon weakened the most immediate connection that existed between the national security state and average citizens."[8] And fourth, although most of the Gates Commission's recommendations were to prove remarkably sound, especially given the complicated nature of the problem, several of the arguments against the AVF noted in the report emerged over time as more serious than anticipated. Chief among these are the issues of declining political ownership of the U.S. military and diminished oversight of the armed forces by both Congress and the media.

Regarding the issue of political ownership of the American military, the historical record indicates over 330 conflict-related military deployments since 1798, although about half of these were after World War II when the United States had become a superpower with global security interests.[9] And though it is difficult to make a robust empirical case that the cessation of the draft contributed to more frequent use of the U.S. armed forces abroad, the evidence is suggestive.

A more appropriate measurement might be restricted to the post-1945 era, between the periods when the United States maintained conscription (1946–1973) and subsequently relied on an entirely volunteer formation (1973–2012). Nineteen overseas military deployments occurred in the twenty-seven-year draft period versus more than 144 during the thirty-nine-year course, to date, of the AVF. This translates into an AVF-deployments-per-annum ratio five times higher than that of the draft force. Even here, however, precise comparisons are difficult. Many post-1973 uses of military forces were repeated interventions in the Balkans, Haiti, and Iraq, and a large number were in conjunction with UN and NATO operations, not necessarily indicative of the U.S. "military adventurism" adumbrated in the Gates Commission report. Still, the manifestly increased frequency of foreign military deployments after the establishment of the AVF (again, by a factor greater than five) is worrisome.

Of course, the two AVF interventions unique in breadth and scope are Iraq and Afghanistan. Together they are the longest in duration of any American war (the Afghanistan conflict alone enjoys this distinction); the seventh-most-lethal American conflict measured in fatalities; second in fatalities (after the Mexican-American War) of those conflicts fought entirely with volunteer forces; and second only to World War II in expense, and perhaps soon to become the most costly armed intervention in U.S. history.[10]

Here a reasonable argument can be made that the absence of those domestic political constraints inherent in a draft force may have freed otherwise cautious U.S. government decision makers to carry out large-scale extended military operations in both Iraq and Afghanistan. When I have spoken on this topic to various audiences around the country, I have asked: "If we had a conscripted military good enough to accomplish the same missions assigned our current volunteer forces—admittedly a bold assumption—would the United

States have invaded Iraq in 2003 and have had one hundred thousand troops stationed in Afghanistan one decade after 9/11?" Never more than one or two participants offer an affirmative response.[11]

Concerns that a political decoupling of the military from the American people might open the door to military adventurism, noted but dismissed by the Gates Commission, were very much on the minds of some civilian and military leaders during the early years of the AVF. Prominent among this group was the chief of staff of the Army, General Creighton Abrams, who served as the commander of Military Assistance Command, Vietnam, from 1968 to 1972. Abrams sought to keep the military connected to the Congress, states, and public by ensuring the forces were structured so that a large-scale protracted conflict (such as those in Iraq and Afghanistan) would require significant mobilization of reserves and National Guard, an act generally not free of political risk.[12]

General John Vessey, a former chairman of the Joint Chiefs of Staff, recalled about Abrams:

> He thought about [the kind of nation America was] an awful lot, and concluded that whatever we're going to do [we should not] build an Army off here in the corner someplace. The armed forces is an expression of the nation. If you take them out of a national context, you are likely to screw them up. That was his lesson from Vietnam. He wasn't going to leave them in that position ever again. And part and parcel of that was that you couldn't go to war without calling up the reserves.[13]

Reserves have, in fact, been substantially employed in both Iraq and Afghanistan, but not in sufficient numbers to give real pause to government leaders ordering their deployments.[14] Thus, with well-resourced and capable volunteers supplemented by generally willing reservists, America's politicians have not faced significant organized and sustained domestic grassroots opposition to the unpopular conflicts in Iraq and Afghanistan, quite unlike the Vietnam War experience.[15]

The framers of the U.S. Constitution believed that Congress should have extensive authority to take the country to war, and this is so codified in Article I, Section 8, paragraph 11. Yet Congress has exercised its constitutional prerogative to declare war only five times in America's history. The reassertion of congressional war-making authority in the War Powers Resolution has been ignored by every president since its enactment in 1973.[16]

Congress has even fewer incentives under the AVF model to assert its constitutional responsibilities against the executive, especially in the preliminary and initial stages of a military intervention. Without sizable numbers of organized constituents fretting about the personal and family costs of a conflict, the legislator's preferred strategy is to discount the future and avoid casting a vote against waging war during the flag-waving stage of a crisis. (Consider, for example, the many politicians who survived their 2002 votes in favor of the Iraq War Resolution, simply claiming later they were misled by the Bush administration.) Most members of Congress, always with an eye on reelection, will give pause before contesting strong executive appeals to commit forces abroad in the stated defense of the national interest. However, by such abdication of responsibility, Congress is failing to serve as the check on executive power envisioned by the drafters of the Constitution.[17]

The Gates Commission also concluded that adoption of an all-volunteer force would "actually increase democratic participation in decisions concerning the use of military force," contending, in part, that "if tax increases are needed or military spending claims priority over other public spending, a broad public debate is likely. Recent history suggests that increased taxes generate far more public discussion than increased draft calls."[18] For at least three reasons this prediction proved inaccurate.

The first is a matter of scale. U.S. defense outlays today, massive though they are (constituting an estimated 45 percent of the global total in 2011), consume a much smaller percentage of total federal spending than in 1970 when the Gates Commission report was published.[19] Some comparisons: In 1968 (the height of the Vietnam War), defense-military spending accounted for 45.1 percent of federal outlays; in 2008 (the year marking the maximum combined level of effort in the Iraq and Afghanistan Wars) defense-military spending was only 19.9 percent of the federal budget, a percentage exceeded by Health and Human Services (23.5 percent), Social

Security (21.7 percent), and almost equaled by Treasury's debt financing (18.4 percent).[20] In 1968, defense spending stood at 9.4 percent of GDP, whereas in 2009 it composed 4.6 percent.[21] And unlike during the era of the Gates Commission, advocates of robust military spending now argue that defense should be largely immune from the ongoing budget debates, the real deficit threats being posed by entitlement programs and mounting interest payments on our national debt.

The second is a matter of context. For now at least, our nation's unprecedented extended deficit spending spree has removed from the public agenda any serious discussion about current expenditure levels. Thomas Gates, who served as a secretary of defense under the fiscally conservative president Dwight Eisenhower, could never have imagined our current state of affairs. With U.S. federal deficits as a percentage of GDP reaching levels not experienced since the immediate aftermath of the Second World War, the quest for budget discipline that Gates took as a given has been all but abandoned.[22] The problem was made more acute during the course of the Iraq and Afghanistan conflicts as the Bush administration, supported by Congress, actually reduced taxes and made housing credit more plentiful.[23] American citizens could be forgiven for making no connection between their individual tax payments and the real cost of two distant wars.[24]

The third reason is structural. The extraordinary and unprecedented use of civilian contractors in conflict zones has obscured the actual price of war from the American people, who tend to measure costs in number of troops deployed. The use of contractors on battlefields proliferated during the first decade of the twenty-first century. It is estimated that between 2007 and 2011, on average contractors outnumbered deployed military personnel in both Iraq and Afghanistan, a huge increase when compared with Operation Desert Storm in 1991, when only about four thousand were employed.[25] It might be argued that the Department of Defense could also employ numerous contractors to augment a conscript force, but the point is that their large-scale use in support of our volunteer armed forces not only conceals the real scope of conflict from the American people, but also reduces pressure on the military's leadership either to recommend strategies that can be implemented by the extant force or alternatively to request a large expansion of the AVF, which might, in turn, open a debate about conscription.[26]

If there has been an erosion of political constraints on the employment of U.S. military forces since the establishment of the AVF, our nation's particular historical circumstances constitute another structural feature that may also contribute to the forces' frequent dispatch abroad. Whereas America has been the sole global military superpower since the end of the Cold War, the same is not true in the economic domain. Today's world is militarily unipolar and economically multipolar. With the collapse of the Soviet Union, the United States gained and has maintained a huge comparative advantage in the use of coercive power (versus economic and soft power), and its application is perhaps now often seen as the most cost-effective of the available instruments of the national will. Such a hypothesis is speculative, but is also consistent with historical theories of change in world politics that posit economically declining hegemonic powers often overreaching militarily to preserve global systems whose maintenance is considered a matter of vital prestige.[27]

Having discussed some of the unintended consequences of the adoption of the all-volunteer force model in terms of eroding democratic political ownership of the U.S. military, we turn to the issue of accountability.

Among the objections to the end of conscription identified and rejected by the Gates Commission was that it would lead to "the growth of a separate military ethos, which could pose a threat to civilian authority, our freedom, and our democratic institutions."[28] As yet, no such direct sustained and organized threat has materialized. However, the commission stopped short of speculating on the possible impact of the AVF on the quality of both civilian oversight and on the willingness of senior military officers to take appropriate responsibility for their organization's failures. I believe both have suffered, though it should be noted that the views I offer here are admittedly more informed by personal experience than by quantitative analysis.

The two most important external sources of imposed accountability on the American military are Congress and the media. Neither has performed with distinction in recent decades.

First, consider Congress. The number of serving members of Congress with military experience has decreased significantly since the end of conscription in 1973. In the 91st Congress (1969–1971), 398 members had served in the military; in the 112th Congress (2011–2013), only 118, a drop in percentage from over 73 percent to about 22 percent.[29] Moreover, Congress now has very few members who have sons or daughters serving in the armed forces, and is therefore even further removed from the military.[30]

With the attendant loss of expertise, family ties, and perhaps interest, Congress appears disinclined to rigorously challenge the advice of senior military officers or to question their management practices. Indeed, nearly abject congressional deference to the military has become all too common. A usual response of politicians when asked their views on the prosecution of an ongoing conflict is to routinely assert that they will give the generals and admirals whatever they need—hardly a strong affirmation of civilian control of the military. Concerned about potential political fallout from charges of "not supporting the troops" and lacking confidence in their own knowledge, members tread cautiously before publicly disagreeing with ranking professional soldiers and the strategies that they advocate.[31]

I had an opportunity when serving as the U.S. ambassador to Afghanistan to witness this reticence firsthand. Visiting members of Congress generally were passive and supportive when receiving briefings from uniformed military leaders. They placed a hefty premium on photo opportunities with troops throughout their visits. By contrast, they were always skeptical and occasionally confrontational when in similar sessions with the embassy's civilian team in Kabul. Having previously served twice as a military commander in Afghanistan, I could plainly see the contrast.

To be clear, I think the congressmen were right to challenge our civilian team. We were spending a huge amount of taxpayers' money, war aims were hard to define, and progress was difficult to measure. Congress' job is to exercise oversight, and members owed their constituents informed judgments. However, by not subjecting the military—which in Afghanistan was consuming over twenty times the amount of funds spent by the civilian team—to the same

rigorous standards of scrutiny, these legislators were applying a
double standard and not faithfully executing their constitutional
responsibilities.[32]

A vignette aptly illustrates the impact of the all-volunteer force
on congressional oversight of the military. Over an eighteen-month
period (from early 2011 through July 2012), some forty-six coalition soldiers were murdered by their supposed allies in the Afghan
National Army and Police in twenty-nine reported attacks.[33] We
could assume that with a draft force, families of those killed would
have clamored for congressional hearings, and that Congress would
have eventually obliged, or perhaps even preempted any calls for
hearings by acting to review the matter without public prompt-
ing. Yet during that period, only one congressional hearing was
held on this topic. It lasted ninety-five minutes, with two civilian
deputy assistant secretaries of defense and two Army brigadier generals (neither serving commanders in the field) representing the
Department of Defense and armed forces.[34] The hearing received
scant media attention. In seeking a balance between displays of def-
erential respect for the military and the exercise of sober, demanding oversight, members have often found political expediency in
weighting the former.

The performance of the media has, like that of Congress, been
uneven in shining a spotlight on the all-volunteer force. I say "uneven"
because occasionally excellent press exposés, well-researched books,
and analytical think tank reports have led to a tightening of accountability. It might also be argued that the lack of tough media reporting on the military may simply reflect the high standards achieved
by the American armed forces; perhaps the good news has crowded
out the bad. This is, however, a dubious proposition, especially given
the fantastic amounts of money being spent by our military in chaotic expeditionary environments where efficiencies are impossible to
achieve and massive amounts of waste, fraud, and corruption are all
but unavoidable.

Media interest and focus have diminished over time for several
reasons. First, most media compete in a relentlessly time-constrained
news cycle. The loss of access to senior-level military officials is a
high-risk business proposition in a combat zone; hence reporters

have been careful to avoid burning bridges with critical reporting that challenges the views of command headquarters. Add to this their need to spend most of their time on the story of the day or week, and it becomes evident why some of the most insightful, frank, and surprising stories about senior military commanders and their strategies often appear only intermittently, authored by the handful of non-mainstream media outlets and by reporters on special assignments.

Second, the decline in resources many major media outlets devote to investigative journalism has meant, in turn, fewer hard looks at the military, not to mention other subjects of national concern. This is especially true given that the armed forces, as an all-volunteer organization, elicit less reader or viewer interest than, say, scandals involving domestic politicians or titillating revelations about government officials and Hollywood luminaries.[35]

Financially strapped major media also attempt to provide "I was there" frontline reporting through the relatively recent innovation of embedding journalists with combat units. For the immediately engaged parties, embedding is a clear win-win; reporters have access to dramatic stories of hardship and heroism, and commanders are better able to control the message. However, as journalist and novelist David Ignatius writes,

> embedding comes at a price. We are observing these wars from just one perspective, not seeing them whole. When you see my byline from Kandahar or Kabul or Basra, you should not think that I am out among ordinary people, asking questions of all sides. I am usually inside an American military bubble. That vantage point has value, but it is hardly a full picture. I fear that an embedded media is becoming the norm, and not just when it comes to war.[36]

Ignatius's argument can be taken even further; the reporter embedded in an all-volunteer unit manned entirely by those concerned about professional reputations and future careers is acquiring less ground truth than he or she might perhaps realize or admit.

Third, the well-funded Department of Defense and armed forces have, over time, developed long-term relationships with various think tanks, analysts, and retired military consultants whom they periodically ask or encourage to visit theaters of war and provide assessments. Arrangements in the conflict zone, entirely orchestrated by the military, include logistics, security, travel, and scheduling. Not surprisingly, when the travelers return to the United States, they generally support their sponsor's views in written op-eds and appearances on news shows.

What is extraordinary is that although no other government agency has the autonomy or resources to engage in such taxpayers-subsidized self-promotion, the Department of Defense and military have not been taken to task. Again, as ambassador from 2009 to 2011, I marveled at how Defense Department–sponsored consultants would spend weeks at a time in Afghanistan and often conclude that while the military dimension of the then ongoing surge was supposedly achieving intended results, it was shortcomings on the civilian side of the equation that jeopardized overall mission success.

The need for extensive, rigorous, and dispassionate oversight of our armed forces is manifest enough. The expenditures involved are immense, the national security stakes high, and the potential moral and political degradation associated with warfare extreme. And despite the importance of oversight in our civil society, with the connective tissue between the U.S. military and society weakened by the AVF construct, two critically important gatekeepers— Congress and the media—have reduced their vigilance. When a reporter who has written and reported skillfully on Afghanistan and Pakistan, Dexter Filkins, was asked during an interview on National Public Radio where all the billions spent on the Afghan army have gone, he replied, "The first is, you know, it's Afghanistan and…it's hard to imagine unless you see it, but if you can imagine a place on the moon, trying to build a base on the moon."[37] Whether the U.S. military was manned by volunteers or conscripts, Congress as well as the media would be moved to praise the daring and courage required to metaphorically build bases on the moon. But only with a conscript force might Congress, reinforced by the media, feel compelled to question why they were attempting to do so in the first place.

Last, I turn to the topic of accountability among senior U.S. military leaders. Samuel Huntington, in his classic work on civil-military relations, *The Soldier and the State*, wrote that key professional attributes of officership include expertise in the management of violence, acceptance of responsibility, and motivation derived from "technical love for his craft and the sense of social obligation to utilize this craft for the benefit of society."[38] Rigorous adherence to these attributes, in turn, is critical if the profession is to self-limit its behavior in ways that reinforce internal accountability and objective civilian control of the military.

The attribute of expertise has, in a sense, been undermined by ever-expanding boundaries of claimed professional military competence. As our volunteer armed forces have been increasingly employed in counterinsurgency (COIN) operations, Huntington's concise expression that the professional officer's "peculiar skill...is the management of violence" has lost its bite.[39] The breathtaking scope of COIN operations, as conceived in current U.S. military doctrine, makes this so.

The U.S. Army and Marine Corps doctrinal guide to COIN, *Field Manual (FM) 3-24*, states:

> The military forces' primary function in COIN is protecting [the] populace....Durable policy success requires balancing the measured use of force with an emphasis on nonmilitary programs. Political, social, and economic programs are most commonly and appropriately associated with civilian organizations and expertise; however, effective implementation of these programs is more important than who performs the tasks. If adequate civilian capacity is not available, military forces fill the gap....Counterinsurgents take upon themselves responsibility for the people's well-being in all its manifestations. These include the following: Security from insurgent intimidation and coercion, as well as from nonpolitical violence and crime; provision for basic economic needs; provision of essential services, such as water, electricity, sanitation, and medical care; sustainment of key social and cultural institutions; [and] other aspects that contribute to a society's basic quality of life.[40]

Our military rises to this self-defined overarching COIN challenge by generating ever new capabilities simply because no other civilian department can do so at the speed and scale of a powerful and loosely controlled Pentagon. As a result, our armed forces have taken on ever more tasks not directly related to war fighting. Some examples from the wars in Iraq and Afghanistan:

- Since 2004, U.S. military commanders have spent over $8 billion in rebuilding and reconstruction projects as part of the Commander's Emergency Response Program (CERP).[41] Senior officers contend that "money is ammunition," and "depending on the state of the insurgency, Soldiers and Marines should prepare to execute many nonmilitary missions to support COIN efforts since everyone has a role in nation building, not just Department of State and civil affairs personnel."[42] Congress has been magnanimous in its support. The money involved is massive in absolute and comparative terms. For example, in fiscal year 2011, military CERP spending in Afghanistan roughly equaled U.S. foreign development assistance for education and social services globally.[43]

- Military commanders in 2010 carried the day with their argument that key to the Taliban's defeat in southern Afghanistan was the provision of massive amounts of diesel-generated electricity to Kandahar city residents. Senior officers confidently predicted that as more lights came on, "COIN effects" would be achieved on a grand scale. Again, Congress, eager to support the troops in the field, appropriated $800 million in fiscal years 2011 and 2012 to DOD as part of the Afghan Infrastructure Fund in a combined effort with USAID to deliver sustainable power to southern Afghanistan over a several-year period.[44]

- As the military poured ever greater sums of money into the Afghan economy, hugely contributing (along with their civilian counterparts) to corruption and Taliban revenue, it established in 2010 "Task Force Transparency," a military-led interagency organization commanded by a brigadier general and based in Kabul with branches throughout the country. Its stated mission was to work "with Afghan leaders to expand the rule of law, fight criminal networks, and break 'a culture of impunity.'"[45] The U.S. military, marshaling its considerable assets, has enthusiastically become the visible tip of the foreign anticorruption spear throughout Afghanistan, confidentially briefing President Karzai on its findings and attempting to elicit his support. Yet permitting American Army general officers, not civilian authorities, to lead massive, comprehensive, rule-of-law and anticorruption efforts in a fledgling impressionable democracy, such as is Afghanistan, undermines by poor example the principle of civilian control of the military both in Kabul and Washington.

- In 2009, the chairman of the Joint Chiefs of Staff put into effect the "Afghan-Pakistan Hands Program" designed to build a bench of hundreds of linguistically proficient and culturally savvy military men and women who could help increase mutual understanding with the host nation populace and reduce the friction of military operations, especially in Afghanistan.[46] A much more ambitious effort to create in-country expertise than anything attempted on the civilian side of the civilian-military equation (the civilian side simply not having the resources and scales of economy possessed by the armed forces), "AfPak" hands, as they are nicknamed, frequently walk on paths far removed from Taliban insurgent enemies. One such hand, reflecting on his experience in Afghanistan, said he "did a lot of stuff trying to engage with small village elders, adopting local schools...facilitating closer ties...putting together school field trips, etc." He emphasized how "his most memorable moments were spent with his Afghan military counterparts with whom *he worked so hard to better the quality of life in very poor rural areas.*"[47] Looking to the future, the joint staff director of the program commented, "As conventional NATO forces are withdrawn, Afghan Hands will play an increasingly vital role as the 'connective tissue' between [the government of Afghanistan], Afghan civil society, international organizations, nongovernmental organizations, the U.S. interagency, and NATO's enduring force."[48]

I do not debate the rationale or logic behind most of the nontraditional programs and projects undertaken by the military as it has endeavored to creatively apply its COIN doctrine. Indeed, both as a commander and as an ambassador in Afghanistan, I advocated for some of these programs myself and was never wont to look a gift horse in the mouth. Yet, as the armed services have become major stakeholders in ever-expanding areas of our government, Huntington's implicit civilian-military contract that grants a degree of autonomy to military officers "to manage violence" in return for their profession's monopolization by the state has been emptied of content.[49] With the erosion, over time, of agreed-upon professional boundaries for the appropriate exercise of military influence, strict military accountability has been diluted, and the officer corps' emphasis on essential war-fighting skills has been diminished. Huntington emphasized that, as in most professions, the quality of officership is characterized by responsibility. Once again, the protracted messy conflicts that our volunteer legions have been thrust into in recent years have seemed to chip away at standards of accountability appropriate to the military strategy being pursued.

The unique nature of twenty-first-century conflicts and its relevance to the contemporary art of command was made clear in 1999 by General Charles Krulak, then commandant of the Marine Corps, who authored an article that popularized the term "strategic corporal." He explained how in the course of modern complex wars a single member of the armed forces, even at the most junior levels, can become "the most conspicuous symbol of American foreign policy [who potentially influences] not only the immediate tactical situation, but the operational and strategic levels as well. His actions, therefore, will directly impact the outcome of the larger operation; and he will become...the *Strategic Corporal*."[50]

The term became popularized in military circles. Indeed, *FM 3–24* explicitly affirms the concept by noting: "so-called 'strategic corporals'—often make decisions at the tactical level that have strategic consequences. Senior leaders set the proper direction and climate with thorough training and clear guidance; then they trust their subordinates to do the right thing."[51]

Of course, during large-scale conventional wars of the past, conflicts that more resembled the Clausewitzian theoretical extreme, there were no "strategic corporals."[52] A breach of the law of land warfare by an infantry squad of ten soldiers during the battle for Normandy was a matter handled at lower echelons of command and strategically inconsequential. General Eisenhower, the theater-level commander, was not held to account for such acts of misconduct, because they were not relevant to the conduct of the war at his level.

Yet, consistent with the term "strategic corporal," we have seen how similar violations of discipline and regulations have had catastrophic consequences during the wars we have waged in the twenty-first century. Fallout from the Abu Ghraib scandal, murders of civilians, and violations of enemy corpses are illustrations. On the one hand, I believe the conduct of the American armed forces over the course of the two protracted campaigns in Iraq and Afghanistan has been extraordinary; it testifies to the quality of the force that in a decade of hard fighting, there have not been more criminal acts or lapses that reverberated at the strategic level. But on the other hand, if singular failures of the strategic corporal can and do have strategic consequences, at what point must the strategic commander also be held accountable?

In other words, should not strategic commanders, in offering courses of action to their civilian leaders, make explicit the risk of plan failure that stems from the inevitable lapses of those fighting in the trenches? And if the risk is deemed too great, should not the approach be changed? And if the risk is to be absorbed, who should absorb it? When the president of the United States has to repeatedly apologize for the misdeeds of members of our armed forces on the global stage, we are not being well served. Either the doctrine is too problematic and needs to be reconsidered, or there must be accountability at the level of theater commanders when there are frequent failures at the strategic level.[53]

In no small measure, the amount of trust American society places in the officer corps is founded upon the corps' reputation for selfless national service. Huntington defined the American military profession as one in which the life of the officer "subordinates man to duty for society's purposes." He goes on to say that "modern man may well find his monastery in the Army."[54] However, in contrast with this ideal, the tendency in recent years has been for ever-more-senior retired officers to leverage their military experience and networks to earn considerable incomes after hanging up the uniform.

A comprehensive late-2010 *Boston Globe* study of the post-military careers of some 750 three- and four-star generals and admirals who retired from active duty over the past two decades found that from 2004 through 2008, 80 percent went to work as consultants or defense executives, compared with less than 50 percent who did so ten years earlier.[55] Bryan Bender, the author of an article explaining the study, wrote: "The revolving-door culture of Capitol Hill—where former lawmakers and staffers commonly market their insider knowledge to lobbying firms—is now pervasive at the senior rungs of the military leadership."[56] Senator Jack Reed (D-RI), himself a West Point graduate, was quoted by Bender as saying, "When I was an officer in the 1970s, most general officers went off to some sunny place and retired. Now the definition of success of a general officer is to move on and become successful in the business world."[57]

Using Huntington's metaphor, it would be the equivalent of overwhelming numbers of retired abbots somehow capitalizing on their long service to their religious orders and finding ways to earn substantial wealth and gain considerable policy influence the moment they cast off their robes.

My point in examining the American military profession's attributes of well-demarcated expertise, responsibility, and social obligation is *not* to criticize practices that are legally sanctioned and publicly accepted (though perhaps not deeply understood). Rather, it is to offer for consideration the proposition that the kind of officership described in the Huntington ideal differs in important ways from that found within our volunteer armed forces in the twenty-first century.

In the end, if the establishment of the AVF in 1973 did entail unanticipated and rarely acknowledged costs in terms of political ownership and accountability, does it even matter? I contend it most profoundly does and conclude with three reasons why this is so.

First, as previously discussed, the great expense and frequent employment of the all-volunteer force have become givens within our body politic. The U.S. military, ever versatile and ready to confront new security challenges, has become a Thor's hammer that makes increasing numbers of foreign policy problems appear to be nails.

It has not always been this way in the United States, not even during the first full decade of the Cold War. As Leslie Gelb has written:

> Truman and Eisenhower carried out their [economic] reforms while holding military spending in check—Pentagon budgets came last, not first. Both presidents allocated defense outlays using the "remainder method," whereby they subtracted necessary domestic spending from tax revenues and gave the leftovers (the "residual," as Eisenhower called it) to defense.... [They] were particularly conscious of the ill effects of being a debtor nation.[58]

Yet today, while the domestic implications of our mounting fiscal woes seem evident to most Americans, the long-term impact on our international security standing does not. Our relatively insulated defense spending is rarely included in serious debates about a comprehensive security strategy that must be founded upon economic strength and human capital.

Second, to the extent that the inception of the all-volunteer force has allowed and tempted America to frequently deploy its superbly trained and well-equipped troops into harm's way, there have been unintended consequences. One is reminded of the tale of the knight who returns to the castle after a long, hard day of battle and reports proudly to his king, "Sire, I have been defeating the soldiers and burning the towns of your enemies in the west all day on your behalf." The king, taken aback, exclaims, "But I have no enemies to the west!" The knight, crestfallen, replies, "Well, you do now, Sire!" Sober national assessments about opportunity and reputational costs associated with the use of force have not been sufficiently rigorous in recent decades.

Third and perhaps most significant is the effect that the end of the obligation of military service has had on the civic virtue necessary to sustain a republic. We collectively claim the need for robust armed forces given the multifaceted foreign threats our country faces, and yet as individuals, we do not wish to be troubled with any personal responsibility for manning the frontier. The merits of the volunteer force are clear, and few Americans have a strong desire to return to a draft.[59] Moreover, it may be possible to address certain negative consequences of the all-volunteer force through various policy means and approaches separate from reinstating conscription. In fact, given the stakes, we must find a way to deal explicitly with the shortcomings of the all-volunteer force in an incremental, politically pragmatic fashion. But that process must begin with an honest acknowledgment of the serious challenges posed by an all-volunteer force.

Still, as social and cultural historian Beth Bailey noted at the conclusion of her superb study of the AVF: "In a democratic nation, there is something lost when individual liberty is valued over all and the rights and benefits of citizenship become less closely linked to its duties and obligations."[60] As the world's leading power, priding itself on a willingness to employ its vast military might in the defense of universal democratic values, there is a truth and irony here that should at least be acknowledged.

Notes

1 A 2012 Gallup survey noted: "Americans are most confident in the military (75 percent), which has finished first each year since 1989 except 1997, when small business edged it out." In the same 2012 survey, small business was second to the military at 63 percent, and Congress stood at the bottom of the list at 13 percent. See "Confidence in U.S. Public Schools at New Low," June 20, 2012, http://www.gallup.com/poll/155258/Confidence-Public-Schools-New-Low.aspx (accessed August 5, 2012).

2 Bernard Rostker, *I Want You! The Evolution of the All-Volunteer Force* (Santa Monica, CA: Rand Corp., 2006), 23–32.

3 Daniel Webster, "On Conscription," speech delivered in the U.S. House of Representatives on December 9, 1814, http://www.constitution.org/dweb-ster/conscription.htm (accessed June 29, 2012).

4 Donald Vadergriff, *Manning the Future Legions of the United States: Finding and Developing Tomorrow's Centurions* (Westport, CT: Praeger Security International, 2008), 62.

5 *The Report of the President's Commission on an All-Volunteer Armed Force* (New York: Macmillan, 1970), 125.

6 This paper does not address these mounting all-volunteer costs, but they are of increasing concern. The health care portion of the defense budget climbed from $19 billion in 2001 to about $55 billion in 2011 and continues to balloon. See Robert Fenn, "Robert Gates Says Health Care Costs Hurt Defense Budget," *U.S. News & World Report*, February 24, 2011,

http://www.usnews.com/opinion/blogs/Peter-Fenn/2011/02/24/robert-gates-says-healthcare-costs-hurt-defense-budget (accessed July 2, 2012). Retirement costs have increased from about $4.4 billion in 1973 (the first year of the AVF) to over $50 billion in 2011. See Department of Defense Office of the Actuary, *DOD Statistical Report on the Military Retirement System,* May 2011, 20, http://actuary.defense.gov/Portals/15/Documents/statbook11.pdf (accessed July 2, 2012).

7   Colonel William Raymond Jr., *Uncle Sam Says, "I Want You!"—the Politics of the Draft and National Service* (monograph) (Fort Leavenworth, KS: School of Advanced Military Studies, 2005), 38.

8   Julian E. Zelizer, *Arsenal of Democracy* (New York: Basic Books, 2010), 235.

9   Richard F. Grimmett, *Instances of Use of United States Armed Forces Abroad, 1798–2009* (Washington, DC: Congressional Research Service, January 27, 2010), 1–30. Grimmett indicates that his list of overseas military ventures is "without reference to the magnitude of the given instance noted" and that "the instances differ greatly in number of forces, purpose, extent of hostilities, and legal authorization."

10 "America's Wars" (fact sheet), Department of Veterans Affairs, Washington, DC, November 2011, http://www.va.gov/opa/publications/factsheets/fs_americas_wars.pdf (accessed July 1, 2012); Amy Belasco, *The Cost of Iraq, Afghanistan, and Other Global War on Terror Operations since 9/11* (Washington, DC: Congressional Research Service, March 29, 2011), 3; Stephen Daggett, *Costs of Major U.S. Wars* (Washington, DC: Congressional Research Service, June 29, 2010), 1–3; and Joseph E. Stiglitz and Linda J. Bilmes, "The True Cost of the Iraq War: $3 Trillion and Beyond," *Washington Post,* September 5, 2010, http://www.washingtonpost.com/wp-dyn/content/article/2010/09/03/AR2010090302200.html (accessed July 1, 2012). Actually, the number of combat deaths (killed in action and died of wounds) suffered in Iraq and Afghanistan to date is the highest of any war in American history fought exclusively with volunteers; during the Mexican-American War battle deaths were fewer than two thousand, while those attributed to disease and accidents were over twelve thousand. See John S. D. Eisenhower, *So Far from God: The U.S. War with Mexico, 1846–1848* (New York: Anchor Books, 1989), 369.

11 Two such occasions were at Stanford University on December 7, 2011, while participating on an American Academy of Arts and Sciences–sponsored panel discussing the future of the American military (see the *American Academy of Arts and Sciences 2012 Spring Bulletin,* http://www.amacad.org/publications/bulletin/spring2012/military.pdf [accessed July 2, 2012]) and on May 3, 2012, when delivering the Frank E. and Arthur W. Payne Lecture, "The Future of the American Military" (the presentation is available at http://fsi.stanford.edu/events/recording/7140/1/720 [accessed July 2, 2012]).

12 Richard W. Stewart, general ed., *Army Historical Series, American Military History,* vol. 2, *The United States Army in the Global Era, 1917–2003* (Washington, DC: United States Army Center for Military History, 2005), 376.

13 Lewis Sorley, *Thunderbolt: General Creighton Abrams and the Army of His Times* (New York: Simon & Schuster, 1992), 364.

14 Reservist contributions to manning the total force in Iraq and Afghanistan peaked in fiscal year 2005 at 68.3 million military duty days. By comparison, during fiscal 1991 (Operation Desert Storm) the total was 44.2 million, and in the late 1980s about 0.9 million per annum; see John Nagl and Travis Sharp, *An Indispensable Force: Investing in America's National Guard and Reserves* (Washington, DC: Center for a New American Security, September 2010), 22. Against this, reservists generally deployed far less frequently than their active-duty counterparts, from rates between 25 percent and 50 percent in fiscal 2008, to even lower today. See Amy Belasco, *Troop Levels in the Afghan and Iraq Wars, FY2001–FY2012: Cost and Other Potential Issues* (Washington, DC: Congressional Research Service, July 2, 2009), 42. Additionally, some research would suggest that many, but by no means all, reservists had net income gains during deployments, which could potentially decrease any aversion to serving. See James Hosek, *How Is Deployment to Iraq and Afghanistan Affecting U.S. Service Members and Their Families?* (occasional paper) (Santa Monica, CA: Rand Corp., 2011), 29–31.

15 In 2008, a Gallup poll reported 63 percent of those Americans surveyed thought it had been a mistake to send troops to Iraq, while in 1971 a Gallup survey recorded 61 percent of its interviewees holding the same view of the Vietnam intervention. See http://www.gallup.com/poll/106783/Opposition-Iraq-War-Reaches-New-High.aspx_(accessed July 2, 2012). Discontent with the Afghanistan War is not reflected in questions relating to the original decision to deploy troops, since this was done in the aftermath of the 9/11 attack on the American homeland. In March 2012, however, Gallup reported half of those Americans surveyed believed that the United States should speed up its planned troop withdrawals from Afghanistan. See http://www.gallup.com/poll/153260/Half-Say-Speed-Afghanistan-Withdrawal.aspx (accessed July 2, 2012).

16 James A. Baker III and Warren Christopher, *National War Powers Commission Report* (Charlottesville, VA: Miller Center of Public Affairs, July 3, 2008) http://web1.millercenter.org/reports/warpowers/report.pdf (accessed July 3, 2012), 7.

17 James Madison notably wrote, "The constitution supposes, what the History of all [governments] demonstrates, that the [executive] is the branch of power most interested in war, & most prone to it. It has accordingly with studied care, vested the question of war in the [legislature]." Letter from James Madison to

Thomas Jefferson, April 2, 1798, http://www.thefederalistpapers.org/founders/madison/james-madison-letter-to-thomas-jefferson-1798.

18 *Report of the President's Commission on an All-Volunteer Armed Force*, 152.

19 International Institute for Strategic Studies, *The Military Balance 2012* (London: Routledge, 2012), 31.

20 Office of Management and Budget, "Historical Tables: Budget of the U.S. Government Fiscal Year 2011," http://www.whitehouse.gov/sites/default/files/omb/budget/fy2011/assets/hist.pdf (accessed July 2, 2012), 84 and 89.

21 Ibid., 127 and 132.

22 Jeffrey D. Sachs, *The Price of Civilization* (New York: Random House, 2011), 17.

23 Ibid.

24 See Robert D. Hormats, *The Role of Liberty: Paying for America's Wars* (New York: Henry Holt, 2007), for an in-depth discussion of this point.

25 Deborah Kidwell, *Public War, Private Fight: The United States and Private Military Companies* (monograph) (Fort Leavenworth, KS: Combat Studies Institute, 2005), 19; and Moshe Schwartz, *Department of Defense Contractors in Afghanistan and Iraq: Background and Analysis* (Washington, DC: Congressional Research Service, May 13, 2011), 2, http://www.fas.org/sgp/crs/natsec/R40764.pdf (accessed July 2, 2012).

26 To this argument must be added a consideration of the very mixed performance of contractors during the extended conflicts in Iraq and Afghanistan. If the AVF will be dependent upon private military and security companies to wage future large-scale protracted wars, as seems likely, then the liabilities associated with the employment of contractors must be considered a cost. See Deborah D. Avant and Renée de Nevers, "Military Contractors and the American Way of War," *Daedalus* 140 (Summer 2011): 88–99.

27 See, for example, Robert Gilpin, *War and Change in World Politics* (New York: Cambridge University Press, 1990), and Paul Kennedy, *The Rise and the Fall of the Great Powers* (New York: Random House, 1987).

28 *Report of the President's Commission on an All-Volunteer Armed Force*, 14.

29 Jennifer E. Manning, *Membership of the 112th Congress: A Profile* (Washington, DC: Congressional Research Service, March 1, 2011), 7–8.

30 In a conversation on this subject, Professor David M. Kennedy at Stanford University stated (in April 2012) that his research indicated about ten children of members were currently serving in the military. As he pointed out, although the methodology was imperfect, even if the figure is doubled, the number is still low. Kennedy contrasted this figure with a 2007 U.S. Army survey that indicated that some 304 active-duty generals had among them an astonishing 180 sons and daughters serving in the military.

31 American politicians have historically made congressional votes on wartime appropriations litmus tests on "supporting the troops." President Bush famously said during the Iraq War, "I often hear that war critics oppose my decisions but still support the troops. Well, I take them at their word,

and here's their chance to show it. It's unconscionable to deny funds to our troops in harm's way because some in Congress want to force a self-defeating policy." Against this, the late Lieutenant General William Odom argued, "Now, if you can say that getting your troops out of a strategically ill-advised deployment is not supporting the troops, then I don't understand the common sense of supporting the troops." See Guy Raz, "Congress Funds War to Support Troops," National Public Radio, December 21, 2007, http://www.npr.org/templates/story/story.php?storyId=17495023 (accessed July 8, 2012).

32 For spending estimates, see Belasco, *Cost of Iraq*, 17.

33 "Man in Afghan Army Uniform Wounds 5 US troops Outside Eastern Base," *Washington Post*, July 3, 2012, http://www.washingtonpost.com/world/asia_pacific/nato-says-man-in-afghan-army-uniform-attacks-coalition-troops-wounding-several/2012/07/04/gJQAhKHRMW_story.html (accessed July 8, 2012). Only attacks by Afghan soldiers and police resulting in the deaths of coalition soldiers are routinely reported by NATO ISAF headquarters in Afghanistan, so the total number of attacks and coalition soldiers wounded is unknown.

34 Chairman of the House Armed Services Committee Representative Buck McKeon chaired this hearing on February 1, 2012. See http://armedservices.house.gov/index.cfm/hearings-display?ContentRecord_id=60f15690-7e58-4f99-a1dd-63f96bd1f441 (accessed July 8, 2012).

35 For a discussion on the challenges faced by the media in adequately supporting investigative journalism, see Mary Walton, "Investigative Shortfall," *American Journalism Review*, September 2010, http://www.ajr.org/Article.asp?id=4904 (accessed July 8, 2012).

36 David Ignatius, "The Dangers of Embedded Journalism in War and Politics," *Washington Post*, May 2, 2010, http://www.washingtonpost.com/wp-dyn/content/article/2010/04/30/AR2010043001100.html?sid=ST2010043001134 (accessed August 6, 2012).

37 Transcript of Terry Gross interview of Dexter Filkins, "After Troops Leave, What Happens to Afghanistan?" National Public Radio, July 10, 2012, http://www.npr.org/templates/transcript/transcript.php?storyId=156504634 (accessed July 17, 2012). Filkins shared a Pulitzer Prize in 2009 for his reporting from Afghanistan and Pakistan while with the *New York Times*.

38 Samuel P. Huntington, *The Soldier and the State: The Theory and Politics of Civil-Military Relations* (Cambridge, MA: Belknap Press of Harvard University Press, 1957), 11–15.

39 Ibid., 13.

40 *FM 3–24 / MCWP 3–33.5 CounterInsurgency* (Washington, DC: Department of the Army and Marine Corps Combat Development Command, December 15, 2006), 2–1 and 2–2.

41 Belasco, *Cost of Iraq*, 34.

42 *FM 3–24 / MCWP 3–33.5 CounterInsurgency*, 1–27.

43 In fiscal year 2011, the Department of Defense requested CERP spending of $1.3 billion, and USAID reported in calendar year 2011 spending $1.34 billion worldwide on assistance for education and social services. See Belasco, *Cost of Iraq*, 34; and http://foreignassistance.gov/ObjectiveView. aspx?FY=2011&tabID=tab_sct_Peace_Planned&budTab=tab_Bud_ Planned (accessed August 7, 2012).

44 Office of the Inspector General for Afghanistan Reconstruction, "Fiscal Year 2011 Afghanistan Infrastructure Fund Projects Are behind Schedule and Lack Adequate Sustainment Plans," July 30, 2012, http://www.sigar.mil/pdf/ audits/2012-07-30audit-12-12Revised.pdf.

45 John Ryan, "Units Aim to Root Out Corruption in Afghanistan," *Army Times*, February 16, 2012, http://www.armytimes.com/news/2012/02/army-task-forces-fight-afghanistan-corruption-021612w/ (accessed August 7, 2012).

46 Joint Chiefs of Staff, "AFPAK HANDS Management Element," http://www. jcs.mil/page.aspx?id=52 (accessed August 7, 2012).

47 Natela Cutter, "Afghanistan/Pakistan Hands Program Ensures Stronger Bonds," CNN iReport, August 1, 2011, http://ireport.cnn.com/docs/ DOC-644756 (accessed August 7, 2012). Italics added.

48 Mark Porter, "Afghan Hands Helping to Reshape Afghanistan," US Forces Afghanistan, posted July 13, 2012, http://www.dvidshub.net/news/ printable/91588 (accessed August 7, 2012).

49 Huntington, *Soldier and the State*, 11 and 15.

50 General Charles C. Krulak, "The Strategic Corporal: Leadership in the Three-Block War," *Marines Magazine*, January 1999, http://www.au.af.mil/ au/awc/awcgate/usmc/strategic_corporal.htm (accessed July 10, 2012).

51 *FM 3–24 / MCWP 3–33.5 CounterInsurgency*, 1–28.

52 Carl von Clausewitz, *On War*, ed. and trans. Michael Howard and Peter Paret (Princeton, NJ: Princeton University Press, 1976), 77.

53 See David Rothkopf, "A New Challenge for Our Military: Honest Introspection," *Foreign Policy*, March 19, 2012, http://www.foreignpolicy. com/articles/2012/03/19/a_new_challenge_for_our_military_honest_ introspection?page=0,1 (accessed July 11, 2102).

54 Huntington, *Soldier and the State*, 465.

55 Bryan Bender, "From the Pentagon to the Private Sector," *Boston Globe*, December 26, 2010, http://www.boston.com/news/nation/washington/articles/2010/12/26/ defense_firms_lure_retired_generals/?page=1.

56 Ibid.

57 Ibid., 2.

58 Leslie H. Gelb, "GDP Now Matters More Than Force: A U.S. Foreign Policy for the Age of Economic Power," *Foreign Affairs* 89, no. 6 (November–December 2010): 39.

59 An October 2011 Pew survey found that more than eight in ten post-9/11 veterans and 74 percent of the public believed the United States should not return to the draft. See Pew Research Center, *War and Sacrifice in the Post-9/11 Era: The Military-Civilian Gap* (October 5, 2011), http://pewresearch.org/pubs/2111/veterans-post-911-wars-iraq-afghanistan-civilian-military-veterans (accessed July 13, 2012).

60 Beth Bailey, *America's Army: Making the All-Volunteer Force* (Cambridge, MA: Belknap Press of Harvard University Press, 2009), 260.

11 :: Military Justice

Charles J. Dunlap Jr.

Abstract: Military justice has never been intended as an exact replica of civilian justice. Historically, the need to maintain discipline under the enormous stress of combat and the high stakes of war impelled all militaries to create a separate and, in many ways, unique justice system. The result is a criminal law process in which military needs sometimes must take precedence over certain rights-centered formalisms of a nation's civilian justice system. However, beginning with the adoption of the Uniform Code of Military Justice in 1951, the two U.S. systems have become increasingly close, with the importation into the military realm of many of the procedural protections of the civilian system. Military justice retains its distinctive features, including the criminalization of absence, cowardice, and insubordination, as well as other offenses without civilian counterpart but which are indispensable for what the Supreme Court calls the armed forces' "separate society." In addition, some procedural differences continue to exist, including command selection of military "juries," as well as an appellate court system empowered to review de novo factual findings of a court-martial. Recently, the use of military commissions—which are separate from courts-martial—have been revised to address war crimes committed by nonstate actors. Today, issues have arisen about the ability of the military justice system to operate independently and effectively. In part, this is the result of well-intended efforts over several decades to "civilianize" and "judicialize" its processes—modifications that have often proven ill-suited to combat zones. Even more problematic is the tendency of political leaders and interest groups to encroach on the role of commanders in military justice matters, and to inject other political influences that threaten the military justice system's independence and effectiveness.

Groucho Marx, so the story goes, once quipped that "military justice is to justice what military music is to music." To the distress of many in the armed forces, as well as to admirers of its justice system, that wisecrack continues to describe the military's criminal jurisprudence in the minds of many Americans.

As with much humor, however, there is some truth in Marx's jest. Just as military music has served a martial purpose for eons—trumpets did a pretty good job for Joshua and the Israelites at the battle of Jericho—so too has military justice served war fighters since virtually the beginning of organized conflict, because it plays a central role in establishing the discipline indispensable for martial success. In the *Anabasis*, Xenophon observed that "if discipline is held to be of saving virtue, the want of it has been the ruin of many ere now."[1] Maurice de Saxe, in his 1732 treatise on war, *Mes Rêveries*, contends that the "Romans conquered all peoples by their discipline. In the measure that it became corrupted their success decreased." For his part, George Washington bluntly insisted that "discipline is the soul of an army. It makes small numbers formidable; procures success to the weak, and esteem to all."

All of this suggests that military justice is not—and never has been—intended to be simply a doppelgänger for a civilian criminal justice system. Unlike its civilian counterpart, it is designed to help execute, if necessary, the difficult—and melancholy—task of getting human beings to kill, in the name of the state, and do so under circumstance where their opponents are bent upon doing the same to them. The current *U.S. Manual for Courts-Martial* (MCM) puts this stark purpose more delicately and rather more elliptically when it explains that "the purpose of military law is to promote justice, to assist in maintaining good order and discipline in the armed forces, to promote efficiency and effectiveness in the military establishment, and thereby strengthen the national security of the United

States."[2] Across nations, cultures, and time, military discipline has typically been unapologetically and, indeed, often necessarily, draconian. Throughout history, misbehaving soldiers have been punished in a variety of frightening ways, to include at times torture, maiming, and even summary execution. During the Revolutionary era, for example, the British army would impose punishments of up to one thousand lashes for relatively minor offenses.

In a way, it is not hard to understand why such harsh measures were needed: the tactics and weapons of the eighteenth century required troops to march shoulder to shoulder to within seventy-five yards of their adversary. At that point the infantrymen would fire volley after volley into the similarly packed ranks of their adversary to achieve the effect of mass fire with their oft-inaccurate muskets. Additionally, the crammed-together troops might also face withering exchanges of cannon fire from almost point-blank range. Anyone injured in such blasts faced, at best, the horrifying prospect of rudimentary medical care, including the high probability of amputation. It took uncompromising discipline to steel soldiers for this terrifying environment.

Given such verities, it is unsurprising that the Continental army adopted Britain's military justice code, the Articles of War, with relatively few changes. That system, with periodic adjustments and improvements, largely persisted through World War II. In that conflict, which saw sixteen million Americans serving in uniform, over two million courts-martial of U.S. troops took place. Most of those trials were conducted without lawyers or legally trained personnel, and this and other deficiencies led to much criticism after the war. As one commentator put it,

> Many of these citizens also had some very unpleasant experiences with the military justice system. At that time, the military justice system looked quite different than it does today and did not offer accused the protections afforded by the civilian courts system. It was a system that was foreign to many American citizens and they disapproved of the way criminal law was being applied in the military.[3]

To address these concerns, Congress passed major reform legislation in 1951 that replaced the Articles of War with the Uniform

Code of Military Justice (UCMJ).[4] The new law regularized disciplinary processes throughout the several service branches, provided
for consistent rules of evidence, and embedded legally trained participants more deeply into the system. In addition, it established
the all-civilian Court of Military Appeals (CMA), which is now
known as the Court of Appeals for the Armed Forces (or CAAF).
Importantly, this tribunal—like the entire military justice system—
was established by Congress as an "Article I" court under its constitutional powers,[5] as opposed to a part of the judicial branch of
government, which is governed by Article III of the Constitution.

Later, the Military Justice Act of 1968, again drawing much from
civilian jurisprudence, added additional modernizing procedures,
to include the mandatory use of a military judge for all but the most
minor trials.[6] Moreover, the adoption in the 1980s of the Military
Rules of Evidence from the Federal Rules of Evidence was—and
is—considered an important step in ensuring fairness of military
trials and promoting the sense that military courts are "just as
good" as civilian trials because, after all, it is often said, the rules
and procedures much mirror each other.

While such changes certainly address criticisms of the military
justice system, it is not evident—as is discussed below—that all of
the changes were actually constitutionally required or have, necessarily, facilitated the administration of military justice, especially
in the field where it is so needed.[7] The founding fathers, whose
recent experience with the Revolution left them well aware of wartime exigencies, seemed to have recognized that all the particu-
lars of Article III trials are not necessary or practical for a military
disciplinary process, which may require administration in austere
conditions. Continuing concern about the viability under field
conditions of an increasingly complex military criminal justice
system led then secretary of defense Leon Panetta in July 2012 to
commission a panel to examine the efficacy of the military justice
system in deployed areas.[8]

For its part, the Supreme Court frequently made it clear that it
suffers no illusions about the need for special considerations as to
how justice is administered in the military realm. In his superb book
on military justice, retired Army colonel Larry Morris maintains

that the Supreme Court and other courts have a "strong inclination" to "defer to the military as a separate society and to set a lenient standard of review for decisions that are within the judgment of commanders, leaders, and policymakers."[9]

Nevertheless, there have been biting critiques. In the 1969 case of *O'Callaghan v. Parker*[10] Justice William O. Douglas remarked that while "the Court of Military Appeals takes cognizance of some constitutional rights," courts-martial "as an institution are singularly inept in dealing with the nice subtleties of constitutional law." He added, with ill-concealed contempt, that "a civilian trial ... is held in an atmosphere conducive to the protection of individual rights, while a military trial," Douglas asserted, "is marked by the age-old manifest destiny of retributive justice."

Despite that unflattering assessment, the actual holding of *O'Callaghan* did not dismantle the military justice system. Instead, it merely determined that only those offenses that had "service connection" were suitable for military courts. The result of *O'Callaghan* was, however, near chaos in military practice, as courts at both the trial and appellate levels struggled to address a myriad of factual situations to determine if they were sufficiently related to military service for resolution at a court-martial.

At the same time a process began, much driven by the Court of Appeals (perhaps smarting from Douglas's rebuke), to "judicialize" the system away from its traditional commander-centric focus toward one more akin to civilian courts. As then captain (later brigadier general) John Cooke wrote in 1977, a core principle of this effort was embodied in the decisions by the Court of Military Appeals that "substantially shifted the balance of power in the system by invalidating or restricting powers previously exercised by commanders and other line personnel, and by depositing greater ultimate authority in the hands of lawyers and judges."[11]

In his dissent in *O'Callaghan*, Justice John Harlan warned that "the infinite permutations of possibly relevant factors [establishing court-martial jurisdiction] are bound to create confusion and proliferate litigation over the [court-martial] jurisdiction issue." That proved to be exactly the case, and in 1987 the Supreme Court overruled *O'Callaghan* in *U.S. v. Solario*.[12] In *Solario* the Court abandoned the "service connection" test in favor of essentially "green card" jurisdiction (in reference to the then green identification cards that members of the armed forces carried). It reestablished personal jurisdiction in courts-martial based exclusively on the military status of the accused.

Perceptions about the supposed callousness of the system, and even questions about its legitimacy, continue to haunt military jurisprudence. As recently as 2009, Chief Justice John Roberts cited with approval the 1957 case of *Reid v. Covert* for the proposition that "traditionally, military justice has been a rough form of justice emphasizing summary procedures, speedy convictions and stern penalties with a view to maintaining obedience and fighting fitness in the ranks."[13] What is remarkable about his comment is that what is apparently believed to be a "rough form of justice" is, nevertheless, acceptable in the military of a democratic superpower.

Actually, the notion that the military system is a "rough form of justice" is not borne out by most objective analyses. A 2012 study by the Congressional Research Service amply demonstrates that military courts generally provide the same procedural safeguards as those found in civilian federal criminal trials.[14] In a comparison to state court criminal proceedings using a hypothetical case arising in the state of Virginia as an example, two military attorneys found that in nearly every instance the armed forces provided as much as or more due process for a defendant. In particular, the greater resources available to military defense counsel were highlighted.[15]

Rather ironically, it is not altogether clear that the founding fathers ever intended courts-martial to involve the elaborate procedures they employ today. For example, the Constitution specifically exempts the military from the Fifth Amendment requirement for a grand jury indictment. Furthermore, the Court in *Covert* observed that "it has not been clearly settled to what extent the *Bill of Rights* and other protective parts of the Constitution apply to military trials."[16] That 1957 dictum remains largely true today, as a CAAF judge explicitly noted in her 2005 dissent in *U.S. v. Mizgala*.[17]

Thus, it can be argued that the rights of service members in disciplinary matters are much dependent upon the largesse of Congress.[18] As the Supreme Court said in the 1953 case of *Burns v. Wilson*:

> The rights of men in the armed forces must perforce be conditioned to meet certain overriding demands of discipline and duty, and the civil courts are not the agencies which must determine the precise balance to be struck in this adjustment. The Framers expressly entrusted that task to Congress.[19]

However, for its part, CAAF claims rather inexplicably that "the Supreme Court has assumed the Bill of Rights applies to the military" and insists it applies "absent military necessity or operational needs."[20] As a practical matter, the effectiveness—and fairness—of the system depends upon those who practice in it. These are principally military lawyers called JAGs (the acronym for their formal title of "judge advocates"). JAGs are not just licensed lawyers, but today are among the best and brightest the legal profession has to offer; in recent years only one in twenty applicants has been accepted by the service JAG corps.

Once a lawyer is licensed in a U.S. jurisdiction and commissioned into one of the services, the UCMJ requires the judge advocate general (the senior lawyer of each of the services) to certify the individual as competent to defend persons in courts-martial. In addition, the judge advocate general of each of the services has statutory responsibilities to supervise his assigned JAGs and to provide oversight of the administration of military justice throughout the armed forces. As a check on abuses in the field, JAGs are entitled by law to communicate directly with senior JAGs, notwithstanding any efforts by field commanders to the contrary.[21]

Many offenses prosecuted in the military justice system involve the same sort of crimes (e.g., assault, larceny, DWI) denounced in any criminal code. Indeed, the third clause of Article 134 of the UCMJ (the "catchall" article[22]) permits the assimilation of virtually the entire federal criminal code into military law. There are, however, limits to integrating civilian law into the code. In the 2012 case of *U.S. v. Hayes*, CAAF refused to permit bootstrapping *state* criminal codes into the UCMJ.[23]

Even among "conventional" offenses there are some differences based on the special considerations of military service. For example, Article 134 criminalizes deaths that are the result of simple negligence, a standard of culpability commonly found in civil lawsuits but not in the criminal courts. In the 1979 case of *U.S. v. Kick*, the Court of Military Appeals explained,

> There is a special need in the military to make the killing of another as a result of simple negligence a criminal act. This is because of the extensive use, handling and operation in the course of official duties of such dangerous instruments as weapons, explosives, aircraft, vehicles, and the like. The danger to others from careless acts is so great that society demands protection.[24]

Of course, the UCMJ contains a variety of offenses that are unique to the military. Absence offenses are a good example. Desertion—which is quitting one's post with the intent to stay away permanently—carries the death penalty if done in time of war. Quite obviously, no armed force can tolerate troops abandoning their duties, especially in the face of combat. Lesser absences are also criminalized. In the military, being even a minute late for work during peacetime is a crime punishable by up to a month in jail. Of course, that measure of punishment is rarely imposed, but "failure to repair" (as lateness is termed in the military) commonly results in an administrative forfeiture of pay or even a reduction in rank.

The criminalization of absence offenses is one illustration of how the UCMJ helps create a mind-set of obedience and attention to detail that is so necessary for success in war. Another example—and one that often perplexes civilians—is dereliction of duty. There are several dereliction offenses, depending on whether the failure to execute an assignment was willful, negligent, or the result of culpable inefficiency.

The MCM does, however, make it clear that when the failure to complete that task is genuinely the result of inability—such as when a soldier repeatedly fails to pass his marksmanship test despite earnest effort—he is not criminally liable (although he may find himself required to put in many extra hours of practice, to include time that otherwise might have been off-duty). Still, when a military member's failure to do his duty is, in fact, willful or negligent, then the punishment is more severe than for someone who fails to complete a project for a civilian company or organization.

The UCMJ also lists a number of offenses designed to help control the natural terror that combat can produce in individuals. Besides desertion in wartime, capital punishment may also be imposed for behaviors that may seem rather innocuous or even inexplicable to civilians, but is understandable given the paramount interests of a military organization at war. Thus, "sleeping on post," failing to do the "utmost" to "encounter the enemy," and "shamefully" surrendering are all death penalty offenses. Additionally, execution is authorized for "cowardly conduct," which the MCM defines as "misbehavior motivated by fear."[25]

To be sure, a serviceman's mental state can exonerate him if—as is typical in civilian jurisprudence—he suffers from "a severe mental disease or defect" and as a result of that he is "unable to appreciate the nature and quality" of the act or its "wrongfulness."[26] Post-traumatic stress disorder (PTSD), for example, does not, per se, excuse misconduct, absent a showing it has the effect discussed above; it may, however, be raised as a matter of mitigation of any sentence.[27]

Despite the rather large number of UCMJ offenses that carry the death penalty, no service member has been executed since 1961. Six soldiers are currently on death row at the U.S. Disciplinary Barracks in Fort Leavenworth, Kansas,[28] but none is there for a conviction for uniquely military offenses; all are sentenced for crimes that include premeditated murder as at least one of the charges.

The armed forces necessarily place a premium on the obedience of orders. In the 1890 case of *In Re Grimley*, the Supreme Court noted that an "army is not a deliberative body.... [Its] law is that of obedience. No question can be left open as to the right to command in the officer, or the duty of obedience in the soldier."[29] In the 1983 case of *Chappell v. Wallace*, the Court was equally unambiguous when it said, "The inescapable demands of military discipline and obedience to orders cannot be taught on battlefields; the habit of immediate compliance with military procedures and orders must be virtually reflex, with no time for debate or reflection."[30]

Nonetheless, military law imposes no obligation to obey an unlawful order. Although all orders are presumed lawful, and soldiers disobey them at their peril, there are limits to the "orders" defense. In the infamous Vietnam-era My Lai massacre case, Army lieutenant William Calley claimed his murderous behavior was in response to superior orders he had allegedly received. The Court of Military Appeals, after noting that Calley was "convicted of the premeditated murder of 22 infants, children, women, and old men" who were his prisoners, rejected out of hand the assertion that Calley's intelligence was such that he might not have known that the supposed order was unlawful. The court dryly observed that "whether Lieutenant Calley was the most ignorant person in the United States Army in Vietnam, or the most intelligent, he must be presumed to know that he could not kill the people involved here."[31]

However, when an order is not actually unlawful, the fact that it may be unreasonable or contrary to one's personal belief does not excuse disobedience. Indeed, the MCM explicitly states that the "dictates of a personal conscience, religion, or personal philosophy cannot justify or excuse the disobedience of an otherwise lawful order."[32] Thus, in U.S. v. Rockwood, an Army captain's conviction for offenses related to his departure from his base against his superior orders during the 1994 Haiti relief mission was sustained on appeal despite his claim that he had a moral and legal obligation under international human rights law to inspect the admittedly deplorable conditions of Haiti's National Penitentiary.[33] Such decisions, the court found, were the prerogative of command, not of individual subordinate soldiers.

Among the more fascinating aspects of the UCMJ are the provisions related to commissioned officers. Subordinates can be punished not just for disobeying officers, but also for being disrespectful in acts or language. In this regard, the MCM pointedly states that "truth is no defense." At the same time, however, officers are held accountable in ways enlisted personnel are not. In finding that officers can be sent to trial for offenses that are typically handled administratively when involving enlisted personnel, the CMA observed that the Armed Services comprise a hierarchical society, which is based on military rank. Within that society commissioned officers have for many purposes been set apart from other groups. Since officers have special privileges and hold special positions of honor, it is not unreasonable that they be held to a high standard of accountability.[34]

One of the special restrictions placed on officers is the prohibition in Article 88 against "contemptuous words" against the president, the secretary of defense, and other civilian officials. Though the MCM cautions that "private conversations should not ordinarily be charged" and that adverse criticism "even though emphatically expressed" ordinarily should not be alleged, speech is criminalized in a way that would be unconstitutional in civilian society.[35]

In one of the rare instances where an Article 88 violation was prosecuted, Lieutenant Henry H. Howe was convicted for attending a demonstration in 1965 in El Paso, Texas, while carrying a sign that said "LET'S HAVE MORE THAN A 'CHOICE' BETWEEN PETTY, IGNORANT, FACISTS IN 1968" and, on the other side, "END JOHNSON'S FACIST AGGRESSION IN VIETNAM." The CMA upheld the conviction against First Amendment challenges, finding that what Article 88 properly sought to "avoid is the impairment of discipline and the promotion of insubordination by an officer" and that under the circumstance the conduct constituted "a clear and present danger to discipline within our armed services."[36]

Unlike Article 88, which is rarely alleged, Article 133—which denounces "conduct unbecoming an officer and a gentlemen"—is not infrequently included on charge sheets involving officers. In another Vietnam-era case, *Parker v. Levy*, the Supreme Court examined whether "conduct unbecoming an officer" was too vague a standard to which to attach criminal liability.[37] Levy, an Army doctor and commissioned officer, was convicted for making statements to enlisted troops such as that he did not "see why any colored soldier would go to Viet Nam: they should refuse to go to Viet Nam and if sent should refuse to fight" and that "Special Forces personnel are liars and thieves and killers of peasants and murderers of women and children."

In rejecting Levy's habeas corpus petition,[38] the Supreme Court observed that it had "long recognized that the military is, by necessity, a specialized society separate from civilian society" and that the "military has ... by necessity, developed laws and traditions of its own." Those differences, the Court said, arose from the fact that "the primary business of armies and navies is to fight or be ready to fight wars should the occasion arise."

Thus, the Court believed that notwithstanding the broad language of Article 133, Levy could have no reasonable expectation that using the words he did under the circumstances would be anything other than violative of the UCMJ provision. In so concluding, the Court pointed out that the "fundamental necessity for obedience, and the consequent necessity for imposition of discipline, may render permissible within the military that which would be constitutionally impermissible outside it." Today, Article 133 charges often incorporate the elements of a wide range of offenses, to include relatively minor ones. Although prosecutors are required to prove the additional element that the misconduct was "conduct unbecoming an officer," any conviction permits the dismissal of the officer (the equivalent of a dishonorable discharge for an enlisted person).

Of course, not all violations of the UCMJ automatically result in a court-martial. Commanders are urged to attempt to resolve misbehavior at the lowest possible level, and most disciplinary measures are administrative, not judicial. For example, commanders and supervisors will employ corrective measures to include oral and written counselings, admonitions, and reprimands. For the vast majority of troops, these administrative tools are sufficient for correcting behavior.

More aggravated situations, yet still "minor offenses," can be handled by a commander via a nonjudicial procedure under Article 15 of the UCMJ.[39] These are summary administrative proceedings, often conducted by commanders without the involvement of legal personnel, that permit the imposition of limited fines, restrictions, extra duties, and—where facilities are available—correctional custody. Correctional custody is designed to be akin to confinement, but more of a reversion to the strict regime of boot camp in order to reinstill military virtues in the offender and return him to duty. (It is reported that punishment pursuant to Article 15 is what is being recommended in the December 2011 incident involving the burning of Korans in Afghanistan.[40]) In cases where an individual is deemed unsuitable for further service, but not for reasons warranting a court-martial, administrative discharge may be directed.

If a particular disciplinary situation appears to warrant more than administrative disposition, criminal charges are "preferred" on the accused as the first step in the court-martial process. While military law permits any person "subject to the Code" to prefer charges, it usually falls to the immediate commander to do so. Depending upon the seriousness of the allegation, the commander may decide—with the advice of his or her JAG—to dismiss the charges or to resolve them administratively. The commander, if authorized to convene courts-martial, can also "refer" the case to a summary or special court-martial. If, however, the charges are serious enough, he may order a formal investigation pursuant to Article 32 of the UCMJ.

Article 32 investigations are often considered to be a statutory substitute for the grand jury process, even though the Constitution explicitly exempts military cases from that requirement. In practice, Article 32 hearings are much different from grand jury proceedings in that they are usually public proceedings with the accused present and accompanied by counsel. The accused (or, more likely, his lawyer) is permitted to interrogate government witnesses and call his own.

In many ways, the Article 32 hearings have evolved into mini-trials where allegations are sometimes "litigated," even though the hearings are, technically, merely investigations. The hearing officer, ordinarily a JAG, will draft a report that will be forwarded to the commander along with the assembled evidence and transcripts of testimony. The hearing officer will make a nonbinding recommendation as to how the charges should be resolved.

Several types of courts-martial exist to which a commander can refer charges: summary, special, and general. They are mainly distinguished by the maximum punishments that can be imposed.[41] A summary court can jail a soldier for thirty days, but not impose a discharge. A special court-martial can confine a defendant for up to a year, and the sentence can include a bad conduct discharge. A general court-martial can adjudge any punishment up to the maximum authorized for the crime, to include death and a dishonorable discharge. Besides the stigma attached to a "bad conduct discharge" and a "dishonorable discharge" (called a "dismissal" when imposed upon an officer), these punitive separations can cause the loss of eligibility for many federal and state veterans' benefits.

The court-martial itself draws much from civilian trial processes. One key difference is that the "jurors" (called "members" in military parlance) are not randomly selected, as they generally are in civilian cases, but rather selected by the commander, based, as the UCMJ requires, on a determination that the officers are "best qualified by reason of age, education, training, experience, length of service, and judicial temperament."[42] Though the concern is often understandably raised that a commander could "pack" a court panel to achieve a desired result, in practice such is rarely the case.

There are a number of reasons for this, beginning with the fact that the independence of the officers selected (the panel may include up to one-third enlisted members if an enlisted accused so requests) is protected by Article 37 of the UCMJ, which prohibits any effort to coerce or unlawfully influence the members or, for that matter, the military judge or counsel for either side. In addition, the appellate courts, and especially CAAF, have been exceptionally rigorous in their effort to root out "unlawful command influence," which it has long condemned as the "mortal enemy of the military justice system."[43]

Court-martial panels also differ from most civilian courts in their size, as well as the manner in which they come to their findings. Summary courts-martial consist of a single officer, while special courts need at least three members, and general courts must have at least five. If the accused does not choose to be tried by military judge alone, his case will be decided by a secret written ballot of the members during their closed deliberation. In military cases, however, a conviction requires only a two-thirds agreement of the panel; there are no "hung juries" in military trials. In addition, the sentence also is decided by the members (if the accused does not elect trial by military judge alone). Like the finding, a sentence requires a two-thirds vote, unless the sentence includes confinement for more than ten years (requiring a three-fourths vote) or death (unanimous agreement is mandated).

Besides incarceration, military sentences can include reprimands, fines and forfeiture of pay, hard labor without confinement, reduction in grade, and a punitive discharge. Although not yet tested for constitutionality, death is the only authorized punishment for spying in violation of Article 106 of the UCMJ. Other military death penalty cases usually require procedures similar to those found in civilian jurisprudence, including the presentation of aggravating factors.

The appellate process for court-martial convictions is more elaborate than that typically available in civilian settings. Although its extent largely depends upon the severity of the punishment imposed, it typically begins with review by the commander who convened the court-martial. That review, aided by the advice of a judge advocate, cannot result in a reversal of acquittal to any charge or any increase in sentence, but only in the approval of the adjudged findings and sentence, or a mitigation of either in some way.

Again, depending upon the severity of the sentence, the next level of review ordinarily is conducted by the court of review of each individual service. What is unusual about these courts is that they are empowered not only to act on errors of law, but also to conduct a fresh (de novo) review of the facts and overturn the case—even in the absence of legal error—if they find the proof insufficient. Moreover, they may reassess the appropriateness of the sentence and diminish it if they wish. Essentially, they can only affirm the decision or act in some way to the defendant's benefit.

The next level of appeal is to the Court of Appeals for the Armed Forces. As already noted, the CAAF is empowered to review only errors of law (except in the Coast Guard, the judges in service courts of review are military appellate judges). Unlike the service courts of review, however, CAAF's powers are limited to errors of law. Beyond CAAF, appeal can be made to the Supreme Court, but only in limited circumstances. As the Congressional Research Service put it,

> [The Supreme Court's] power to review military cases generally extends only to cases that the CAAF has also reviewed. For this reason, the CAAF's discretion over the acceptance or denial of appeals often functions as a gatekeeper for military appellants' access to Supreme Court review. If the CAAF denies an appeal, the U.S. Supreme Court will typically lack the authority to review the decision. In contrast, criminal appellants in Article III courts have an automatic right of appeal to federal courts of appeals and then a right to petition the Supreme Court for review.[44]

An issue related to military justice—but very separate—is the matter of military commissions. Military commissions have a long history in the United States. They were used during the Mexican War, and thousands of Americans were tried by military commission during the Civil War, including anti-Lincoln conspirators. However, in 1866 the Supreme Court in the case of *Ex Parte Milligan* found unconstitutional the domestic use of military commissions against nonbelligerents in areas where the courts were still functioning.[45]

During World War II, civilians in Hawaii were tried by military tribunals under the authority of the Hawaii Organic Act, which permitted declarations of martial law. However, the Supreme Court applied its *Milligan* precedent in finding that despite the statutory authorization, such trials were unconstitutional where U.S. civilian courts were able to function.[46]

Nevertheless, when German saboteurs—including a naturalized American citizen, Herbert Haupt—were delivered to U.S. shores by a Nazi submarine in 1942, the Court distinguished *Milligan*. In denying the saboteurs' petition for habeas corpus, the Supreme Court concluded in *Ex Parte Quirin* that "those who, during time of war, pass surreptitiously from enemy territory into our own, discarding their uniforms upon entry, for the commission of hostile acts involving destruction of life or property, have the status of unlawful combatants punishable as such by military commission."[47]

As to the American citizen among the saboteurs, the Court said:

> Citizenship in the United States of an enemy belligerent does not relieve him from the consequences of a belligerency which is unlawful because in violation of the law of war. Citizens who associate themselves with the military arm of the enemy government, and with its aid, guidance and direction enter this country bent on hostile acts are enemy belligerents within the meaning of the Hague Convention and the law of war.

Those "consequences" included being subject to trial by a military commission. Six of the eight—including Haupt—were executed within weeks of their conviction.

Following World War II, General Tomoyuki Yamashita, the Japanese commander in the Philippines, where horrific atrocities were committed by his troops, was tried by military commission. Charged not with personally committing or ordering war crimes, but rather with "unlawfully disregarding and failing to discharge his duty as a commander to control the acts of members of his command by permitting them to commit war crimes," he was tried and convicted by military commission. In denying his application for leave to file a petition for a writ of habeas corpus and writ of prohibition, the Supreme Court found his commission trial lawful, even though hostilities had ended.[48] Yamashita was hanged on February 23, 1946.

The case has been widely criticized, but still stands for the important principle of command accountability, *respondeat superior*, the concept that commanders are responsible for the actions of their subordinates. Today, command responsibility incorporates requirements for some "information of knowledge that triggers a duty to act" with respect to "ongoing or anticipated law of war violations by subordinates," as well as a "causal relationship between the commander's omission and the war crimes committed by the subordinate."[49]

In the aftermath of 9/11, military commissions took on something of an unprecedented role when President George W. Bush issued his "Military Order" concerning detention of terrorism suspects, as well as their potential trial by military commission.[50] It seems as if the design for the commission process used an improved version of the much-respected Nuremberg trials as the template. Those proceedings were not, however, military commissions conducted under U.S. law, but rather were international tribunals.

Regardless, it is doubtful that the processes used at Nuremberg could survive scrutiny today (e.g., the Nuremberg defendants did not have the right to remain silent, or challenge the impartiality of the fact-finding judges). Indeed, William Shawcross argues that Nuremberg offered defendants fewer rights than did the military commissions created by the Bush administration. According to Shawcross, any "German in the dock at Nuremberg would be astonished to learn of his rights, privileges, and entitlements, if he were suddenly transferred by time machine to the court in Guantanamo."[51]

In any event, in 2006 the Supreme Court in *Hamdan v. Rumsfeld*[52] held that the military commissions devised by President Bush violated both the UCMJ and international law. This generated a number of statutory and regulatory changes, which ended with the implementation of the Military Commission Act of 2009.[53] Although some scholars remain dissatisfied with commissions as formulated today,[54] a comparison with courts-martial under the UCMJ suggests that the commissions are generally on firm legal footing, even as issues such as the scope of the charges triable by military commissions persist.[55]

While courts-martial remain distinct from military commissions, an issue has emerged with them that relates to a fundamental concern of the commission cases: When can military authorities try a civilian who is not an enemy belligerent? As Professor Stephen I. Vladeck points out, "The Supreme Court repeatedly recognized categorical constitutional limits on the military's power to try civilians (including contractors), at least during 'peacetime.'"[56] Additionally, Vladeck notes that the CMA invalidated trials of contractors during the Vietnam War: because the conflict was never formally "declared" a war, it did not fit the statutory construct permitting the trial of "civilians accompanying the force" as provided by the UCMJ.[57]

However, after a *foreign* contract employee of the Army assaulted another contract employee in Iraq in 2008, the alleged offender found himself tried by a U.S. court-martial. In discussing jurisdiction, the Army court of review observed that the law had changed since the Vietnam-era cases:

> In 2006, Congress amended Article 2(a)(10), which had long authorized UCMJ jurisdiction over "persons serving with or accompanying an armed force in the field" during "time of war." This amendment was effected by replacing the temporal requirement of a "time of war" with "time of declared war or contingency operation."[58]

Because of the statutory revision, the Army court concluded that since the incident occurred at an overseas combat outpost during actual hostilities, court-martial jurisdiction was properly found. CAAF agreed and affirmed the conviction,[59] but the case is likely to make its way to the Supreme Court.

Military law today is a well-developed corpus of jurisprudence, but one not without controversy. Incidents from the wars in Iraq and Afghanistan indicate an erosion of discipline.[60] Allegations that soldiers engaged in the killing of civilians for "sport" in 2010[61] were followed by accounts in late 2011 and 2012 of other acts of indiscipline, including reports of troops burning Korans,[62] urinating on Taliban corpses,[63] and posing with body parts of enemy fighters,[64] not to mention the shocking allegations of the cold-blooded murder of seventeen Afghans civilians by a U.S. Army sergeant.[65]

Senior military officers and defense officials admit they are deeply troubled by the events,[66] because they keenly understand the destructive effect of indiscipline on the military's ability to accomplish its mission. Secretary of Defense Leon Panetta told troops recently that "these days, it takes only seconds for one picture to suddenly become an international headline … and those headlines can impact the mission we're engaged in, they can put your fellow service members at risk, they can hurt morale, and they can damage our standing in the world."[67]

Panetta is echoing a point that former commandant of the Marine Corps General Charles C. Krulak made in 1999: that given the enormous power of instant, worldwide media, every act carries potentially strategic consequences, even those committed by very junior troops in remote locations. Krulak presciently explained,

> In many cases, the individual Marine will be the most conspicuous symbol of American foreign policy and will potentially influence not only the immediate tactical situation, but the operational and strategic levels as well. His actions, therefore, will directly impact the outcome of the larger operation; and he will become ... the *Strategic Corporal*.[68]

Clearly, misconduct can have a real effect on operational success in the twenty-first century. Many defense strategists cite the collapse of discipline that led to the detainee abuse scandal at Abu Ghraib as one of the worst setbacks the U.S armed forces suffered since 9/11, much because of the propaganda victory that it handed the insurgents. General David Petraeus has said that "Abu Ghraib and other situations like that are non-biodegradable. They don't go away. The enemy continues to beat you with them like a stick."[69]

There can be many explanations for erosion in discipline, but one aspect may be the military justice system itself, and the outcome of the 2005 Haditha incident in Iraq could be illustrative. This case arose from a situation where twenty-four innocent Iraqi civilians were killed by U.S. Marines in a botched response to an improvised explosive device attack on a convoy. Of the eight original suspects, six had charges dropped, one was tried and acquitted, and the last accused—Staff Sergeant Frank Wuterich—negotiated a plea agreement in 2012 that limited his punishment to a demotion but no jail time. Many military justice experts were at a loss to explain the apparent leniency in his case, as well as the apparent inability to convict any of the others allegedly involved.[70]

However, the complex evidentiary rules—almost identical to those applicable in the most staid federal courtroom in an American suburb—may have also played a role. The *New York Times* reported that beyond missteps by military prosecutors and a reluctance of decision makers to second-guess the actions of troops in combat, "collecting physical evidence and finding witnesses can be difficult because the killings often occur in unstable and dangerous areas, and the cases often come to light only after time has passed."[71] It is no surprise, therefore, that after reports of the killing of seventeen Afghan civilians in March 2012, CNN reported that "critics are questioning the military's ability to conduct the transparent, speedy investigation demanded by Afghanistan in the case."[72]

Decades of "civilianizing" and "judicializing" of the military justice system may have altered the system beyond what the Constitution would require for military jurisprudence, and certainly far beyond the "rough justice" of Chief Justice Roberts's belief. Indeed, as suggested above, the process today may be too cumbersome and complex for the battlefield environments where it is needed to function.[73] Major Franklin Rosenblatt presents a disturbing picture of the current situation in a 2010 article, "Non-Deployable: The Court-Martial System in Combat from 2001–2009."[74] According to Rosenblatt, "After-action reports from deployed judge advocates show a nearly unanimous recognition that the full-bore application of military justice was impossible in the combat zone."[75]

Rosenblatt cites a catalog of reasons for the troubles in applying the UCMJ in remote areas, ranging from logistical difficulties to procedural shortcomings to attitudinal issues, and warns that "deployed courts-martial may someday become a relic of military history rather than a viable commander's tool."[76] Saddling commanders in austere locations with adhering to many of the same intricacies of a domestic judicial system may be proving to be too much. Lieutenant Colonel Michael Stahlman, a Marine JAG, admits that "commanders often perceive the military justice system as a roadblock instead of an effective leadership tool."[77]

Whether UCMJ complexities and burdens are the cause or not, it appears that commanders may be avoiding taking the disciplinary action they should, and this can create a dangerous attitude among the troops. In fact, a new Army report suggests commanders are "opting out" of the system:

> The rise in crime in contrast to the decline in disciplinary action (e.g., court martial, summary court martial, Article 15), retention of multiple felony offenders and the deliberate change in terms of reference

regarding criminal misconduct all point to a softening in the perception of criminality.... Subtle changes in policy language (e.g., removing the term "criminal" from "serious criminal misconduct"), which may inadvertently shift leader perception of criminality, will not change the nature of the criminal act or alter its impact on victims, good order and discipline, and unit readiness.[78]

Still, some experts insist that the system can work, even in the field. In a recent article, Major E. John Gregory cites his own Army experiences in Iraq and argues that they demonstrate that

when a proper emphasis is placed on military justice in theater by both the command and military justice practitioners, the court-martial system is a fully deployable system of justice which is not overly burdensome, meets the command's disciplinary needs, and is highly protective of an accused's rights.[79]

Encouraging words for sure, but the trick is obtaining the "proper emphasis" under circumstances where there are multiple operational demands on a commander's time and resources. The answer is not, however, to ship miscreants home, as some have suggested, but rather to examine the "civilianized" processes to determine which ones are truly constitutionally required—or prudent normatively— and streamline the system accordingly to make it compatible with the needs of discipline in the twenty-first century.

The ability to impose discipline, in situ, is vitally important to any military organization in combat, as otherwise misconduct can become a ticket out of a war zone. At the height of the Vietnam War in 1968, a court-martial was conducted in an underground bunker at Khe Sanh. As recorded by Gary Solis in his masterly *Marines and Military Law in Vietnam: Trial by Fire*, all the proceedings were conducted as the enemy poured intense artillery, rocket, and mortar fire onto the isolated outpost.[80] The court-martial acquitted the accused of smoking marijuana, but convicted him of sleeping on post and sentenced him to reduction in grade and forfeitures. The prosecutor aptly noted that the "sentence was appropriate" because the "accused was not sent back to the brig or otherwise allowed to escape the confines of Khe Sanh."[81]

Interestingly, some nations—including especially heirs to the British military justice system—are increasingly civilianizing their systems even more than the United States has done, often with reference to resolving military disciplinary matters in civilian courts.[82] Casting cases to civilian courts does not, however, necessarily provide the desired justice. Consider the case of former Marine sergeant Jose Luis Nazario.

Although retired military members may be subject to court-martial, military jurisdiction generally terminates at the end of an enlistment or when a military member is otherwise discharged without retirement.[83] Thus, Nazario, who was discharged before allegations related to the killing of four civilians in Iraq were resolved, had to be tried in a civilian court. Following his acquittal in 2008, news reports related that "several jurors acknowledged that they also did not feel qualified to judge a Marine's actions in the midst of a battle."[84] One juror said "she hoped the verdict would send a message to the troops in Iraq" to the effect that they would "realize that they shouldn't be second-guessed, that we support them and know that they're doing the right thing."[85]

Another challenge to the military justice system today relates to the handling of sexual assault allegations. In 2006, Congress, spurred primarily by heartrending but anecdotal claims of mishandled cases, and dissatisfied with the military's efforts to address these alleged incidents, revised the sexual assault offense found in Article 120 of the UCMJ. The result was such a bloated and confusing statute that in 2011 CAAF found key provisions unconstitutional,[86] necessitating a complete legislative replacement (which itself may be subject to challenge).[87]

The military's difficulty in dealing with sexual assault cases may seem to be a manifestation of the victimization of women in an organization overwhelmingly populated by males (women compose only 14.6 percent of the 1.4 million active-duty service members[88]). The New York Times, for example, claims that it "is even harder for military women to get away from abusers they work with or for; they can't just quit their jobs or leave a combat zone."[89] This misperceives the issue. A 2010 Department of Defense study did show that a higher *percentage* of women (4.4 percent) than men (0.9 percent) reported "unwanted sexual contact."[90] However, the translation of those percentages into actual *numbers* shows that considerably more men (approximately 11,288) perceived themselves as victims of "unwanted sexual contact" than did women (approximately 9,433).

The armed forces have made an extraordinary effort to crack down on sexual assaults, establishing a web of victim's resources, special policies and reports, training, and—significantly—an increased emphasis on prosecution.[91] However, criticism—especially in Congress—continues unabated.[92] Accordingly, further legislation is now before Congress, a proposal called the "STOP Act."[93] This legislation has a number of features, including the establishment of a Sexual Assault Oversight and Response Council, separate from the military chain of command, who would, in turn, appoint a "director of military prosecution" with authority over sexual offenses in the armed forces.[94]

This proposal to remove field commanders from acting in this particular class of offenses is controversial. Army major general Gary Patton, the newly appointed head of the military's Sexual Assault Prevention and Response Office, warns that "if you were to take the disciplinary component and put it into some external, centralized, whatever, body, independent, apart from the chain of the command, you've just removed the commander from the problem and tied the commander's hands."[95] His predecessor, Air Force major general Mary Kay Hertog, agreed with having more senior commanders take the initial action in these cases but added,

> Some have argued that allegations of sexual assault are best addressed outside the chain of command. I disagree.... [Keeping the] initial disposition of these cases within the military chain of command ... will ensure that the military itself remains responsible for addressing this critically important issue. Experience has shown time and again that strong internal leadership is effective in bringing about major change. The chain of command must ensure justice and be held to account for the consequences.[96]

Furthermore, the STOP Act proposal seems to assume that the military's difficulties with sexual assault prosecution are somehow uniquely the result of command indifference (or worse). Indeed, in its proposed "findings," the STOP Act does cast aspersions on military officers by stating that the "great deference afforded command discretion raises serious concerns about conflicts of interest and the potential for abuse of power." However, the American public—if not Congress—rates military officers second only to nurses as the profession having the highest honesty and ethics.[97] (Members of Congress were rated the lowest.) Similarly, an April 2012 poll showed the U.S. public had the most confidence in military leaders, and the least in those of Congress.[98] Thus, whatever negative view Congress may have as to the potential for abuse by military commanders, it would not seem to be shared by the public.

Moreover, the military's challenges with sexual assault cases are hardly unique: the Department of Justice, while citing increasing civilian prosecutions, concedes that in the United States *generally*, "sexual assault cases have been underreported and had low prosecution rates."[99] In any event, reports in December 2011 indicate that "military commanders sent about 70 percent more cases to courts-martial that started as rape or aggravated sexual-assault allegations than they did in 2009."[100] Additionally, Reuters reported in August 2012 that military "commanders routinely lack sufficient evidence to prosecute [sexual assault] cases."

Importantly, as in any justice system, it is a "fundamental right" of a service member to be subject to court-martial only where the evidence reasonably establishes that he or she has committed a triable offense.[101] Clearly, prudence is necessary, especially when there are a growing number of cases where, but for DNA technology, persons wrongly convicted of sexual assault would continue to languish in jail. The National Registry of Exonerations compiled by University of Michigan Law School and Northwestern University recently reported, for example, that there have been more than two thousand wrongful convictions for serious crimes since 1989 (the year DNA exonerating evidence became readily available).[102] Issues can also arise about misidentification and, occasionally, false reports.[103] It is simply counterfactual to blame military commanders for the difficulties associated with sexual assault cases, as these same matters would, one would assume, similarly impact the special directorate the draft legislation proposes to establish.

In addition, referring cases to an office with an obvious agenda to increase prosecutions and, presumably, convictions, raises serious questions not just about impartiality, *qua* impartiality, but also regarding the special "enemy" of the military justice system: unlawful command influence.[104] As a matter of law, improper influences on the military justice system can arise just as readily from politicians and others as from commanders formally part of the process.[105] Reports are already emerging that "the politics of rape are tainting [the] military justice system," with one defense counsel claiming that "reality is they're charging more and more people with bogus cases just to show that they do take it seriously."[106]

In fact, a McClatchy Newspaper analysis "found that the military is prosecuting a growing number of rape and sexual assault allegations, including highly contested cases that would be unlikely to go to trial in many civilian courts."[107] Concerns have been raised, it is reported, "that the anti-rape campaign of advocacy groups and Congress is influencing" commanders to send undeserving cases to trial.[108] According to Charles Feldmann, a former military and civilian prosecutor turned civilian defense attorney, a military officer is "not going to put his career at risk on an iffy rape case by not prosecuting it," because if he "dismisses a case and there's political backlash, he's going to take some real career heat over that dismissal."[109]

Efforts, such as the STOP Act, to diminish the role of commanders in military justice matters need to be approached with great caution, as doing so upends thousands of years of military practice and tradition built on hard-won experience. Those countries that have taken similar steps in recent years have found themselves struggling with disciplinary processes that are out of sync with battlefield realities, as well as the overall needs of armed organizations responsible for the nation's defense.[110] It should not be forgotten that, as the Supreme Court said in *Haig v. Agee*, "It is obvious and unarguable that no governmental interest is more compelling than the security of the Nation."[111]

The U.S. military justice system, despite many challenges, can, will—and must—continue to sustain the most powerful armed force the world has ever known. While its legitimacy, especially in an era of an all-volunteer military, depends upon the perception as well as the fact of fairness, it also needs to be effective and efficient. Achieving that aim requires thoughtful prudence, well grounded in the pragmatism generated by operational experience, and tempered by the values and principles of a liberal democracy. The importance of this responsibility cannot be overstated. As the renowned Roman military thinker Vegetius sagely warned, "No nation can be happy or secure that is remiss and negligent in the discipline of its troops."

Notes

1 Xenophon, *Anabasis,* book 3, chap. 1, http://ancienthistory.about.com/library/bl/bl_text_xenophon_anabasis_3.htm.
2 *Manual for Courts-Martial, United States,* pt. 1, 3 (2012) (hereinafter "MCM"), http://www.loc.gov/rr/frd/Military_Law/pdf/MCM-2012.pdf. Italics added.
3 U.S. Marine Corps, *The Military Justice System,* http://www.marines.mil/unit/judgeadvocate/Documents/JAM/Mil_Justice_Materials/Resources/MJFACTSHTS.html.
4 Codified in Title 10, U.S. Code § 801 et seq.
5 The UCMJ is established under Congress's authority "to make Rules for the Government and Regulation of the land and naval Forces," as found in Article I, Section 8, cl. 14 of the U.S. Constitution.
6 The Military Justice Act of 1968 was much in reaction to issues that arose during the Vietnam War. See, generally, William Thomas Allison, *Military Justice in Vietnam: The Rule of Law in American War* (Lawrence: University Press of Kansas, 2007).
7 See notes 74 to 82 below, and accompanying text.
8 See U.S. Secretary of Defense, Memorandum for the Secretaries of the Military Departments, Chairman of the Joint Chiefs of Staff, and Chair, Defense Legal Policy Board, Subject: Military Justice in Combat Zones, July 30, 2012, http://www.caaflog.com/wp-content/uploads/Military_Justice_in_Combat_Zones.pdf.
9 Laurence J. Morris, *Military Justice: A Guide to the Issues,* 9 (2010).
10 *O'Callaghan v. Parker,* 395 U.S. 258 (1969).
11 Captain John S. Cooke, "The United States Court of Military Appeals, 1975–77: Judicializing the Military Justice System," *Military Law Review* 76, no. 43 (1977).
12 *U.S. v. Solario,* 483 U.S. 435 (1987).
13 *U.S. v. Denedo,* 556 U.S. 904, 918 (2009) (Roberts, J., concurring in part and dissenting in part).
14 See, generally, R. Chuck Mason, *Military Justice: Courts-Martial, an Overview,* Congressional Research Service, March 14, 2012, http://www.fas.org/sgp/crs/natsec/R41739.pdf.

15 Major General Jack L. Rives and Major Stephen J. Ehlenbeck, "Civilian versus Military Justice in the United States: A Comparative Analysis," *Air Force Law Review* 52, no. 213 (2002), http://www.afjag.af.mil/shared/media/document/AFD-081204-027.pdf.

16 *Reid v. Covert*, 354 U.S. 1, 37 (1957).

17 *U.S. v. Mizgala*, 61 M.J. 122, 130 (CMA 2005).

18 Article I, Section 8, cl. 14 of the U.S. Constitution.

19 *Burns v. Wilson*, 346 U.S. 137, 140 (1953) (citations omitted), cited with approval in *Solario*, at 440.

20 *U.S. v. Khamsouk*, 57 M.J. 282, 297 (CAAF 2002),

21 10 U.S.C § 806.

22 10 U.S.C § 934, art. 134, UCMJ, provides as follows: "Though not specifically mentioned in this chapter, all disorders and neglects to the prejudice of good order and discipline in the armed forces, all conduct of a nature to bring discredit upon the armed forces, and crimes and offenses not capital, of which persons subject to this chapter may be guilty, shall be taken cognizance of by a general, special, or summary court-martial, according to the nature and degree of the offense, and shall be punished at the discretion of that court."

23 *U.S. v. Hayes*, __M.J.__ (CAAF 2012).

24 *U.S. v. Kick*, 7 M.J. 82, 84 (CMA 1979).

25 MCM.

26 Ibid., at Rules for Courts-Martial 916 (k)(1).

27 For a discussion of a proposed change to the military justice system's approach to PTSD, see Major Evan R. Seamone, "Reclaiming the Rehabilitative Ethic in Military Justice: The Suspended Discharge as a Method to Treat PTSD and TBI and Reduce Recidivism," *Military Law Review* 208, no. 1 (2011), http://www1.spa.american.edu/justice/documents/3605.pdf.

28 The Disciplinary Barracks is the main U.S. military prison. See, generally, U.S. Army Combined Arms Center, "U.S. Disciplinary Barracks," November 10, 2011, http://usacac.army.mil/cac2/usdb/.

29 *In Re Grimley*, 147 U.S. 147, 153 (1890).

30 *Chappell v. Wallace*, 462 U.S. 296, 300 (1983).

31 *U.S. v. Calley*, 48 C.M.R. 19, 29 (CMA 1973).

32 MCM, pt. IV, 14c(2) (a).

33 *U.S. v. Rockwood*, 52 M.J. 98 (CAAF 1999).

34 *U.S. v. Means*, 10 M.J. 162, 166 (CMA 1981).

35 MCM, pt. IV, 12c.

36 *U.S. v. Howe*, 37 C.M.R. 429, 438 (CMA 1967).

37 *Parker v. Levy*, 417 U.S. 733 (1974).

38 For a discussion of habeas corpus actions, see, generally, Legal Information Institute, Cornell University School of Law, "Habeas Corpus," August 19, 2010, http://www.law.cornell.edu/wex/habeas_corpus.

39   10 U.S.C § 815.

40   David S. Cloud, "Discipline Recommended in Afghanistan Koran Burning," *Los Angeles Times*, June 19, 2012, http://www.latimes.com/news/nation-world/nation/la-na-koran-burning-20120620,0,33470.story.

41   See, generally, Mason, *Military Justice*.

42   10 U.S.C § 825(d)(2).

43   *U.S. v. Thomas*, 22 M.J. 388, 393 (CMA 1986).

44   Mason, *Military Justice*.

45   *Ex Parte Milligan*, 71 U.S. 2 (1866).

46   *Duncan v. Kahanamoku*, 327 U.S. 304 (1946).

47   *Ex Parte Quirin*, 317 U.S. 1 (1942).

48   *In Re Yamashita*, 327 U.S. 1 (1946).

49   Geoffrey S. Corn et al., *The Law of Armed Conflict: An Operational Approach* (2012), 535.

50   White House, President George W. Bush, "Detention, Treatment, and Trial of Certain Non-Citizens in the War against Terrorism," November 13, 2001, http://georgewbush-whitehouse.archives.gov/news/releases/2001/11/20011113-27.html.

51   William Shawcross, *Justice and the Enemy: Nuremberg, 9/11, and the Trial of Khalid Sheikh Mohammed* (2011), 101.

52   *Hamdan v. Rumsfeld*, 548 U.S. 557 (2006).

53   See, generally, Jennifer K. Elsea, *Military Commission Act of 2009: Overview and Legal Issues*, Congressional Research Service, April 6, 2010, http://www.fas.org/sgp/crs/natsec/R41163.pdf.

54   See, for example, Jordan J. Paust, "Still Unlawful: The Obama Military Commissions, Supreme Court Holdings, and Deviant Dicta in the D.C. Circuit," *Cornell International Law Journal* 45, no. 2 (2012), 367.

55   See, for example, *U.S. v. Al Bahlul*, 820 F. Supp. 2d 1141 (CMCR 2011) (en banc).

56   Steve Vladeck, "Can the Military Court-Martial Civilian Contractors? Reflections on the Oral Argument in *United States v. Ali*," *Lawfare* (blog), April 12, 2012, http://www.lawfareblog.com/2012/04/can-the-military-court-martial-civilian-contractors-reflections-on-the-oral-argument-in-united-st ates-v-ali/.

57   *U.S. v. Averette*, 41 C.M.R. 363 (CMA 1970).

58   *U.S. v. Ali*, 70 M.J. 514 (ACMR 2011).

59   *U.S. v. Ali*, No. 12-0008/AR, 2012 CAAF LEXIS 815 (July 18, 2012), http://www.armfor.uscourts.gov/newcaaf/opinions/2011SepTerm/12-0008.pdf.

60   See, for example, Anna Mulrine, "Command Failure?" *Christian Science Monitor*, April 30, 2012, p. 10.

61   Mark Boal, "The Kill Team: How U.S. Soldiers in Afghanistan Murdered Innocent Civilians," *Rolling Stone*, March 27, 2011, http://www.rollingstone.com/politics/news/the-kill-team-20110327.

62 Cloud, "Discipline Recommended."

63 Graham Bowley and Matthew Rosenberg, "Video Inflames a Delicate Moment for U.S. in Afghanistan," *New York Times*, January 12, 2012, http://www.nytimes.com/2012/01/13/world/asia/video-said-to-show-marines-urinating-on-taliban-corpses.html?pagewanted=all.

64 David Zucchino, "U.S. Troops Posed with Body Parts of Afghan Bombers," *Los Angeles Times*, April 18, 2012, http://articles.latimes.com/2012/apr/18/nation/la-na-afghan-photos-20120418.

65 Matthew Rosenberg, "U.S. Sergeant Charged with 17 Counts of Murder in Afghan Killings," *New York Times*, March 23, 2012, http://www.nytimes.com/2012/03/24/us/staff-sgt-robert-bales-faces-murder-charges-in-afghan-killings.html.

66 Andrew Tilghman, "Officials Troubled over Behavior of U.S. Troops," *Army Times*, May 3, 2012, http://www.armytimes.com/news/2012/05/military-panetta-discipline-problems-050312w/.

67 Brian Bennett, "Defense Chief Leon Panetta Implores U.S. Troops to Avoid Misconduct," *Los Angeles Times*, May 4, 2012, http://articles.latimes.com/2012/may/04/nation/la-na-nn-panetta-military-discipline-20120504.

68 General Charles C. Krulak, "The Strategic Corporal: Leadership in the Three-Block War," *Marines* magazine, January 1999, www.au.af.mil/au/awc/awcgate/usmc/strategic_corporal.htm.

69 Joseph Berger, "US Commander Describes Battle of Marj as First Salvo in Campaign," *New York Times*, February 21, 2010 (quoting General David H. Petraeus), http://www.nytimes.com/2010/02/22/world/asia/22petraeus.html.

70 Charlie Savage and Elisabeth Bumiller, "An Iraqi Massacre, a Light Sentence and a Question of Military Justice," *New York Times*, January 27, 2012, http://www.nytimes.com/2012/01/28/us/an-iraqi-massacre-a-light-sentence-and-a-question-of-military-justice.html.

71 Ibid.

72 Chelsea J. Carter, "Missteps, Closed Culture Undermine Confidence in Military Justice System," CNN, March 27, 2012, http://www.cnn.com/2012/03/24/world/meast/afghanistan-bales-perception/index.html.

73 Secretary of Defense, Memorandum for the Secretaries, July 30, 2012.

74 Franklin D. Rosenblatt, "Non-Deployable: The Court-Martial System in Combat from 2001–2009," *Army Law*, September 2010, p. 12.

75 Ibid.

76 Ibid., 22.

77 Lieutenant Colonel Michael R. Stahlman, USMC, "Advocacy Outside of the Courtroom: Dispelling Common Misperceptions Held by Commanders," *Army Lawyer*, March 2002, 55, http://www.loc.gov/rr/frd/Military_Law/pdf/03-2002.pdf.

78 Department of the Army, *Army 2020: Generating Health and Discipline in the Force, Report 2012*, 163, http://usarmy.vo.llnwd.net/e2/c/downloads/232541.pdf.

79 Major E. John Gregory, "The Deployed Court-Martial Experience in Iraq 2010: A Model for Success," *Army Lawyer*, January 2012, p. 6, http://www.loc. gov/rr/frd/Military_Law/pdf/01-2012.pdf.

80 Lieutenant Colonel Gary B. Solis, *Marines and Military Law in Vietnam: Trial by Fire* (1989), 108.

81 Ibid.

82 See, generally, Stephen Strickey, "Civilianization and the Eroding Role of the Commanding Officer in the Court Martial Process: A Comparative View of Australia, Canada, and the United Kingdom and the United States," May 4, 2012 (unpublished manuscript; copy on file with the author).

83 See *U.S. v. Watson*, 69 M.J. 415 (2010).

84 Tony Perry, "Marine Acquitted in Killings of 4 Iraqis," *Los Angeles Times*, August 29, 2008, http://articles.latimes.com/2008/aug/29/local/me-marine29.

85 Ibid.

86 *U.S. v. Prather*, 69 M.J. 338 (CAAF 2011).

87 Michael Doyle and Marisa Taylor, "Congress Tries Again to Get Military Sexual Assault Laws Right," McClatchy Newspapers, December 13, 2011, http://www. mcclatchydc.com/2011/12/13/133000/congress-tries-again-to-get-military.html.

88 Women in Military Service for America Memorial Foundation, *Statistics on Women in the Military*, November 30, 2011, http://www.womensmemorial. org/PDFs/StatsonWIM.pdf.

89 "Sexual Violence and the Military," editorial, *New York Times*, March 8, 2012, http://www.nytimes.com/2012/03/09/opinion/sexual-violence-and-the-military.html.

90 Department of Defense, *Annual Report on Sexual Assault in the Military Fiscal Year 2010*, March 2011, p. 2, http://servicewomen.org/SAPRO%20 Reports/DoD_Fiscal_Year_2010_Annual_Report_on_Sexual_Assault_in_ the_Military.pdf.

91 See, generally, Department of Defense, Sexual Assault and Response Office, http://www.sapr.mil/ (last visited June 21, 2012).

92 See, for example, Jackie Speier, "Why Rapists in Military Get Away with It," CNN, June 21, 2012, http://www.cnn.com/2012/06/21/opinion/ speier-military-rape/index.html.

93 HR 3435, 112th Cong,. 1st sess., http://www.gpo.gov/fdsys/pkg/BILLS-112hr3435ih/ pdf/BILLS-112hr3435ih.pdf.

94 Ibid. According to Rep. Speier, "H.R. 3435, the Sexual Assault Training Oversight and Prevention Act (STOP Act), has 125 co-sponsors. It would take these cases out of the normal chain of command and place the jurisdiction, still within the military, in the hands of an impartial office staffed by experts—both military and civilian."

95 Lauren French, "Army General: Don't Hobble Commanders in Sex Assault Cases," Reuters, August 6, 2012, http://www.reuters.com/article/2012/08/06/ us-usa-military-assault-idUSBRE8751HE20120806.

96 Mary Kay Hertog, "The Pentagon: Assault Cases Must Go through Chain of Command," *USA Today*, April 24, 2012, http://www.usatoday.com/news/opinion/editorials/story/2012-04-24/military-sexual-assault-Panetta/54514466/1.

97 Gallup, *Honesty/Ethics in Professions*, November 19–21, 2010, http://www.gallup.com/poll/1654/honesty-ethics-professions.aspx.

98 Harris Poll, "Confidence in Congress Stays at Lowest Point in Almost Fifty Years," PR Newswire, May 21, 2012, http://www.prnewswire.com/news-releases/confidence-in-congress-stays-at-lowest-point-in-almost-fifty-years-152253655.html.

99 Philip Bulman, "Increasing Sexual Assault Prosecution Rates," U.S. Department of Justice, National Institute of Justice, November 2009, http://www.nij.gov/journals/264/SANE.htm.

100 Marisa Taylor and Chris Adams, "Military's Newly Aggressive Rape Prosecution Has Pitfalls," McClatchy Newspapers, November 28, 2011, http://www.mcclatchydc.com/2011/11/28/131523/militarys-newly-aggressive-rape.html.

101 *United States v. Hardin*, 7 M.J. 404 (CMA 1979).

102 David G. Savage, "Registry Tallies over 2,000 Wrongful Convictions since 1989," *Los Angeles Times*, May 20, 2012, http://articles.latimes.com/2012/may/20/nation/la-na-dna-revolution-20120521.

103 See Stewart Taylor Jr. and K. C. Johnson, *Until Proven Innocent: Political Correctness and the Shameful Injustices of the Duke Lacrosse Rape Case* (2007), 373–76.

104 See *U.S. v. Thomas*, 22 M.J. 388, 393 (CMA 1986).

105 See, generally, Michael La Marca, *Did the President and Secretary of Defense Commit Unlawful Command Influence? The Upcoming Cases of Nidal Hasan, Bradley Manny, and Robert Bales*, May 1, 2012 (unpublished manuscript; copy on file with the author).

106 Taylor and Adams, "Military's Newly Aggressive Rape Prosecution."

107 Ibid.

108 Ibid.

109 Ibid.

110 See, generally, Strickey, "Civilianization."

111 *Haig v. Agee*, 453 U.S. 280, 307 (1981).

12 :: Women in the U.S. Military

THE EVOLUTION OF GENDER NORMS AND MILITARY REQUIREMENTS

Michelle Sandhoff and Mady Wechsler Segal

Abstract: Though service in the military traditionally has been a masculine endeavor, women have played important roles in the military throughout history. In the United States, women have participated in every war. In this chapter, we consider the history of women's service in the U.S. military, which has increased dramatically over time. We analyze the reasons for the changes in women's participation in the armed forces. Enabling factors, those that can set the stage for increases in women's military participation, include changes in gender norms relating to family and labor force participation. Driving factors, such as legislative or judicial decree or changes in military needs, can quickly reshape women's military roles. We use this framework to describe the historical changes in women's service in the U.S. military, including an in-depth discussion of the roles of women in the conflicts in Afghanistan and Iraq.

Introduction

Service in the military—in the United States and most other nations—traditionally has been a masculine endeavor. Indeed, the military has been a gender-defining institution, functioning as a proving ground for masculinity. The masculine military culture, built on denigration of femininity and homosexuality, has long limited women's participation both formally and informally, through formal prohibitions on the participation of those deemed less than "real men," and informally through cultures of harassment and professional closure.[1] The emphasis on the masculine nature of military service has served to justify the exclusion of women and open homosexuals.[2] The exclusions reinforce the idea that service in the military, especially in offensive combat roles, is a masculine pursuit.[3]

This chapter shows how women's involvement in the United States armed forces has changed over time and analyzes the reasons for these changes. Although official roles open to women have changed in recent years, women have participated in every U.S. war. However, women's military roles and representation have increased dramatically over time, and recent changes have continued that evolution.

From nurses to Female Engagement Teams, from combat support to fighter pilots, women have helped meet the demands of varied military missions. Changes in the character of the U.S. military (including military personnel needs), civilian social conditions, and social norms regarding gender and sexual orientation have influenced women's military participation. This chapter describes the social processes that have shaped this evolution and presents a history of the changes in response to those processes.

What Shapes Women's Participation in the Military?

Both enabling factors and driving forces have facilitated the participation of women in the armed forces of the United States and other nations.[4] Enabling factors are those that work slowly to provide the background for women's involvement. Driving forces are those that serve as turning points that affect women's participation more quickly and directly.

Among enabling factors are changing gender roles in family, employment, and the military itself. Lesser family responsibilities for women increase their representation in the armed forces. Later age of marriage, later age at birth of first child, and fewer children have set the stage for increases in women's military participation.

Given the historical relationship between citizenship and service in the military, the granting of citizenship rights to women serves as a precursor to women's greater participation in all aspects of society, including civilian labor force participation and opportunities (and perhaps ultimately responsibilities) for military service.

Women's increased involvement in the civilian labor force has facilitated their increasing participation in the military. According to Mady Segal, "women's greater involvement in the workplace brings structural and cultural changes in the society that make military service more compatible with women's roles, thereby making their exclusion less justifiable."[5] In general, increased gender integration in the civilian sector increases women's military participation (though, with high gender segregation, women by necessity are employed by the armed forces to fill female-specific positions, as occurred in the United States during World War I, with women used as telephone operators).[6]

The changing missions of the military are also important: the less aggressive the role of the military (e.g., peacekeeping and homeland defense), the greater the opportunities are for women's participation.[7]

Driving forces have increased women's military roles dramatically. Changes in military structure and the national security situation (including the need for personnel), legislation increasing voluntary participation of women (or even requiring women's involvement), and judicial decisions prohibiting discrimination in the military on the basis of sex have directly increased women's military involvement.[8]

As nations have shifted from systems of conscription to voluntary service, women's military roles have increased because of personnel shortages.[9] Changes in military technology also have facilitated women's participation by changing the organization of warfare or women's social roles (or both). Most military jobs now are considered support rather than offensive combat and require less brawn and more brain.[10]

The national security situation and the need for personnel affect the participation of women nonlinearly. High levels of threat require more personnel, including women. At a low level of threat, countries that value gender equality include women in their armed forces, as there is little danger of actual armed conflict. At a medium level, threat perceptions are not high enough to mobilize women, yet the threat is credible enough that women in the armed forces seem to be in danger; these conditions seem to reduce women's military roles.[11]

What follows is a brief history of women's roles in the U.S. military, with reference to the reasons for changes—that is, the specific enabling factors and driving forces at the time. These include some examples from other nations to show that these social processes are not limited to the United States, but are more universal in their applicability. We give special attention to the current issues regarding women's military roles and experiences and the rapid evolution of social norms regarding gender and sexual orientation.

Women in the U.S. Military before 1973

Women have participated in the U.S. military throughout history, although permanent military roles for women were not legally recognized until 1948. Barred from military service because of their gender, women disguised themselves as men and boys and fought in the American Revolution, the War of 1812, the Mexican War, and the Civil War. Some women openly took on combat duties as replacements for their husbands, while other women served in noncombat positions as nurses and spies.[12] Women also performed support roles, such as cooking and laundry.[13] Social roles of women in civilian society dictated that combat tasks were viewed as masculine, while support tasks could be feminine. Although not recognized as members of the military, women served important support functions, doing what was needed to keep the military, and their men in it, going.

Women were first allowed official roles in the military as nurses, in the Civil War and later in the Spanish-American War. In 1901, based on these experiences, Congress formed the Army Nurse

Corps,[14] providing a model for incorporating the labor of women into wartime military activity.[15] While women were excluded from combat by both military policy and social norms, women nurses were actively recruited to meet wartime needs, thereby creating a distinct feminine role deeply entwined with otherwise masculine notions of war and combat.

Responding to the demands of World War I, women were employed by military forces of the warring nations (including Germany, Russia, the United Kingdom, and the United States) in both nursing and non-nursing capacities in unprecedented numbers. The U.S. Navy and Marine Corps established women's units in 1917 and 1918, respectively. These uniformed women were granted military status and were assigned to jobs women normally held in civilian society, such as telephone operator and clerk; some were stationed overseas. Because these units were created to meet specific personnel needs, they were temporary, and the women were demobilized after the war.

In World War II a major shift occurred in the nature of women's military participation. Not only did women serve in large numbers, but their roles expanded. Congress created women's organizations, with their original designations implying their intended temporary nature (e.g., Women's Army Auxiliary Corps, later changed to Women's Army Corps). Although women were assigned mainly to traditional fields (health care, administration, and communications), small numbers served in almost every specialty, excluding direct combat. For example, some were airplane mechanics, parachute riggers, and weapons instructors.[16]

Although servicewomen faced negative stereotypes and some civilian social opposition,[17] their service—and the military's positive evaluation of their performance and contributions—paved the way for the acceptance of women as a permanent part of the military. In 1948 the Women's Armed Services Integration Act officially created a permanent place for women in the U.S. military, though women's roles were tightly constrained. Women could constitute no more than 2 percent of the force, they could not be permanently promoted above the rank of lieutenant colonel / commander (O-5), and they were barred from service aboard navy vessels (with the exclusion of hospital ships and transports) and from service in aircraft on combat missions.

In 1967, Congress modified the laws concerning women's military service. The 2 percent ceiling was removed, and limits on women's promotion were lifted.[18] Limits on women's career opportunities remained, as did a policy of automatic discharge for pregnancy, and husbands of servicewomen were required to demonstrate dependency in order to receive family benefits automatically granted to wives of servicemen (in 1972 this was struck down by the Supreme Court in *Frontiero v. Richardson*).[19]

Throughout the 1960s and 1970s, gender roles and norms in civilian society were undergoing dramatic transformation, which enabled these changes in women's military roles. Women were increasingly entering higher education and employment, including fields that previously had been exclusively male or male dominated. Civilian women broke barriers in occupations such as law enforcement, coal mining, science, medicine, and law. As employment opportunities for women increased and contraception gave women control over reproduction, social norms and roles began to change. Marriage and childbearing were delayed, and dual-earner households became more common. These shifts in gender norms in civilian society set the stage for even more changes in women's military roles as the U.S. military underwent structural change in the 1970s.

End of Conscription and Increased Roles for Women

The end of conscription has played a role in increasing women's military participation in several Western countries. Abolition of the U.S. draft in 1973, coupled with enabling social forces such as delays in childbearing and increases in women's labor force participation, drove sharp increases in women's military involvement.[20]

Facing personnel shortfalls with the end of conscription, the military opened new occupations to women.[21] In the wake of congressional approval of the Equal Rights Amendment and anticipating its ratification by the states, the military began preparing to equalize service opportunities. In addition, the opening of the military to increased participation by women was preceded by the prominence of civil rights issues, the emergence of a new feminist movement, and, again, increased women's labor force participation.[22] Title IX, a portion of the Education Amendments of 1972, mandated equal treatment of males and females in all programs of educational organizations receiving federal funding; this included equal access to sports participation, which had implications for women's preparation for the physical requirements of the military. Women became aviators in the Navy, Army, and Air Force, and in 1976 Congress opened the service academies to women.[23] Policy changes allowed women to command organizations with both men and women, ended automatic discharges for pregnancy, equalized family benefits, and increased training opportunities for women.[24] In 1978, following judicial intervention, women were allowed permanent assignment to noncombatant ships, and the navy instituted the Women in Ships program, which opened up additional positions for women.[25]

Between 1971 and 1981 women's share of the force jumped from 1.6 percent to 8.9 percent. In 2011, women composed 14.5 percent of the U.S. military, 7.3 percent of general/flag officers, and 10.9 percent of the senior enlisted force.[26] Women have remained between 10 and 15 percent of military personnel throughout the 1990s and early 2000s.[27]

In 2011, U.S. military policy allowed women to serve in all positions except enlisted submarine jobs and offensive ground combat slots below the brigade level. Almost 80 percent of active component positions were open to women, though with substantial variation by branch. The air force was the most accessible, with 99 percent of positions open to women and women composing 19 percent of the air force. The Marine Corps was the least accessible to women, owing to its emphasis on ground combat and its reliance on the navy for support services, to which women gravitate. Only 68 percent of positions in the Marines were open to women, and women composed only 7 percent of the Marine Corps. On February 9, 2012, the Department of Defense announced changes in assignment policy that would open over fourteen thousand additional positions to women, increasing the positions open to women to 81 percent.[28]

In January 2013, the Department of Defense officially rescinded the direct combat exclusion in place since 1994. This will potentially open all or almost all positions to women. The services are to submit implementation plans by May 15, 2013, and complete the process by January 1, 2016. The process of integrating women will follow "guiding principles developed by the Joint Chiefs of Staff," including "preserving unit readiness" and "validating occupational performance standards, both physical and mental, for all occupational specialties (MOS), specifically those that remain closed to women." For those "specialties open to women, the occupational performance standards must be gender-neutral." Although the branches may request that certain positions remain closed to women, such closures will require the personal approval of the chairman of the Joint Chiefs of Staff and must be based on empirical data.[29]

In spite of prior formal limitations on their service in offensive combat, women have been involved in combat in Iraq and Afghanistan. As of February 2012, women composed about 12 percent of the troops who have served in operations in Afghanistan in the past ten years. In Iraq and Afghanistan, 144 women have been killed and 865 wounded;[30] women account for about 2 percent of U.S. military deaths.[31]

The Gradual Opening of Additional Roles for Women

The participation of women in the U.S. military has been a gradual process. As women in the military demonstrated their competence and ability, military leaders and the American public have questioned assumptions behind gender-based exclusion. Eventually, both Congress and military policy makers have lifted most restrictions on women's military service, and the latest policy change may remove the last exclusions. Yet the experience of the United States offers but one possible model for the integration of women in the armed forces. For example, Germany's integration of women was, in theory, swift and complete. For decades after World War II, women were barred from service in the Bundeswehr with the exception of the medical and musical corps.[32] Then, in 2000, a ruling of the European Court of Justice prompted Germany to open all military positions to women.[33] Although on paper the Bundeswehr is highly accessible to women, women remain concentrated in traditionally feminine roles, such as medicine and administration. While women compose 10 percent of all military personnel, they are 37 percent of the medical branch.[34]

In the United States, gender integration of navy ships involved a gradual opening of different kinds of vessels to women, first with hospital ships and transports, then temporary duty on other ships on noncombat missions, then regular assignment to surface combat ships, with the latest development being the assignment of women officers to submarines. In contrast, United Kingdom policy makers rejected a similar strategy on the grounds that all ships were combat ships in war (a lesson learned from the casualties aboard supply vessels during the Falklands conflict), and they opened all classes of ships to women at the same time.[35]

Mission changes also mattered. Following the end of the Vietnam War, the U.S. military began increasingly taking on humanitarian and peacekeeping missions. During these missions, women demonstrated their competence and ability. In 1983 women soldiers participated in the invasions of Grenada to free U.S. medical students and in bombing raids in Libya. In 1989 women soldiers participated in the invasion of Panama, where a female military police officer commanded troops in a firefight and women pilots came under fire and were subsequently awarded the Air Medal.[36] In 1988 the Department of Defense issued the "Risk Rule,"[37] which standardized across the services the criteria for exclusion of women from positions because of the risk of combat involvement. As a result, thirty thousand new positions opened to women.[38]

Women's service in Operations Desert Shield and Desert Storm in 1990–1991 again demonstrated women's capabilities and led to several important changes in women's military roles. During the conflict, 40,872 women were deployed to the Gulf theater. The mass media highlighted the diverse roles of military women. The performance of women soldiers under wartime conditions led to a reevaluation of the assumptions that had been made about women's participation.[39] Despite resistance from civilian detractors and some military leaders, Congress repealed the ban on women in combat aviation and the ban on women serving on combat ships. In 1994 the Risk Rule was lifted, opening tens of thousands of positions to women. A concern with women in offensive ground combat remained, and from 1994 until 2012 policy limitation barred women from being assigned to units below the brigade level whose primary mission was ground combat.[40] The exclusion of women was also permitted in cases where it was cost prohibitive to provide appropriate berthing and privacy arrangements, where the unit or positions were required to co-locate with direct ground combat units closed to women, in long-range reconnaissance operations and Special Operations Forces missions, and where physical requirements would exclude most women service members.[41]

The restriction that prevented women from serving on submarines was lifted in 2010, though enlisted positions on submarines remained closed to women until a cohort of women submarine officers could be developed.

In February 2012, the Department of Defense notified Congress that it intended to change the policies barring women from positions required to co-locate with ground combat units and open select jobs in direct ground combat units to women at the battalion level. These changes went into effect May 2012 and opened an additional fourteen thousand slots to women.[42] This change was a direct result of the recognition that the contemporary battlefield is nonlinear, with no clearly defined front/rear.[43] The policy announcement by the Defense Department in January 2013 removing the direct ground combat exclusions may be the last phase of this gradual evolution.

During the process of gradual integration of women in the U.S. military, the military, Congress, and the public have discussed the appropriate military roles for women. Two frequent rationales used in arguments both for and against expanding women's roles in the military are "military effectiveness" and "citizenship rights and responsibilities."[44] Citizenship arguments are a mainstay of those favoring increased participation of women. Military service has long played a role in increasing the social standing and citizenship rights of minority groups. Military service is seen as a meaningful way to fulfill duties of citizenship as well as an avenue for gaining recognition of citizenship rights,[45] a path of social mobility, and a source of tangible benefits such as training, stable employment, and post-service education.[46]

Those opposing women's military participation often argue that women's presence will interfere with military effectiveness, either by virtue of women's lesser capabilities for military performance or because their integration will degrade unit cohesion. The common wisdom is that units with higher cohesion are more effective, especially in combat. Yet recent research evidence has challenged these assumptions. The accumulated evidence shows that there is sometimes a relationship between cohesion and group effectiveness, but there are three very important qualifiers to this relationship. First, the direction of causality is not established. Some evidence indicates that causality works in the direction opposite to what is usually assumed—that is, it is group success that produces cohesion.[47]

Second, the evidence for a relationship between cohesion and group performance shows that task cohesion, not social cohesion, is related to success.[48] Indeed, high social cohesion sometimes negatively affects performance.[49] Task cohesion is the extent to which group members are able to work together to accomplish shared goals. It includes the members' respect for the abilities of their fellow group members. For combat situations, it translates into the trust that group members have in each other, including faith that the group can do its job and thereby protect its members from harm. Task cohesion can be horizontal or vertical. The latter is the unit members' respect for and confidence in their leaders' competence. Social cohesion is a more affective dimension and includes the degree to which members like each other as individuals and want to spend time with them off duty. Vertical social cohesion would include the extent to which unit members believe that their leaders care about them.

Third, there is evidence that vertical cohesion (i.e., effective leadership) affects both horizontal cohesion and performance. Groups in which members have confidence that their leaders are competent and care about what happens to them are more likely to be successful in various ways. Good leaders by definition organize task activities within the unit in ways that foster task effectiveness, respect, and caring among group members. Thus, even if performance is enhanced by cohesion (and the evidence is not clear on this), it is likely to be task cohesion, not social cohesion, that provides the positive effects. There is no research evidence showing that gender-integrated units have lower task cohesion.

Women, Combat, and Contemporary Operations

The conflicts in Iraq and Afghanistan have made it clear that formal restrictions on women's service do not always match the realities of service in a war zone. Unlike conventional historical wars, the conflicts in Iraq and Afghanistan witness no clear distinction between rear and forward positions in the battle space. Women in combat support jobs are routinely exposed to risk. For example, many deaths and severe wounds of service members have resulted from improvised explosive devices planted on or near the roads. Women serve as truck drivers and are passengers in vehicles on these dangerous roads.

Additionally, a mission dedicated to "winning the hearts and minds" of the local peoples requires cultural sensitivity to gender norms and requires that women soldiers be available to interact with (and sometimes search) local women. Of necessity, military women have served on missions with combat units. Despite policy prohibiting women to be "assigned to" combat units, the practice developed of servicewomen being "attached to" combat units. Outspoken civilian opponents of military women's expanded roles seized on this to expose what they saw as a violation of policy and thereby further exclude women from the support roles in the combat theater.[50] The outcome of the policy reevaluation, however, went in the other direction: the military ground services recognized the essential functions of women in these situations and established new jobs.

The new positions in the war zone include the Female Engagement Teams in the Army and the Marine Corps (the latter beginning with the "Lioness" units of women Marines). These teams of specially trained women soldiers and Marines currently accompany combat units (including Army National Guard units) and work with Afghan women, serving various functions.[51] U.S. military women meet with the local women to discuss many topics, including issues of women's rights, education, security, health care, and violence against women.[52] These women's units are important sources of information about the local population, and their work can lead to medical and social service delivery to respond to unmet needs.[53] The creation and use in the Army of women's units called "Cultural Support Teams" places them in "special operations" and co-locates them with male Special Operations Forces.[54] The reality of military operations in Iraq and Afghanistan has been a driving force in the creation of these women's units and the evolution of policy regarding women serving with ground combat units.

It appears that American civilians are ready not only for American women to be in these kinds of military roles, but also for them to be part of direct combat units. Fully 73 percent of respondents to a 2011 *Washington Post* public opinion poll supported giving women direct combat roles, an astounding figure that may be attributed to media coverage of the situations and successful performance of U.S military women in the recent combat theaters.[55] These developments show that the needs of military missions drive changes in women's military roles.

In their various roles, military women have been exposed to combat, even though officially barred from assignment to offensive combat positions. Women's combat exposure has increased since the 1990s because of changes in military policy and the nature and length of the conflicts in Iraq and Afghanistan. While about 7 percent of pre-1990 women veterans reported combat exposure, for post-1990 women veterans this has risen to 24 percent.[56] Combat brings with it not just the threat of physical injury or death, but also stress and trauma, which can take a mental and emotional toll on service members. As women's military roles change, the effects of combat-related trauma, and possible gender differences in coping with trauma, become increasingly relevant. Overall, women are more likely than men to experience PTSD following traumatic experiences;[57] however, it is unclear if there are gender differences in mental health outcomes of military service. Studies considering the effects of combat exposure have mixed results; some find that combat exposure may have a slightly more negative effect on women than men, but other studies find no difference by gender. Gender differences in mental health outcomes are difficult to determine because men and women experience military service and combat in different roles. For example, women may be more likely than men to experience certain aspects of the aftermath of battle, such as handling human remains, while men are more likely to prepare for and participate in firefights. How these different roles may affect mental health is uncertain at this time.[58]

In addition to combat, exposure to sexual harassment and violence (termed "military sexual trauma," or MST) contributes to PTSD. Rates of PTSD are higher for those who have experienced MST than for those who have experienced other types of trauma.[59] MST is particularly relevant to the experiences of women service members and veterans. In the first attempt to measure the prevalence of MST, data from veterans who deployed to Iraq and Afghanistan were examined.[60] Within this population, 15.1 percent of women reported MST.[61] In these data, a history of MST was significantly correlated with a diagnosis of PTSD, other anxiety disorders, depression, and substance-use disorders.

Gender and Sexuality

For seventeen years after 1993, the service of homosexual service members was limited under the policy of "Don't Ask, Don't Tell" (DADT). In December 2010 this policy was repealed. Repeal came after almost a year of study that took into account the views of current service members and family members, the testimony of currently serving gay and lesbian soldiers, and the experiences of other militaries in integrating openly homosexual service members.

The masculine nature of military culture has long affected the acceptance of homosexual service members. Like women, homosexual men have been viewed as threats to the masculine nature of the institution. The masculine nature of the military is also evident in that the debates about the inclusion of homosexuals are concerned almost exclusively with military men. Concerns about privacy revolve around the comfort of heterosexual military men and focus on the effects of having known gay men serve. The perspectives of women—heterosexual or homosexual—are rarely a part of these discussions.[62]

Despite this, DADT had a disproportionate effect on women in the military, and it is too soon to know what effect the repeal may have on women's military participation. Although the debates about DADT largely focused on privacy and other concerns of heterosexual men, women accused of being lesbians were most likely to be discharged.[63] For example, 31 percent of discharges under DADT in 1999 were of women, although women composed only 14 percent of the force.[64] One reason for this is that discharges of men for homosexuality have tended to be individual, whereas suspicions that there are lesbians in a unit have led to discharges of multiple women. It may also be that the social pressures on military women have led them to appear masculine, leading to suspicions of homosexuality. Of course, it is also possible that a higher proportion of military women than men are homosexual.

As with increased participation of women, revisions to DADT have been affected by changing civilian social norms around homosexuality and gay rights as well as the increased need for personnel during the recent conflicts.[65]

Conclusion

Women have played crucial roles in the U.S. military throughout history. Although the military is a social institution built on ideas of masculinity, women are an integral part of the total force; and while the military remains a deeply masculine culture, women's service increasingly shapes the character and capabilities of the U.S. military. Women's labor, as nurses, in support roles, and most recently on the ground in Iraq and Afghanistan, enables the U.S. military to carry out its missions. The demands of these missions have played a central role in shaping the participation of women. As a driving force that can quickly change the legal and social acceptance of women's military roles, military needs affect the roles in which women serve. These changes, however, also rely on changes in civilian society. Enabling factors such as changes in gender norms relating to family and work set the stage for women's increased military participation. When enabling and driving factors meet, as they did with the end of conscription in 1973, and again with the recent conflicts, the role of gender and sexuality in determining military roles changes quickly and often dramatically. This can be seen in the recent creation of special roles for women in combat zones, as well as the latest policy change that is likely to open at least some offensive ground combat specialties to women. In addition to the factors noted above for this development, such as recognized outstanding performance by military women in the combat zones, a lawsuit brought by servicewomen against the extant combat exclusion has been another driving force for the new policy. However, the services still have to develop scientifically valid and legally acceptable gender-neutral standards for each combat job. It is likely that some attempts will be made to continue to exclude women from some specialties and units, but those efforts will depend upon the evidence of the extensive testing of standards.

As women's formal roles in the military change, debates and discussions about the role of gender in the military and in civilian society change. The military is beginning to renegotiate its masculine culture to create a (hopefully safe) space where women's service can be best utilized. As more combat positions open to women, and larger numbers of women fill these roles, we can anticipate continued discussion of gender and PTSD and the role of gender in providing quality care for wounded warriors. As larger numbers of women serve in the military, increased attention is also needed on those issues unique to women veterans, and how best to provide for their needs. Much of the structure in place to support veterans assumes masculine bodies and social roles. While the military is learning how to incorporate women most effectively into service, society is learning how to support female veterans whose social, family, and occupational roles may differ from their male colleagues'. Women may not be able to avail themselves of services, such as homeless shelters, designed with only men in mind. [66]

With the end of DADT, the open integration of homosexual service members into the force will likely raise questions about the diversity of military families. Changing military needs will likely affect women in the military. Will a drawdown in total force strength lead to a decrease in the representation of women, as happened following the Cold War, or will the lessons learned in these wars about the utility of well-equipped women service members be retained?[67] Regardless of what future missions of the U.S. military entail, it is certain that women will have an important role to play.

Notes

1 Laura L. Miller, "Not Just Weapons of the Weak: Gender Harassment as a Form of Protest for Army Men," *Social Psychology Quarterly* 60 (1997): 32–51; David R. Segal and Meyer Kestnbaum, "Professional Closure in the Military Labor Market: A Critique of Pure Cohesion," in *The Future of the Army Profession*, ed. Lloyd J. Matthews (Boston: McGraw-Hill Primis Custom Publishing, 2002).

2 Darlene Iskra, "Attitudes toward Expanding Roles for Navy Women at Sea," *Armed Forces & Society* 33 (2007): 203–23; M. C. Devilbiss, "Best Kept Secrets: A Comparison of Gays and Women in the United States Armed Forces (the Hidden Life of Uncle Sam)," in *Gays and Lesbians in the Military*, ed. Wilbur J. Scott and Sandra Carson Stanley (New York: Aldine De Gruyter, 1994).

3 William Arkin and Lynne R. Dobrofosky, "Military Socialization and Masculinity," in *Making War / Making Peace: The Social Foundations of Violent Conflict*, ed. Francesca M. Cancian and James William Gibson (Belmont, CA: Wadsworth, 1990).

4 We use the model presented in Michelle Sandhoff, Mady Wechsler Segal, and David R. Segal, "Gender Issues in the Transformation of an All-Volunteer Force: A Transnational Perspective," in *The New Citizen Armies: Israel's Armed Forces in Comparative Perspective*, ed. Stuart Cohen (New York: Routledge, 2010). They integrate and expand on the models in Mady W. Segal, "Women's Military Roles Cross-Nationally: Past, Present, and Future," *Gender & Society* 9 (1995): 757–75, and Darlene Iskra, Stephen Trainor, Marcia Leithauser, and Mady Wechsler Segal, "Women's Participation in Armed Forces Cross-Nationally: Expanding Segal's Model," *Current Sociology* 50 (2002): 771–97.

5 Segal, "Women's Military Roles," 767.

6 Jeanne Holm, *Women in the Military: An Unfinished Revolution* (New York: Presidio Press, 1982): 9–15.

7 Iskra et al., "Women's Participation in Armed Forces Cross-Nationally."

8 *Tanja Kreil v. Bundesrepublik Deutschland*, judgment of European Court, January 11, 2000, http://eur-ex.europa.eu/LexUriServ/LexUriServ.do?uri=C ELEX:61998J0285:EN:HTML.

9 See Sandhoff, Segal, and Segal, "Gender Issues," for documentation of the increased participation of women in the military following the end of conscription in Belgium, France, and the United States.

10 Robert L. Goldich, *U.S. Army Combat-to-Support Ratios: A Framework for Analysis* (Washington, DC: Congressional Research Service, 1989).

11 Segal, "Women's Military Roles."

12 Lory Manning and Jennifer E. Griffith, *Women in the Military: Where They Stand*, 2nd ed. (Washington, DC: Women's Research and Education Institute, 1998); Lory Manning, *Women in the Military: Where They Stand*, 6th ed. (Washington, DC: Women's Research and Education Institute, 2008); Holm, *Women in the Military*.

13 Holly A. Mayer, *Belonging to the Army: Camp Followers and Community during the American Revolution* (Columbia, SC: University of South Carolina Press, 1996): 138–42.

14 Manning and Griffith, *Women in the Military*.

15 Martha A. Marsden, "The Continuing Debate: Women Soldiers in the U.S. Army," in *Life in the Rank and File: Enlisted Men and Women in the Armed Forces of the United States, Australia, Canada, and the United Kingdom*, ed. David R. Segal and H. Wallace Sinaiko (Washington: Pergamon-Brassey's, 1986).

16 Holm, *Women in the Military*; Mattie E. Treadwell, *The Women's Army Corps* (Washington, DC: Office of the Chief of Military History, 1954); D'Ann Campbell, *Women at War with America* (Cambridge, MA: Harvard University Press, 1984).

17 Marsden, "Continuing Debate."

18 Manning and Griffith, *Women in the Military*, 3.

19 Marsden, "Continuing Debate."

20 Sandhoff, Segal, and Segal, "Gender Issues."

21 Mady W. Segal, "Women in the Military: Research and Policy Issues," *Youth and Society* 10 (December 1978): 101–26.

22 Ibid.

23 Manning and Griffith, *Women in the Military*.

24 Marsden, "Continuing Debate."

25 Manning and Griffith, *Women in the Military*.

26 Office of the Under Secretary of Defense Personnel and Readiness, "Report to Congress on the Review of Laws, Policies and Regulations Restricting the Service of Female Members in the U.S. Armed Forces" (February 2012), http://www.defense.gov/news/WISR_Report_to_Congress.pdf.

27 Department of Defense, *Selected Manpower Statistics*, fiscal year 2005; Department of Defense, *Population Representation in the Armed Forces*, fiscal years 2006 and 2007.

28 Office of the Under Secretary of Defense Personnel and Readiness, "Report to Congress."

29 Department of Defense, Office of the Assistant Secretary of Defense (Public Affairs), News Release No. 037–13, "Defense Department Rescinds Direct Combat Exclusion Rule; Services to Expand Integration of Women into Previously Restricted Occupations and Units" (Washington, DC: Department of Defense, January 24, 2013. http://www.defense.gov/releases/release.aspx?releaseid=15784.

30 Casualty rates include combat and noncombat causes. Karen Parrish, "DOD Opens More Jobs, Assignments to Military Women," American Forces Press Service (Washington, DC: Department of Defense, February 9, 2012), http://www.defense.gov/news/newsarticle.aspx?id=67130.

31 "Pentagon's New Rules Deploy Women Closer to Combat," MSNBC, February 9, 2012, http://usnews.msnbc.msn.com/_news/2012/02/09/10366237-pentagons-new-rules-deploy-women-closer-to-combat.

32 Bernhard Fleckenstein, "Germany: Forerunner of a Postnational Military?" in *The Postmodern Military: Armed Forces after the Cold War,* ed. Charles C. Moskos, John Allen Williams, and David R. Segal (New York: Oxford University Press, 2000).

33 *Tanja Kreil v. Bundesrepublik Deutschland.*

34 Gerhard Kümmel, Bundeswehr Institution of Social Research (SOWI), e-mail message to authors, April 24, 2012.

35 Christopher Dandeker and Mady Wechsler Segal, "Gender Integration in Armed Forces: Recent Developments in the United Kingdom," *Armed Forces & Society* 23 (Fall 1996): 29–47.

36 Ibid.

37 Based on the discovery that the existing combat exclusion statutes were being applied inconsistently, the Risk Rule imposed a standard interpretation across services. The rule stated that "risks of exposure to direct combat, hostile fire, or capture are proper criteria for closing noncombat positions or units to women, provided that … such risks are equal to or greater than that experienced by associated combat units in the same theater of operations"; quoted in Holm, *Women in the Military,* 433 (ellipsis is Holm's).

38 Dandeker and Segal, "Gender Integration."

39 *The Presidential Commission on the Assignment of Women in the Armed Forces: Report to the President* (Washington, DC: Government Printing Office, November 15, 1992).

40 Ground combat is defined as "primary mission is to close with and destroy enemy forces." More information can be found in "Information on DOD's Assignment Policy and Direct Ground Combat Definition" (Washington, DC: GAO, October 1998), http://www.gao.gov/archive/1999/ns99007.pdf.

41 Manning and Griffith, *Women in the Military*; Office of the Under Secretary of Defense Personnel and Readiness, "Report to Congress."

42 Jena McGregor, "Military Women in Combat: Why Making It Official Matters," *Washington Post*, May 25, 2012, http://www.washingtonpost.com/blogs/post-leadership/post/military-women-in-combat-why-making-it-official-matters/2012/05/25/gJQAOsRvpU_blog.html.

43 "Department Opens More Military Positions to Women."

44 For an extensive treatment of these values rationales, see Mady W. Segal and Amanda F. Hansen, "Value Rationales in Policy Debates on Women in the Military: A Content Analysis of Congressional Testimony, 1941–1985," *Social Science Quarterly* 73 (1992): 296–309.

45 James Burk, "Citizenship Status and Military Service: The Quest for Inclusion by Minorities and Conscientious Objectors," *Armed Forces & Society* 21 (1995): 503–29.

46 Charles C. Moskos and John Sibley Butler, *All That We Can Be: Black Leadership and Racial Integration the Army Way* (New York: Basic Books, 1996).

47 Brian Mullen and Carolyn Copper, "The Relation between Group Cohesiveness and Performance: An Integration," *Psychological Bulletin* 115 (March 1994): 210–27.

48 Ibid.

49 Carol Burke, "Pernicious Cohesion," in *It's Our Military, Too! Women and the U.S. Military*, ed. Judith H. Stiehm (Philadelphia: Temple University Press, 1996), 205–91; Robert MacCoun and Donna Winslow, *The Canadian Airborne Regiment in Somalia: A Socio-Cultural Inquiry* (Ottawa: Canadian Government Publishing, 1997); Donna Winslow, "Rites of Passage and Group Bonding in the Canadian Airborne," *Armed Forces & Society* 25 (Spring 1999): 429–57.

50 "Army Affirms Its Ban on Women in Combat," *Washington Times*, January 19, 2005, http://www.washingtontimes.com/news/2005/jan/19/20050119-121710-8327r/.

51 Army News Service, "Women Soldiers to Deploy as Afghanistan 'Female Engagement Team,'" June 7, 2011, http://www.army.mil/article/59144/Women_Soldiers_to_deploy_as_Afghanistan__female_engagement_team_/; Ted Roelofs, "West Michigan Army Team Goes to Afghanistan to Engage Other Women, and Win Them Over," *Grand Rapids Press*, January 8, 2012, http://www.mlive.com/news/grand-rapids/index.ssf/2012/01/west_michigan_army_team_goes_t.html.

52 Jeff M. Nagan, "Female Shuras Uncover Hardships Facing Rural Afghan Woman," *Army.mil*, December 22, 2011, http://www.army.mil/article/71272/Female_shuras_uncover_hardships_facing_rural_Afghan_women/.

53 "Female Engagement Team (USMC)," Regional Command Southwest Press Room, http://regionalcommandsouthwest.wordpress.com/about/female-engagement-team-usmc/.

54 U.S. Army John F. Kennedy Special Warfare Center and School, "Cultural Support Program," http://www.soc.mil/swcs/cst/index.htm.

55 Ed O'Keefe and Jon Cohen, "Most Americans Back Women in Combat Roles, Poll Says," *Washington Post*, March 17, 2011, http://www.washingtonpost.com/wp-dyn/content/article/2011/03/16/AR2011031603861.html.

56 Eileen Patten and Kim Parker, "Women in the U.S. Military: Growing Share, Distinctive Profile," *Pew Social & Demographic Trends* (Washington, DC: Pew Research Center 2011), http://www.pewsocialtrends.org/2011/12/22/women-in-the-u-s-military-growing-share- distinctive-profile/.

57 There also may be differences between men and women in their likelihood of reporting PTSD symptoms.

58 Amy E. Street, Dawne Vogt, and Lissa Dutra, "A New Generation of Women Veterans: Stressors Faced by Women Deployed in Iraq and Afghanistan," *Clinical Psychology Review* 29 (2009): 685–94.

59 Deborah Yaeger, Naomi Himmelfarb, Alison Cammack, and Jim Mintz, "DSM-IV Diagnosed Posttraumatic Stress Disorder in Women Veterans with and without Military Sexual Trauma," *Journal of General Internal Medicine* 21 (2006): 65–69.

60 Rachel Kimerling, Amy E. Street, Joanne Pavao, Mark W. Smith, Ruth C. Cronkite, Tyson H. Holmes, and Susan M. Frayne, "Military-Related Sexual Trauma among Veterans Health Administration Patients Returning from Afghanistan and Iraq," *American Journal of Public Health* 100 (August 2010): 1409–12.

61 For men, reported rates of MST are much lower, with only 0.7 percent of men reporting experiences with MST. Likely both men and women are underreporting.

62 Karin De Angelis, Michelle Sandhoff, Kimberly Bonner, and David R. Segal, "Sexuality in the Military," in *International Handbook of the Demography of Sexuality* (New York: Springer, forthcoming).

63 Michelle Beneke and Kirstin S. Dodge, "Military Women: Casualties of the Armed Forces War on Lesbians and Gay Men," in *Gay Rights, Military Wrongs*, ed. Craig A. Rimmerman (New York: Garland Publishing, 1996), 71–108; Kimberly B. Bonner, *Do Lesbians in the Military Pass as Heterosexual?* (master's thesis, University of Maryland, College Park, 2010).

64 Service members Legal Defense Network, *Conduct Unbecoming: The Tenth Annual Report on "Don't Ask, Don't Tell, Don't Pursue, Don't Harass"* (Washington, DC: SLDN, 2004).

65 In 2001, 1,273 service members were discharged under DADT; however, by the next year DADT-related discharges dropped to 906, and to 787 the following year. Ibid.

66 See recent news coverage on problems facing homeless veterans. For example: "Female War Vets Battle Homelessness, Attack Trauma," *San Francisco Chronicle*, April 22, 2012, http://www.sfgate.com/cgi-bin/article.cgi?f=/c/a/2012/04/21/MN141NS65T.DTL.

67 The decrease in women's representation in the military would have been even greater had not the end of the Cold War been followed by the U.S. involvement in the Persian Gulf after Iraq's invasion of Kuwait. Military women's exemplary performance in the Gulf War (surprising to many detractors) helped advocates to spearhead legislation increasing women's military roles to include service on combat ships and aircraft.

13 :: Casualties

Jonathan Shay

Abstract: Privation and disease have mainly killed soldiers until very recently. Now that enemy action predominates, faster and better control of bleeding and infection before and during evacuation spares ever more lives today. This chapter focuses on psychological war wounds, placing them in the context of military casualties. The surgeon's concepts of *primary* wounds in war, and of wound *complications* and *contamination*, serve as models for psychological and moral injury in war. "Psychological injury" is explained and preferred to "post-traumatic stress disorder," being less stigmatizing and more faithful to the phenomenon. Primary psychological injury equates to the direct damage done by a bullet or shell; the complications—alcohol abuse, for example—equate to hemorrhage and infection. Two current senses of "moral injury" equate to wound contamination. As with physical wounds, it is the complications and contamination of mental wounds that most often kill service members and veterans, or blight their lives.

The veterans I served for twenty years were rigorous, generous, and patient teachers on what had wrecked their lives and on what might be done to protect the new generation of American kids who go into harm's way for our sake. They made me their missionary to the U.S. forces on prevention of psychological and moral injury. So, practicing full disclosure, this entire piece has the veterans' missionary agenda as its energy source, and speaks with my personal voice, not detached god-speak from the edge of the universe.

Some history puts current *physical* casualties in context:

In 1861, the French civil engineer Charles Minard published a brilliant, if misleading, graphic of losses from Napoleon's army during its hellish round-trip from the Polish border to Moscow and back, 1812–1813. Most non-historians today know of this chart through Edward R. Tufte's classic, *The Visual Display of Quantitative Information*. The subzero cold prevailing during the retreat from Moscow rivets attention, both because of the black, dramatically thick, but rapidly thinning line drawn westward across a map of Russia to graphically represent troop strength during the winter retreat, and the prominent temperature scale linked to this ever-dwindling line. However, in his "Combat Trauma Overview" for the *Anesthesia and Perioperative Care* volume of the *Textbook of Military Medicine,* Colonel Ronald F. Bellamy, a retired U.S. Army Medical Corps surgeon,[1] points out that Napoleon lost two-thirds of his four-hundred-thousand-plus army primarily to *heat*, disease, and starvation before reaching Borodino, not far from Moscow. You can see this staggering attrition during the approach march in Minard's graphic, if you look for it past the eye-catching, it-was-not-Bonaparte's-fault visual narrative that the Russian winter alone defeated Napoleon.

But one needn't go so far back as Napoleonic warfare to see what a hostile physical environment can do to an army: during World War II in North Africa, far-famed Rommel had *twice* as many troops in hospital for sickness as killed, wounded, or missing.

It is hard for us in the twenty-first century to recall that the main killers of troops throughout history have been the privations of the nonhuman physical environment—heat, cold, dehydration, hunger, and, above all, disease. The fact that Homer's *Iliad* opens with a plague—"and the funeral pyres burned day and night"—is entirely realistic, not merely the poet's evocation of the gods' heavy hands. Americans are brilliant and culturally lavish at logistics, provisioning our troops with *everything material* they need to stay functional, and whisking them away from danger when they are hurt or sick. Today's ever more abundant supply of safe drinking water and food to U.S. troops deployed in the harsh environments of Iraq and Afghanistan probably improves their fate over Rommel's troops in North Africa more than antibiotics and air evacuation. Even so, as of early 2008, the number of service members evacuated from the current theaters of war by air for "diseases / other medical" roughly equaled the number evacuated for physical injuries. War zones *remain* dangerous, unhealthy places.[2]

But beyond illness and accidents, the enemy *does* matter, and in past centuries many, many more combatants eventually died a lingering death from wounds than died immediately. Homer's portrayal of virtually every wound as instantly fatal is one of the very few glaring untruths about war in the *Iliad*. The true medical "miracle" of today's military medicine is how few of the wounded die, if they can be brought alive out of the fight. This miracle continues to evolve, with developments in the ability to call for help, speed of and critical care *during* evacuation to comprehensive treatment, prevention of exsanguination and wound contamination, and concentration on the tedious basics of "damage control" surgery and resuscitation, even while airborne en route to a fully equipped and staffed surgical hospital. To this specialized military medical progress one must above all add recent progress in training *all* troops to be lifesavers, providing them with means to stop bleeding, as well as training, equipping, and empowering the lowest-echelon medics/corpsmen to make critical next steps before the wounded service member's physiology has completely collapsed. As brilliant as American forces are at the logistics of supplying what soldiers need to stay fit in harsh environments, and moving the wounded quickly to surgical treatment and physiological support, there may be no "golden hour" on the battlefield, maybe only a golden five minutes during which self- and buddy-care make all the difference. The addition of an *effective* tourniquet and clotting field dressings to the Improved First Aid Kit carried by every soldier, every Combat Lifesaver (itself an innovation), and every medic or corpsman, and training in their use, have demonstrably saved lives that would have been lost in prior wars. The more effective and ambitious the success at salvage and resuscitation after used-to-be-Killed-in-Action injuries, the more previously unmonitored complications or physiological derangements get added to the prevention list, such as deep vein thromboses and hypothermia (even in hot climates!).[3]

Whether stated as cumulative casualty counts or, more comparably, as rates of wounds and death per hundred thousand per year, the Vietnam War was more deadly and maiming—for example, 1,818 dead per hundred thousand per year in Vietnam, compared to 335 per hundred thousand per year in Iraq.[4] One hopes that a part of this difference is the better training and more rigorous enforcement of the policies that (improved) protective gear be worn at all times. The lifesaving impact of improved communications and of geo-positioning technology is also pervasive but hard to measure. And of course there was the Vietnamese adversary's greater military skill, discipline, and training compared to the Iraqis—and frequently, to our sorrow, compared to ourselves![5]

Every war is hideous, and no injured veteran's or bereaved family's suffering should ever be measured against another's merely by aggregate statistics.

In the 1980s, both ground forces, the Army and Marine Corps, crystallized their conversion to highly mobile, fluid "maneuver warfare" doctrines, which have been fully visible in the most recent wars. The vast spatial sprawl of these operations and the skull-splitting operational tempo pose extraordinary challenges to medical personnel of all sorts at all levels, as well as to line commanders who must consider priorities for scarce resources, such as helicopter lift capacity. All real-world war-fighting presents a conundrum of competing incommensurable goods—for example, how close to the fighting do you locate your surgical personnel and facilities? As close as possible is the obvious answer. But when the forces are moving fast over large distances, exactly how much and whom do you push forward to just behind the point of the spear? How far behind? How secure from enemy actions of what kinds do these personnel and facilities need to be? Close to the fighting is good; doing surgery without being mortared or shot at is good; you can't get both at the same time with the same resources. The balance between security for supporting medical personnel and proximity to the fighting is *always* a work in progress.[6] Once large, kinetic actions end, a new set of conflicting incommensurable goods clamor for attention. The nature of the surgical needs must change, not least because of innovation and adaptation by the *adversary* to the new facts on the ground. These adaptations produce new mechanisms of wounding and new mismatches of needs and resources. Traveling between, supplying, and patrolling around fixed installations create demands and constraints on medical support very different from those of maneuver warfare.

Even laymen know that when a high-velocity bullet or shell fragment takes off a soldier's or Marine's arm, severing arteries, it is not the primary wound that kills, but the *complication* of hemorrhagic shock. If the bleeding is controlled, but nothing further is done, the *complication* of wound infection in this contaminated wound, loaded with foreign bodies and devitalized tissue, will bring death a few days or weeks later. Napoleon's troops knew enough to stop bleeding if they could, as did Agamemnon's troops. Achilles was revered by the troops for his *surgical* knowledge, in addition to his fighting prowess. But Homeric or Napoleonic, the wounded who did not die of hemorrhagic shock were largely doomed by infection.

I draw this distinction between complications and primary injury to segue from physical wounds of war to the psychological wounds of war, where complications and "wound contamination" likewise take greater tolls than the primary injury.

For years I have agitated against the diagnostic jargon "post-traumatic stress *disorder*" (PTSD), because transparently we are dealing with an injury, not an illness, malady, disease, sickness, or disorder. My insistence comes from cultural awareness that within military forces it is entirely honorable to be injured, and that if one is injured and recovers well enough to be fit for duty, there is no real limit to one's accomplishments, even if a prosthesis is employed. Witness the honored career of General Eric Shinseki, who lost a foot in Vietnam, and eventually retired from the U.S. Army as chief of staff. We do not describe him as suffering "missing foot disorder."

To fall ill in the service of one's country is not *dis*honorable, but it sure is *unlucky*. Nobody wants to share a fighting hole or vehicle with an unlucky soldier or Marine, a ship's watch with an unlucky sailor, or aircraft with an unlucky airman. It is stigmatizing in that culture. Among other reasons as well, my agitation has been against the gratuitous stigma conferred in the diagnostic name by its location in the semantic range of *disease*—post-traumatic stress *disorder*—rather than of *wound*. Stigma is a major barrier to military service members asking for help when they have become psychologically injured.

What is the "primary" psychological wound of war? Here I mean "primary" not as "most important," but rather, in the sense of "no complications." Recall how the primary traumatic amputation did not kill the service member, but the complications of hemorrhage and infection did.

In this sense, the primary psychological injury from war is the persistence into civilian life (or life in garrison) of the valid physiological, psychological, and social adaptations that promoted survival in the face of other human beings trying to kill you. Measured against the three clusters of descriptive criteria for the diagnosis "PTSD," the fit is pretty good: the mobilization of the mind and body for lethal danger; the shutting down of activities, thoughts, and emotions that do not directly support survival in the fight; the intrusive hyper-remembering of what the danger looks, smells, or sounds like, to never be taken unprepared.

For example, a primary psychological injury from the current theater in Iraq: A valid survival strategy against roadside improvised explosive devices (IEDs), while driving a vehicle in Iraq, is to drive down the center of the road as fast as possible. This is a rational survival strategy—a rapidly moving vehicle is harder to hit with a command-detonated explosion than a slow-moving vehicle; it is impossible for a driver to know on which side of the road the bomb might be; explosive force declines as the inverse square of the distance; the largest average minimum distance from both roadsides is the center of the road. But upon return to garrison at, say, Camp Lejeune, or Fort Hood, a service member who, while driving (especially if sleep-deprived), momentarily loses the distinction between here-and-now and there-and-then, may well die in a high-speed head-on collision on the roads around Jacksonville or Kileen. In a post-danger setting, the valid adaptation is no longer adaptive, and in this instance fatal, and not only to the service member! Such examples abound, especially when the outcome is less dramatic, often resulting only in inconvenience, other people's puzzlement, or embarrassment.

In the absence of complications, primary psychological injuries from war usually do not wreck veterans' lives. Many adapt to the injury in much the same way as physically injured veterans adapt to injury: they learn skills and work-arounds, they use prostheses. For example, I had a patient who was a Vietnam War Marine infantry veteran who had a nonnegotiable aversion to showing up in the open in a crowd, because it read as "bunching up"—that is, making oneself a target for enemy snipers and mortar men. He could not sit in the stands to watch his son's Little League games, even though he rationally knew there were no snipers. He was simply too uncomfortable to endure it. So his work-around was to watch the game from his truck parked far out the third-base line off left field. This same veteran worked for the gas company. His direct supervisor was also a veteran, and made a "workplace accommodation" to my patient's disability: Instead of requiring him to muster in the open truck yard at 7 a.m. with the other gas service technicians to receive work orders, the supervisor would leave my patient's work orders in a box where he would pick them up at 5 a.m. when no one was around. He would then have breakfast and begin his day's work.

The most common and destructive complications of primary psychological injury from war flow directly from persistence of combat sleep patterns. Soldiers' vigilant sleep—a light doze, instantly ready to respond to danger—is an obviously valid adaptation to an active war zone. If it is not safe to shut out sounds and shadowy movements, they are not shut out, but instead are acknowledged by the soldier's sleep. When this adaptation afterward persists and disrupts sleep, two extremely common complications supervene: first, use, then abuse, of alcohol to promote sleep, and second, loss of emotional and ethical self-restraint and of social judgment. The disastrous pharmacology of alcohol as a sleep medicine is widely known. Less known is impairment of frontal lobe function by sleep loss, per se, which does terrible damage to the lives of veterans and their families. Sleep is fuel for the frontal lobes of the brain. When you are out of gas in your frontal lobes, you become a moral moron and unable to control your behavior in the face of emotions such as anger. Alcohol problems and loss of authority over emotion can thus be seen as complications—akin to hemorrhage and infection—of the primary injury. As with physical wounds, the complications may be far more destructive than the primary injury, such as fatalities connected with alcohol and fatalities in fights connected with loss of authority over anger. Repetitive combat nightmares are prodigious destroyers of sleep. I view traumatic nightmares as an evolutionarily ancient form of remembering about lethal danger, a "primary injury." These nightmares themselves, avoidance of going to sleep because of them, and self-medicating with alcohol to suppress them, are further examples of complications to a primary injury.

One category of psychological injury—moral injury—has recently lit up both in military professional circles and in the clinical literature. I outlined the concept in *Odysseus in America: Combat Trauma and the Trials of Homecoming* (2002):

> When I speak of prevention of moral injury in military service, this Homeric episode [Agamemnon's public dishonor of his most effective and revered subordinate, Achilles, in *Iliad* book 1] is an example of what I want to prevent: betrayal of "what's right" in a high stakes situation by someone who holds power. The consequences for those still on active duty range from a loss of motivation and enjoyment, resulting in attrition from the service at the next available moment, to passive obstructionism, goldbricking, and petty theft, to outright desertion [e.g., Achilles in the *Iliad*], sabotage, fragging [Achilles almost kills Agamemnon in book 1], or treason. In a war, the consequences are catastrophic.[7]

I devote the final fifty pages of *Odysseus in America* to prevention of psychological and moral injury in military service. My current most precise (and narrow) definition has three parts: moral injury is present when (1) there has been a betrayal of what's right (2) by someone who holds legitimate authority (3) in a high-stakes situation. When all three are present, moral injury is present and the body codes it in much the same way as it codes physical attack.

I emphasize the element of *leadership malpractice* because it is something we can *do* something about. The prevalence of leadership malpractice[8] is extremely sensitive to policy, practice, and culture in a military organization. My activities with military forces have been directed that way. They have given me a hearing and appear somewhat receptive,[9] largely because they recognize that expert and ethical leadership are combat strength multipliers. When a leader betrays "what's right," he or she demotivates vast swaths of troops and detaches whole units from loyalty to the chain of command. Stated positively, troops *do* want to know that what they are doing has a constructive purpose, that their direct leaders know their stuff and know their people. Sacrifice falls most heavily on their people.

While I have had bully pulpits before receptive military groups, I cannot point to much change in policy and practice that would significantly reduce the prevalence of leadership malpractice. Some examples of changes not made: change "up-or-out" to "up-or-stay" (subject to rigorous performance evaluation); broaden the "who" and the "how" of performance evaluation (e.g., "360-degree evaluation"); stop imagining officership as a form of "general management," where no specific functional expertise is required.[10]

When the term "moral injury" has recently surfaced in the psychological research literature, it has been used somewhat differently: "Potentially morally injurious events, such as perpetrating, failing to prevent, or bearing witness to acts that transgress deeply held moral beliefs and expectations may be deleterious in the long-term, emotionally, psychologically, behaviorally, spiritually, and socially."[11] The cited clinician-researchers have shown an elevated risk of domestic violence and suicide, if moral injury is present. Our two meanings of "moral injury" differ mainly in whether leadership malpractice is part of the definition. The view of the above researchers could be paraphrased as what happens (1) when someone "betrays what's right," (2) the violator is the self (3) in a high-stakes situation. I have focused where the betrayer of what's right holds legitimate authority. Moral injury in my meaning can lead to moral injury in the above clinician/researchers' meaning. Both forms can occur in the same person. An example would be for a soldier or Marine to be ordered to murder civilians or disarmed, unresisting prisoners (likely a moral injury in my sense), and then, feeling compelled to carry it out, to incur moral injury in their sense. Our junior enlisted fighters do *not* want to know themselves to be murderers. And moral injury in my sense can lead to it in their sense. They both exist and are both destroyers of human flourishing.

Ethical philosophers such as Bernard Williams and Martha Nussbaum have addressed the situation that I and these clinician-researchers report on, under the somewhat opaque term "moral luck." Nussbaum has written with great force on the deteriorating impact of [bad] "moral luck" on good character and connection to others, particularly in her classic *The Fragility of Goodness* and elsewhere. "Annihilation of [ethical] convention by another's acts can destroy ... stable character."[12]

Unfortunately war itself creates an abundance of "moral [bad] luck" that cannot be completely prevented short of ending the human practice of war—which many combat veterans in and out of uniform long for. A recent incident, told to me as having happened in Fallujah, involved a Marine scout-sniper who was supporting an engaged infantry unit, which had losses to a very effective, well-concealed enemy sniper. When the Marine sniper finally discovered and positively identified the enemy sniper, the Marine could see that he had a baby strapped to his front in what we would call a "Snuggli" baby carrier. The Marine interpreted this as use of the baby as a "human shield." Regardless of whether that was true, the Marine understood that the Law of Land Warfare and the Rules of Engagement permitted him to fire on the enemy sniper, and he understood his duty and his loyalty to his fellow Marines to do so. He did fire, and saw the round strike. He will live with that for the rest of his life.

One of my former patients, a well-educated Roman Catholic, opened with the words "I led them into sin," once he became willing to tell the clinical team the most tenaciously painful experience he had had in Vietnam. He and his three-man Marine fire team were left in charge of seventeen disarmed and nonresisting Vietnamese prisoners. As the sergeant was leaving the scene, he said over his shoulder, "We don't need no prisoners," which my patient understood to be an instruction to kill them. My patient discovered that the other Marines were reluctant to murder the prisoners. My patient egged them on and was the first to open fire. He calmly carried the certainty that he personally was damned (his understanding of his religious tradition), but found it impossible to live with the knowledge that he had led the other Marines into mortal sin.

What does leadership malpractice add to the elements visible in betrayal of what's right by the self in a high-stakes situation? Primarily, it *destroys the capacity for social trust* in the mental and social worlds of the service member or veteran. I regard this as a kind of wound contamination in the mind, preventing healing, and leaking toxins.

The above-cited clinician-researchers also note the impairment of trust in patients with their version of moral injury. Further, they note that such patients do not experience physiological activation when they are reminded of the events related to the moral injury, in their sense, differing from PTSD in this regard. My observation has been that moral injury in my sense, which hinges on leader malpractice, *does* involve physiological activation—the body codes moral injury as physical attack.

When the capacity for trust is destroyed, its place is filled by the active expectancy of harm, exploitation, or humiliation. We do not learn one iota more about the human being before us by hanging the psycho-jargon word "paranoid" on this expectancy.

There are three common strategies for dealing with a situation in which harm, exploitation, and humiliation are foreseen: strike first; get away to complete isolation from others; develop effective disguise-deception-concealment.[13] All three of these strategies are formidable destroyers of a flourishing human life. They are also barriers to service members or veterans ever obtaining or keeping meaningful mental health care. In the modern medical setting, this means trusting a clinician on the basis of his or her *credentials*, and *institutional position*. The credentials and institutional position of the original military perpetrator of moral injury were often impeccable, so the situation of being asked to trust someone purely on that basis ("Hello, I'm Dr. Shay. I'm a staff psychiatrist here …") is likely to be a traumatic trigger, a new danger. And if the strike first, run away, or deceive strategies are not enough of an obstacle to obtaining and keeping care, clinicians often take offense at *not* being automatically trusted, and chase the veteran away or retaliate.

Both forms of moral injury—whether leadership malpractice is involved or horrible-bad moral luck—impair the capacity for trust, and increase suicide risk. Officially acknowledged rates of suicide among active-duty personnel have climbed during the wars in Iraq and Afghanistan, generating "news hooks" as various baleful "records" have been broken. The official statistics are biased downward by the fact that suspected suicide deaths in the war zone are investigated by military police detectives (e.g., CID) but only *counted* as suicides when they declare it.[14] If a despairing or drowning-in-guilt-or-shame soldier wants to be dead, and has the slightest inclination to conceal that his or her death is suicide, there is no better place than a war zone to contrive a fatal "accident." In order for CID to be involved, the soldier's commander (probably battalion commander) must initiate the investigation. The *disincentives* for the commander to initiate it or for his or her subordinate commanders to push for one are numerous and powerful. After separation from military service, public health statistical measurement of veteran suicides is poor for the subset of veterans who have connected themselves with the VA, and worse for those who have not. The more severely morally injured a veteran is, the less likely he or she is to have anything to do with the VA, because of mistrust. Or, if the veteran has had criminal convictions—far more probable, in my opinion, if moral injury is in play—the less likely it is for the VA to have anything to do with the veteran.

Retired admiral Mike Mullen, former chairman of the Joint Chiefs of Staff, recently stated at a public appearance at a conference in Aspen, Colorado, that eighteen American veterans per day are killing themselves.[15] This number is drawn from the pool of all veterans, not just current theater veterans. I lack the demographic expertise to comment on this number, but want to mention one observation from an area in which I do have some expertise: psychological injury from war, particularly the Vietnam War. In the twenty years I served the Vietnam veterans population in the clinic, I observed a change in the typical new patient. During the first five years, roughly 1988–1993, the stereotype of the PTSD veteran who could not hold a job because of drink, fighting, problems with authority, having held and lost dozens of them before coming to our program, dominated the flow of new patients. During the final five years, roughly 2003–2008, the typical veteran had had very stable work history, sometimes for the same employer since leaving the service after Vietnam. A characteristic story was that these veterans had been workaholics and that then some event—such as an illness, injury, or the employer going out of business—interfered with this veteran's workaholic adaptation to his combat trauma and he came apart, often culminating in a suicide attempt. In chapter 6 of my *Odysseus in America*, I opined that workaholism was the single most commonly used (and "successful") adaptation to psychological injury from war. Unless you are a member of the immediate family, you would be likely to think, "He's fine." The families are the big psychological bill-payers for this adaptation, even though the veteran often brings home bushels of money—which the veteran typically has little interest in. Vietnam veterans are now typically in their late fifties and early sixties, at a time of stagnation and decline of many sectors of the real U.S. economy, causing large numbers of them to lose their jobs and be unable quickly to find another. So my conjecture is that the shocking statistic cited by Admiral Mullen is driven by the collision of this demographic bulge with economic hard times.

My line of march in the prevention of psychological and moral injury in military service has been to exhort uniformed and civilian leadership on renovating policy, practice, and culture to improve the average ethical performance of military leadership at all levels.[16] Some of these renovations are known as "low-hanging fruit," such as "360-degree evaluation" and replacing "up-or-out." But in this, as in all aspects of human warfare, "the enemy gets a vote." For the insurgent, the creation of moral strain and moral injury is one of his most potent "weapons effects."

The bad old joke about sexually transmitted diseases being "the gift that goes on giving" applies to war, but raised to an exponent. Suicide and all the intergenerational morbidity and mortality that go with family violence are such "gifts."

Many of the veterans I worked with had histories of having done great harms to other, some with heavy criminal careers since Vietnam, often carrying prior diagnoses such as "sociopath," "borderline personality disorder," "character disorder." The general consensus of American mental health has been that no bad experience in adulthood can turn someone with good character into someone with bad character. This is a broadly and deeply held philosophic position, which has a brilliant pedigree going back to Plato, through the Stoics, to Kant, and to Freud. Plato said that if you make it out of childhood with good breeding (we would say, good genes) *and* good upbringing, then your good character, your virtuous behavior, will form as hard, unbreakable, and immovable as rock. American psychiatry has consistently rejected attempts to diagnostically recognize deformities of personality or character arising from bad experience. The American Psychiatric Association has rejected two attempts to get such phenomena recognized in the nosology: "Enduring Personality Change after Catastrophic Experience," and "Disorders of Extreme Stress, Not Otherwise Categorized." The former is currently part of the World Health Organization International Classification of Diseases (ICD-10) nosology; the latter, under a less opaque label, "complex PTSD," is very widely accepted by clinicians who work with morally injured populations, such as incest and political torture survivors, despite its lack of official blessing. "Post-Traumatic Embitterment Disorder," a phenomenon defined and proposed as a diagnostic construct by Professor Michael Linden and his colleagues at the Charité in Berlin, has not (yet) been exposed to the Platonic filter of the APA.

The key to clinical success in working with such veterans and service members is their *peers*. This is a post-service parallel to the psycho-protective benefit *in* the service of unit *cohesion*. Cohesion is military-speak for the concrete face-to-face familiarity, mutual love, reliance, obligation, and visceral sense of being part of each other's future that arise spontaneously in a stable, well-trained, and well-led unit that has been through hard things *together*. Credentialed mental health professionals, myself included, have no business taking center stage in the drama of recovery from moral injury. We can be good stage hands and bit players, but the real stars are other veterans who have walked in their comrades' shoes. Working with veterans carrying such injuries is a constant lesson in humility. We clinicians *earn* trust; we learn to go naked; we listen with the heart as well as the head.

A final public policy item relating to moral injury deserves thoughtful debate: Morally injured veterans are vulnerable to recruitment by tight criminal or coercive religious or political groups. This is not a "liberal anti-military" riff on a supposed association between military service and right-wing extremism. The historical record is clear: German World War I front veterans who were demobilized *together* and returned together to the town in which their division was raised generally settled peacefully back into civilian society, even when their hometowns were now on the *other* side of newly drawn national borders. They rarely gravitated to the *Freikorps*, extremist political gangs of *both* the Left and the Right that sometimes functioned as "death squads." Instead, an "elective affinity" for such groups was discovered by veterans of special *Reichsheer* formations, such as the Jaegers and the Naval Infantry, which recruited individual volunteers from regular army units. Members of these elite units were demobilized *as individuals* and scattered to the winds.

Why raise this historical curiosity here? Because we have a sociologically analogous situation with repatriated "trigger-puller" contractors from the current theaters of war, who have neither home station to return to, nor military unit association, nor clear-cut VA eligibility for treatment and disability pension benefits. The fact that many or most have prior military service will prove a most capricious entitlement, should they wish to call upon it. The piece in this volume by Deborah Avant and Renée de Nevers gives an up-to-date overall picture of military contractors in Iraq and Afghanistan, although the number carrying and using firearms remains very hard to come by.

Who will offer social support and mental health services to trigger-puller contractor veterans? I am not saying that I know that the Weimar Republic would still exist today, with all that implies about a different course to history, if Germany had had Vet Centers and VA mental health clinics. But historians generally agree that the

Freikorps contributed to the weakening of the new German political fabric in the immediate aftermath of World War I. Obviously, not all psychologically and morally injured trigger-puller military contractors will ask for help. But as a matter of public policy, it will be a *very* good investment to make them eligible to receive it, without a lot of hoops to jump through. This is not a handout to the contracting firms, who might be supposed to be obligated to provide medical benefits (including mental health benefits) to injured former employees. Whether or not current law can be construed to compel these firms to provide such coverage, I regard that as *very* imprudent for us as a nation to rely upon. The vet centers, even more than the VA, have the peer tradition to offer meaningful support to this demographic group, although some VA facilities have developed significant peer support and community-of-experience-based programming.

To conclude, I want to dispute the habitual mind-body distinction that I myself implicitly made early in this chapter by distinguishing physical from psychological injuries. This distinction is often useful but, at its root, incoherent. "The body keeps the score," as traumatologist Bessel van der Kolk has so resonantly said. The body codes moral injury as physical attack and reacts with the same massive mobilization. If you doubt that, try the following very unpleasant thought-experiment: Imagine, as vividly as you can, a situation that applies to *your* life circumstances that fits my definition of moral injury—a betrayal of what's right, by someone with legitimate authority, in a situation with high stakes *to you*. I guarantee that your heart rate and guts will respond. We are just one critter: brain/body, mind, social actor, and culture inhabitant at every instant. None of these has ontologic priority.

Notes

1 Thanks to Lieutenant General Patricia D. Horoho, the Army Surgeon General, to Colonel John Lammie of her staff, and to Emily A. Court, reference librarian at the Armed Forces Medical Library, for helping me open the field of view for this chapter beyond psychological and moral injuries in war. The *Textbook of Military Medicine* is a vast multivolume, periodically updated work published by the U.S. Army Surgeon General. I commend the

reader to the whole U.S. Army Medical Department Borden Institute website, http://www.bordeninstitute.army.mil/, where the following are available in their entirety as free pdf downloads: all the massive current volumes of the *Textbook of Military Medicine*; various monographs, such as *Water Requirements and Soldier Hydration*, and *War Surgery in Afghanistan and Iraq, a Series of Cases, 2003–2007*; and the third, 2004 revision of *Emergency War Surgery*.

2 The data in this footnote were current as of January 5, 2008. The number wounded in action (that is, by enemy action) in Operation Iraqi Freedom (OIF) and Operation Enduring Freedom (OEF) was 9,801. This number represents only those severely enough injured to require medical air transport out of theater, which I take as a proxy for the severity of injury; 2.3 times as many were wounded by hostile action, but the wounds could be treated within theater without evacuation (latter proportion for OIF only; OEF, with "more austere" medical facilities, evacuated proportionally more). Adding roughly an equal number of nonhostile injuries severe enough to require medical air transport brings OIF + OEF injured to January 5, 2008, to a total of 19,522. Adding "diseases / other medical" requiring medical air transport brings OIF + OEF air transports to January 5, 2008, to roughly double this total again, to 46,751. That is, this is the total of all who have been medically air transported out of theater for medical/surgical reasons, not as a result of enemy action. Lest the reader speculate that the number of "diseases / other medical" has been inflated by *mental health* evacuations, note two facts: First, current military medical doctrine calls for treating combat stress reactions as close as possible to the service member's unit, using brief and simple interventions, such as "three hots and a cot"—that is, physiological replenishment of food and water (three hots) and sleep (the cot). The doctrine discourages evacuation from theater, because evacuation is believed to freeze the psychological injury in place, at a time it is still reversible. This view has some empirical foundation. Second, the MHAT II (Operation Iraqi Freedom [OIF-11] Mental Health Advisory Team report, January 30, 2005) estimated that all mental health diagnoses together accounted for 6 percent of evacuations, and *of these* 11.7 percent were PTSD and ASD (acute stress disorder), narrowly and strictly diagnosed; 46,751 x 0.06 x 0.117 = 499. A narrow definition of PTSD used by the Department of Defense Task Force on Mental Health produced an estimate that 10 percent of those deployed in OIF/OEF had PTSD (Department of Defense Task Force on Mental Health, *An Achievable Vision: Report of the Department of Defense Task Force on Mental Health* [Falls Church, VA: Defense Health Board, 2007]). Using the Dole-Shalala Commission's round number of 1.5 million service members deployed (the number is now larger), this yielded 150,000 with narrow PTSD. The broad definition, encompassing all significant psychological injuries, including depression, for example, produced an

estimate by the DOD MHTF of 38 percent, or 570,000. The broader definition of PTSD used by the MHTF is closer to that used by the public, the
press, and the Congress: all the bad things that can happen to the mind and
spirit from going to war. If the above numbers of those evacuated for "diseases / other medical" are inflated at all, it is more likely that it is from the
policy of evacuating service members for diagnosis and treatment of conditions for which no appropriate specialist or subspecialist had been deployed
at the time in the theater—for example, gynecologists.

3 Paul R. Cordts, Laura A. Brosch, and John B. Holcomb, "Now and Then:
Combat Casualty Care Policies for Operation Iraqi Freedom and Operation
Enduring Freedom Compared with Those of Vietnam," *J Trauma* 64 (2008):
S14–S20.

4 M. S. Goldberg, "Death and Injury Rates of US Military Personnel in Iraq,"
Military Medicine 175 (2010): 220–26.

5 Other comparisons between Vietnam and Iraq that complicate the comparison: significantly higher "tooth to tail" ratio in Iraq (i.e., excluding contractors in official reporting of casualties, both in numerators and denominators);
higher level of training, skill, and possibly improved small-unit stability and
resultant cohesion in American forces; impact of new communications and
geo-positioning technologies.

6 The reader can get a flavor of what this looks like from an able review,
Major Alec Beekley, "United States Military Surgical Response to Modern
Large-Scale Conflicts: The Ongoing Evolution of a Trauma System," *Surgical
Clinics of North America* 86 (2006): 689–709.

7 Jonathan Shay, *Odysseus in America: Combat Trauma and the Trials of
Homecoming*, with joint foreword by U.S. Senators John McCain and Max
Cleland (New York: Scribner, 2002), 240.

8 Within military circles, the tag "toxic leadership" is commonly used.

9 I still get goose bumps when I recall that during the break at a commanders' conference at the 101st Airborne, where I spoke, several battalion commanders came up to me and told me that they had required their troopers to
read *Achilles in Vietnam* prior to deployment, and that they could overhear
admonishments among them: "Don't betray what's right!"

10 Rivers of ink have been spilled on the Officer Personnel Management System
and related practices and culture. My most important teachers in this area
have been Faris Kirkland, Carl Bernard, Bruce Gudmundsson, Donald
Vandergriff, Franklin "Chuck" Spinney, James N. Mattis, Donn Starry,
Walter Ulmer, Richard Trefry, and my patients at the VA.

11 Brett T. Litz, Nathan Stein, Eileen Delaney, Leslie Lebowitz, William P. Nash,
Caroline Silva, and Shira Maguen, "Moral Injury and Moral Repair in War
Veterans: A Preliminary Model and Intervention Strategy," *Maguen, Shira
Clinical Psychology Review* 29, no. 8 (December 2009): 695–706. Research
data on their construction of moral injury indicates increased suicidality,

impaired trust, and increased domestic violence. To my knowledge, no formal empirical research regarding service members and veterans has been carried out on moral injury involving leadership malpractice, although several of the MHAT studies have collected data that would appear, at least tangentially, to illuminate that.

12 Martha C. Nussbaum, *The Fragility of Goodness: Luck and Ethics in Greek Tragedy and Philosophy* (Cambridge: Cambridge University Press, 1986), 417. An excellent summary of philosophers' handling of "moral luck" can be found in "Moral Luck," by Dana K. Nelkin, in *Stanford Encyclopedia of Philosophy* http://plato.stanford.edu/entries/moral-luck/ (downloaded September 29, 2012).

13 We can recognize Achilles in the first of these strategies, and Odysseus in the third.

14 Suicides are notoriously hard to "measure" for public health statistics, as noted at the end of the nineteenth century by Emile Durkheim in his foundational study. The U.S. Army's policy dated March 26, 2010, "Army Directive 2020–01 (Conduct of AR 15–6 Investigations into Suspected Suicides....")," http://armypubs.army.mil/epubs/pdf/ad2010_01.pdf (downloaded September 29, 2012), strikes me as quite good, *so long as it is actually carried out in practice.* The institutional, cultural, and practical obstacles to this happening on a reliable, routine basis in an active theater of war are enormous.

15 YouTube video, July 1, 2012, http://www.rawstory.com/rs/2012/07/02/mullen-18-veterans-kill-themselves-every-day-in-the-u-s/ (downloaded September 29, 2012).

16 The other two legs of my missionary pitch are *cohesion*—train people together, send them into danger together, and bring them home together with enough time to talk about what they've been through; and *training*—prolonged, cumulative, and highly realistic training for what they really have to do and face.

INDEX